Passing and the Rise of
the African American Novel

Passing and the Rise of
the African American Novel

M. GIULIA FABI

University of Illinois Press

URBANA AND CHICAGO

Library of Congress Cataloging-in-Publication Data
Fabi, M. Giulia (Maria Giulia)
Passing and the rise of the African American novel / M. Giulia Fabi.
p.   cm.
Includes bibliographical references and index.
ISBN 0-252-02667-5 (acid-free paper)
1. American fiction—African American authors—History and criticism. 2. Passing (Identity) in literature. 3. African Americans in literature. 4. Group identity in literature. 5. Race awareness in literature.
6. Race in literature. I. Title.
PS374.N4F34   2001
813.009'353—dc21   00-013099

For
Vanda Landi Forbicini Fabi,
Mario Fabi,
and Barbara T. Christian

Contents

Acknowledgments

It is a great pleasure for me to thank publicly the many friends and colleagues in the United States and in Europe who have followed my scholarly endeavors over the years with supportive interest and critical spirit.

I am deeply grateful to Nellie Y. McKay, William L. Andrews, Elaine H. Kim, Sau-ling C. Wong, Craig Werner, and Genaro Padilla, whose scholarly excellence, teaching skills, critical insights, helpful feedback, and continuing interest in my work have been invaluable sources of intellectual growth for me. I would also like to thank Frances Smith Foster, Henry Louis Gates Jr., Michel Fabre, and Geneviève Fabre for their consistently supportive comments about conference papers in which I presented parts of my manuscript-in-progress. I thank Shelley Sunn Wong, Barry Maxwell, and particularly Arlene Keizer for their critical acumen, rigorous minds, and warm friendship. I am grateful to other longtime friends and colleagues, especially Sandra Gunning, Jacquelyn Y. McLendon, P. Gabrielle Foreman, Harryette Mullen, Gloria Bowles, Anne Goldman, Stephanie Smith, Sharon Johnson, Juliann Martinez, Douglas F. Dowd, and Najuma Henderson; as well as to Deborah Cohen, for being my first friend in California, and Anna Hilbe, for the gift of her advice and affection.

The Department of Ethnic Studies at the University of California at Berkeley has been a constant point of reference for me over the years, and I am grateful to the librarians at Doe Library and especially to Phyllis Bischof. A two-year fellowship at the University of Bologna has been instrumental to the completion of this book.

From among the people who have greatly eased my return to Italy after years of graduate study in the United States, I thank Vita Fortunati for her precious mentoring and contagious scholarly enthusiasm for utopian studies, Guido

Fink for transmitting his love for American literature, Cristina Giorcelli for sharing her knowledge and wit, Rita Monticelli for her intelligence and sense of humor, Paola Boi, Radhouan Ben Amara, and Dominique Marçais for many fascinating discussions, Luciana Tufani for her inspiring intellectual and feminist engagement, and Alessandro Portelli and Annalucia Accardo for welcoming me into the world of African American studies in Italy. I am grateful to my former colleagues at the University of Rome Tor Vergata, especially Lina Unali and Daniela Guardamagna; to my students for their interest in early African American fiction; and to many other supportive friends and colleagues such as Alecia McKenzie, Daniela Corona, Maria Rosaria De Bueriis, Gaetano Schiavo, Sara Antonelli, Peter Gardner, Liana Borghi, Raffaella Baccolini, Alessandra Calanchi, P. A. Skantze, and Matthew Fink.

I thank Willis G. Regier, my editor and the director of the University of Illinois Press, as well as the two anonymous readers for the Press, whose comments have had a significant impact on my revisions of the original manuscript.

Finally, I am profoundly grateful to Michel Huysseune for his unfailing, knowledgeable, and affectionate companionship; to Francesca Fabi for her clever and versatile mind; to Paolo, Francesco, and Elena Fabi for their intelligence and sagacity; and to Bruna Zappieri for presenting me with my first volume of African American literature many years ago.

This book is dedicated to Barbara T. Christian, whose challenging intellect, generous mind, and profound humanity have enriched me more than I can possibly acknowledge, and to my parents, Vanda Landi Forbicini Fabi and Mario Fabi, for their constant support and for putting up with years of long-distance phone calls and a few earthquakes. Their guidance gave me discipline; their trust left me free to choose.

* * *

Earlier versions of portions of chapters 1 and 2 appeared as " 'The Unguarded Expressions of the Feelings of the Negroes': Gender, Slave Resistance, and William Wells Brown's Revisions of *Clotel,*" *African American Review* 27.4 (1993): 639–54; "Frank J. Webb's *The Garies and Their Friends* (1857) and the Unprecedented Fictional Representation of African American Life in the Antebellum North," *Letterature d'America* 60 (1995): 53–79; " 'Race Travels': Towards a Taxonomy of Turn-of-the-Century African American Utopian Fiction," in *Viaggi in utopia,* ed. Raffaella Baccolini, Vita Fortunati, and Nadia Minerva (Ravenna, Italy: Longo Editore, 1996), 335–42; "Reconstructing Literary Genealogies: Frances E. W. Harper's and William Dean Howells' Race Novels," in *Soft Canons: American Women Writers and Masculine Tradition,* ed. Karen L. Kilcup (Iowa City: University of Iowa Press, 1999), 48–66; "Taming the Amazon? The Price of Survival in Turn-of-the-Century African American Women's Fiction," in *The Insular Dream: Obsession and Resistance,* ed. Kristiaan Versluys (Amsterdam: VU Press, 1995), 228–41; and "The Poetics and Politics of a Feasible Utopia: Edward A. Johnson's *Light Ahead for the Negro,"* in *Vite di utopia,* ed. Vita Fortunati and Paola Spinozzi (Ravenna, Italy: Longo Editore, 2000), 303–10.

*Passing and the Rise of
the African American Novel*

Introduction

Nineteenth-century African American fiction has a bad reputation. This reputation is distinctly different from the sense of alienation and distance twenty-first-century readers may feel when approaching the moralism, triumphant poetic justice, imperialist assumptions, and sexual reticence of some Victorian fiction. In the case of African American novels, these critiques are compounded by much more serious accusations of literary incompetence (early African American novelists supposedly were learning how to write fiction), accusations of racial self-hatred (especially in connection with the trope of passing), and accusations of compromises with white literary stereotypes of blacks (as in the depiction of dark-skinned folk characters). Critical common sense holds that early African American literature is of chiefly historical value. The appreciation of its literariness often is overshadowed by the emphasis on the sociohistorical context, and its subversiveness, even when admitted, is reputed to be so covert that no one but the most attentive reader would ever notice it without notes or a detailed introduction. Early African American writers may have had good and important things to say, but they certainly did not have great artistic skills. This void at the origin of African American fiction casts a shadow over its entire tradition that not even Toni Morrison's Nobel Prize has been able to dispel completely.

The bad reputation of nineteenth-century African American fiction contrasts sharply with the celebration of another early genre, the slave narrative, that has taken place especially since the 1970s. Exalting the slave narrative as the foundational genre of the African American literary tradition, as the original repository of what is distinctive and authentic in black literature, has effectively reinforced the critical practice of marginalizing pre–Harlem Re-

naissance fiction. The assumed contrast between the biographical and literary bravery of slave narrators and the supposed narrative caution (and implicit cowardice) of early African American novelists has not been reduced
significantly even by the fact that William Wells Brown, for instance, wrote
both slave narratives and novels. As Carla Peterson notices, in its emphasis
on "the slave narrative as *the* African American literary form from the antebellum period . . . literary criticism of the late twentieth century has come
dangerously close to replicating the historical situation of the early nineteenth
century in its valorization of those African American texts produced under
the direction of white sponsors for the consumption of a white readership"
(*"Doers"* 5).

The critical resistance to pre–Harlem Renaissance fiction traditionally
coalesced around the treatment of all-but-white characters and especially
around what was perceived as their prominence at the expense of visibly black
folk characters.[1] For this reason, *Passing and the Rise of the African American
Novel* focuses precisely on the tropes of miscegenation and passing to outline a literary history of pre–Harlem Renaissance fiction that foregrounds its
sophisticated literary artistry and ideological complexity, its centrality in the
development of the African American novelistic tradition (which can still be
traced, for instance, in Morrison's play with racial indeterminacy in *Paradise*), and its revisionary impact on the study of American literature as a
whole.

To this day, all-but-white characters are considered to be strangely "over-
represent[ed] . . . in black narratives" (V. Smith, "Reading" 57), and this over-
representation has often been read as a symptom of self-loathing. Critics have
had difficulties in accounting for these "whitefaced" novels as the founding
texts of a distinctively African American novelistic tradition, especially because African American scholars have long been confronted with a white-
dominated academic establishment unwilling to recognize the literary value
of black literature as a whole and mostly familiar with white literary stereotypes of the tragic mulatto as neither black nor white, an ill-fated in-between
figure who was nevertheless somewhat "better" than blacks because supposedly genetically closer to whites. These critical difficulties in many cases have
occasioned the summary scholarly disparagement or neglect of the early
novels, which were accounted for as well-meaning but ultimately self-defeat-
ing attempts to revise the tragic mulatto motif that was so popular among
white writers.

It is well known that mulattos and mulattas were popular literary figures
before antebellum African American novelists appropriated them.[2] This historical fact traditionally has led to critical readings that focus on the influence

of white-authored fictions such as Harriet Beecher Stowe's *Uncle Tom's Cabin* on black writers, whose creative contribution has been recognized mostly to be the revision of those antecedent texts. In light of her own borrowings from slave narrators, however, the interracial genealogy of Stowe's novel is too mixed to justify a univocal model of black literary dependence, however revisionary, on white *ur*-texts, as critics such as Frances Smith Foster and Claudia Tate have already demonstrated. Early African American novelists did not merely take over a useful trope or develop its treatment. Rather, in their use of mulatto characters they changed the very nature of the material and of the effect, "as the molecular structure of an element may be changed" (Ellis-Fermor 251). They created multilayered novels that can be read at a variety of "histotextual" (Foreman 329) levels depending on the amount of historical, cultural, and literary knowledge on African America the reader possesses.

Although scholars have often taken for granted and overestimated their similarity, white-authored representations of the tragic mulatto and African American representations of miscegenation and passing constitute profoundly different literary traditions. Of course, this does not mean that they do not share common elements, but rather that those elements have been put to distinctively different uses. No literary tradition is immune from intertextual and intercultural cross-fertilizations, but shared and inherited elements do crystallize in unique literary configurations. For instance, in pre–Harlem Renaissance African American fiction the passers are rarely tragic figures, and even when tragedy does befall them, it is most clearly indicated to be the result of virulent prejudice and discrimination. The lingering suspicion that the mulatto's or mulatta's downfall may stem from some intrinsic, genetic flaw of character (a suspicion that can still be detected even in Mark Twain's or George W. Cable's novels) is conspicuously absent.

These differences notwithstanding, the bad reputation of pre–Harlem Renaissance fiction has survived to this day, as can be gauged by the defensive tone that continues to characterize critical commentaries on early African American fiction, despite the important process of recovery and reinterpretation that has been undertaken in the past thirty years. Black feminist critics in particular have found in the intricate family sagas that generally characterize novels of miscegenation and passing a way to focus on female characters and female concerns and thereby challenge the critical predominance of "the masculinized racial and freedom discourse assumed to characterize the African American novel" (duCille 3). These critics have emphasized the need to "historiciz[e] the racial construction of mulatto" (Tate, *Domestic Allegories* 147) and to read the mulatto as a narrative strategy (e.g., Barbara Christian, Hazel V. Carby, and Ann duCille).

Scholars have also paid great attention to covert practices of literary revision, to what Henry Louis Gates Jr. calls "signifying" strategies of appropriation and subversion of established literary conventions and genres. This critical framework has made it possible to recover the semantic complexity and stratification of pre–Harlem Renaissance African American literature. At the same time, however, the fact that "*signifyin(g)* . . . has emerged as 'the' theory of African-American literature" (Mason, "African-American Anthology" 194) and as the best known interpretive tool for appreciating the African Americanness of African American literature can end up acquiring a double valence. The celebration of covert, coded literary practices of opposition and resistance places the greatest emphasis on the difficulties encountered by African American authors and on their need to negotiate with white audiences. These strong overtones of necessity run the risk of reducing our appreciation for the courageous choices and often extravagant modes of literary rebellion articulated by pre–Harlem Renaissance African American writers.[3] William Wells Brown, Frank J. Webb, Frances E. W. Harper, Pauline E. Hopkins, Sutton E. Griggs, Charles W. Chesnutt, James Weldon Johnson, and the other writers I discuss in this volume were addressing not only a white but also a black audience,[4] and their defiance of dominant literary paradigms often exceeded the boundaries of the necessary, counterpropagandistic, and ultimately defensive revision of stereotypes. They moved into the extravagant, aggressive territories of irony, sarcasm, and parody.

These eruptions into extravagance in pre–Harlem Renaissance African American fiction were systematic, deliberate, and often overt. The loose structure of these novels, the strategic bilingualism whereby characters shift from standard English into the black vernacular as needed, the many metanarrative statements that point directly to the double-voicedness of texts (literary and otherwise), the use of multiple endings, the pervasive presence of black tricksters and a large chorus of visibly black characters who surround and guide the passer are some of the extravagant and distinctive literary strategies discussed in this book.

Building on the important work of recovery and reinterpretation of nineteenth-century fiction that has already been done by such critics as Frances Smith Foster, Barbara Christian, Claudia Tate, Hortense Spillers, William Andrews, Hazel Carby, Henry Louis Gates Jr., Ann duCille, and Deborah McDowell, in *Passing and the Rise of the African American Novel* I argue the distinctiveness of the poetics of passing in pre–Harlem Renaissance fiction, demonstrating its centrality to the rise and development of the African American novelistic tradition. I also highlight how the uses of this trope changed dramatically during the Harlem Renaissance. Although much critical attention has been devoted to tracing the continuities between pre– and post–Harlem Renaissance uses of passing, I argue that such continuities are indirect and mostly to be found in the New Negro novelist's parody of Old Negro fictions. In the absence of an appreciation for this iconoclastic, parodic rejection of previous novels, the comparative study of pre– and post–Harlem Renaissance representations of passing can only continue to lead to the familiar disparagement of the early works.

In early African American fiction, the passer (i.e., a mulatto or mulatta so light skinned as to be able to pass for white) gave literary immediacy and visibility to several crucial issues: the cruelty and immorality of slavery, the hypocrisy of dehumanizing blacks while forcibly consorting with them sexually, and the potential crossing over of racial distinctions and hierarchies supposed to be natural and therefore immutable. The passer, whose body is marked by whiteness and disguises a mixed genealogy, enabled early African American writers to question whiteness as "unmarked category" (Haraway 188), as the invisible standard to racialize others. By capitalizing on the contrast between the brilliant career open to the white-looking passer and the less glamorous conditions of the multiplicity of visibly black characters who as a rule populate these novels, pre–Harlem Renaissance African American writers advanced a pointed and pioneering critique of the "possessive investment in whiteness" (Lipsitz 371).

At the same time, because in early African American fiction many all-but-white characters eventually choose their mothers' race and, so to speak, pass for blacks, the trope of passing provided African American novelists with a means to pioneer a counterhegemonic discussion of blackness as a historically and ideologically changing construct. The passer embodies the reality of cultural difference by containing racial dichotomies: Although his or her liminality is contingent on the existence of recognizably distinct groups, it also turns what was conceived of as a natural opposition into a societal one. In pre–Harlem Renaissance African American fiction the representation of the passer's peculiar status is aimed at drawing attention to the fixity and constrictiveness of the racialized black and white subject positions between which he or she has to choose rather than to the fluidity of personal identity or the pleasures of "experiment[ing] with multiple subject positions" (Ginsberg 16).

The awareness that personal identities are constructed was the starting point of the passer's adventures, not the end result. Early African American novelists used such awareness most obviously to explode white delusions of the naturalness and legibility of race, but they also moved on to a deeper and more complex discussion of "the 'praxis' of identities" (Wald 372) in the making of black culture that was unprecedented in fiction. They celebrated what enslaved and segregated African Americans had been able to construct out of the societally imposed, oppressive confines of their racialized identities. In the hands of early African American authors traditional representations of blackness as a mark of inferiority were transformed and transfigured through the celebratory description of the distinctive history, culture, traditions, and worldview that African Americans had fashioned in the past and continued to fashion in the present. They represented blackness as a consciousness, as well as a condition, more than seventy years before Alain Locke used those terms to hail the New Negro (Locke 7). The novels I discuss in this volume reveal the underestimation from which pre–Harlem Renaissance fiction continues to suffer and the unexpected and unsettling richness of signification that opens up when we stop reading early African American authors through the "hard, distorting glass" (Ellison, *Invisible Man* 3) of their supposed literary inability and approach them with greater critical attention and "respect" (Foster, Introduction xxiv).

1. The Mark Without: Subversive Mulattas and Mulattos in the Fiction of William Wells Brown and Frank J. Webb

William Wells Brown

> And men with a white skin, enjoying all the rights and immunities that their country can give, can scarcely find words with which to denounce this much injured man, who, in fact, had no country as far as they could deprive him of it. . . . He who feels like blaming the negro for calling the Americans tyrants, let him first put himself in the negro's stead. Let him ask himself what would be his own thoughts and feelings were he quitting a land that had made him a slave, before he condemns too harshly the whip-scarred fugitive. (Brown, *Miralda*, February 23, 1861, 1)

William Wells Brown's wife, Annie G. Brown, "so much admired the character of Clotelle as to name [their] daughter after the heroine." The author himself notes the fact in the dedication of the 1867 edition of his novel, underscoring at once the literary effectiveness, inspirational value, and personal significance of his fictional endeavors.

When the first edition of the earliest known African American novel, *Clotel; or, The President's Daughter: A Narrative of Slave Life in the United States,* came out in London in 1853, its author, the ex-slave William Wells Brown, had already become well known both in the United States and in Europe as an antislavery orator. His successful *Narrative of William Wells Brown, a Fugitive Slave* had been issued in 1847 and had gone through several editions, and his travelogue *Three Years in Europe; or, Places I Have Seen and People I Have Met,* the first to be written by a black American, had just been published (1852) and would be well received.[1]

Brown's pioneering status as an experienced prose writer in different genres substantiates the hypothesis that his focus on "white slaves" was a strategic literary choice, rather than solely a symptom of a "psychology of imitation and implied inferiority" (Locke 4), a clue to his "unconscious desire to be white" (Bone 4) and "unabashed allegiance to Anglo-Saxon lineage" (Campbell, *Mythic* 3), or an aberration in the career of an otherwise militant spokesperson for black rights (Gayle, *Black Aesthetic* 386). Although this premise of literary intentionality does not obviate a critical evaluation of Brown's artistic choices, it does open up new vistas on the complexity both of his fictional endeavors and of the process of interpreting them.

In the three book-form editions of *Clotel* (1853, 1864, 1867), Brown's attention is divided and differently partitioned between two competing plots. The first revolves around individual female slaves whose bodies are marked by whiteness. Their very existence constitutes a challenge to rigid racial definitions, and their ability to pass for white represents a genteel form of covert resistance to racial oppression. With some variations in the three editions, this plot follows the adventures of a slave mother who is separated from her daughter. Both pass for white at different times and for different purposes: The mother makes an unsuccessful attempt to rescue her child from slavery, and years later the enslaved daughter succeeds in escaping to Europe.

The second, more original plot centers instead on the slave community and incorporates a wide variety of historical information, anecdotes, folklore, newspaper accounts, and advertisements to document the multiformed life of the slaves and their many diverse, more markedly confrontational forms of communal resistance to slavery. The protagonists of this second plot are most often male and visibly black. The slave women who cannot pass are also subsumed within this community, though without adequate representation: The dichotomy between genteel and confrontational resistance leads Brown to eschew the depiction of active female trickery, a concept extraneous to dominant contemporary ideologies of "true womanhood" as well (Welter 152). The differences between the two plots are also stylistic: The story of the passers is cast within the popular and melodramatic conventions of the sentimental romance, whereas the male communal plot is characterized by "sensationalistic realism" (Andrews, "The 1850s" 47).

The respective relevance of these two narrative modes, as well as of the plots with which they are connected, changes in the various editions of *Clotel*, as Brown makes increasing efforts to contain within more conventional narrative bounds the thematic and formal disruptiveness of his radical interpretation of slave culture. He unifies the action of the novel and diminishes its sketchiness, focusing on his all-but-white protagonists and giving increasing centrality to his revisions of a sentimental plot with which white

American audiences were both familiar and comfortable. Analogously, the significance of *Clotel* in the making of African American fiction changes over time: In the first version, Brown accomplishes the transition from autobiographical to fictional authorship in ways that attest to the conscious artistry that characterizes the African American novelistic tradition since its inception; by the last, Brown's novel emerges as an antecedent of the literary strategies and concerns of post-Reconstruction fiction.

*   *   *

The relationship between autobiographical and fictional authorship that William Andrews discusses with regard to the "novelization" (*To Tell* 272) of slave narratives can also be investigated from the vantage point of Brown's text.[2] The three book-form editions of *Clotel* reveal not only Brown's unfolding assessment of the changes in the condition of African Americans during the momentous decades of the 1850s and 1860s[3] but also the author's attempt to tame the novel's proliferation of characters and events and to accommodate the open-ended real-life "melodrama endemic to American racism" (B. Jackson 337) within the generic boundaries of the sentimental romance.

Despite the higher visibility of the passing plot, the author's most radical and most substantial denunciation of slavery rests on the accretion of mostly male folk characters and stories over which he initially does not impose any fictional order or sense of progression. Brown obliges the reader to experience the incoherence and displacement that he sees as central to slave life. Though never completely edited out of his extensive revisions of the novel, this narrative strategy, which has gained *Clotel* a reputation for "fragmentation" (Heermance 177) and "sketchiness" (Farrison 230), is increasingly tamed and subordinated to the more straightforward movement of the sentimental plot. In the second and third editions, the stronger emphasis on the adventures of the title heroine increases the visibility of the theme of passing. This fact has often been interpreted as a symptom of Brown's greater familiarity with the art of fiction, but it could also be reread as a result of Brown's familiarity with the prejudices of his white American audiences, a familiarity that leads him to deflect attention away from his innovative and frankly oppositional representation of the wealth of communal facts of slave life included in the British edition.

The tensions between the two plots, between melodrama as a theme and as a narrative mode, between the author's desire to portray the life of the slave community and the need to structure the fictional text around the evolution of an individual fate, explain the uneven tone of the novel, which wavers between realism and romance, between a detailed portrayal of slave life and the contrived reunions of long-lost lovers and relatives. These tensions also explain the almost exclusive choice of women as passers. In *Clotel*, Brown presents passing as a genteel, albeit unheroic form of covert resistance that enables female protagonists whose bodies are marked by whiteness to remain traditionally "fragile and well-bred" (Christian, *Black Women* 22). Passing also gives them a strategy to assert their identity in ways that, to paraphrase critic Eva Saks (68), are discontinuous with their status as property: The enslaved mulatta title heroine, among others, resorts to (temporary) passing in the attempt to secure her "rights" to her progeny, freedom, and mobility. Although the figure of the exceptional, often isolated female passer enables Brown to problematize the racial and cultural rationale for slavery by undermining supposedly biological notions of race and appropriating Western notions of beauty and chastity for some of his enslaved characters, passing remains only one (emblematic, more than representative) form of slave trickery and defiance. The slave community (overwhelmingly connoted as masculine) engages in more heroic, because more confrontational, acts of resistance to enslavement: cunning escapes, songs of rebellion, theft, and revolts.

Examining Brown's representation of resistance as gendered makes it possible to reconcile his use of the octoroon as a "narrative device of mediation" (Carby, *Reconstructing* 89) with the often underestimated militancy of his novel. Brown's recipe for manly resistance is grounded in and masked by the portrayal of passing as an unheroic, mostly feminine way to escape, rather than to defy openly, the brutality of slave life. In its first version, the sentimental female plot of *Clotel* is as deceiving as the fabulistic frame of African American folk animal stories. On one hand, the mulatta qualifies as a device of mediation both for her mixed genealogy and her gender: As a "white Negro," she appropriates the qualities of ideal white womanhood and complements them with loyalty, understanding, and support for individual black men. On the other, his male heroes loom in the background as powerful, cunning, and potentially violent freedom fighters: Nat Turner is openly praised in the novel, and other male characters share in varying degrees his manly anger at injustice and his power of defiance.

Evidently conscious that his choice of all-but-white protagonists might (as it did) lead to misinterpretation, Brown makes clear in the novel that his narrative choices do not stem from and are not intended to endorse intraracial color prejudice. He explicitly and repeatedly thematizes the issue of prejudice within the black community, presenting it as a sign of ignorance or a desire for social advancement but ultimately as "the result of the prejudice that exists on the part of the whites towards both mulattoes and blacks" (*Clotel* 130).[4] Through the opposition of whites to both mulattos and blacks, Brown reunites the community on a fictional level and transforms intraracial color prejudice from a divisive issue into a critique of white values. It is significant that Brown, probably unwilling to reduce race to a state of mind, does not erase all somatic markers of blackness from the bodies of his female passers. In Mary's case, for instance, the "iris of her large dark eye had the melting mezzotinto, which remains the last vestige of African ancestry" (84), a description used in many other African American novels before the Harlem Renaissance as a way to reconnect the passers with the visibly black community whose boundaries they skirt and delimit. However, these racial signifiers remain so ambiguous that they do not undermine Brown's representation of race as a sociocultural construct. Rather, in *Clotel* the somatic indecipherability of the "white Negro's" blackness is on a continuum with the initially indecipherable ethnicity of the German woman who was kidnapped into slavery (145–48) or the whiteness of congressperson Thomas Corwin, "one of the blackest white men in the United States" (178), who happens to be mistaken for black.

The first edition of *Clotel; or, The President's Daughter* was published in 1853 in England, where the author was spending a forced exile caused by the Fugitive Slave Law (1850) that threatened to send him back to slavery should he return to the United States. Catering very outspokenly to the "British Christians" (*Clotel* 245) whose abolitionist sympathies he hoped would be "publicly manifested" through recommended boycotts of American slaveholders (*Clotel* 246), Brown articulated a scathingly sarcastic, comprehensive critique of slavery in the American South, race prejudice in the American North, and religious hypocrisy in the American nation as a whole.

Structurally, the volume that contains *Clotel* frames it as an obvious transition from autobiography to fiction. The novel itself is preceded by a shorter, revised version of the author's *Narrative of William Wells Brown, a Fugitive Slave* (1847), retitled *Narrative of the Life and Escape of William Wells Brown* (1853). Critic Robert Stepto's discussion of this procedure as "a successful rhetorical device authenticating his [Brown's] *access* to the incidents, characters, scenes, and tales which collectively make up *Clotel*" (*From Behind the Veil* 30) effectively argues Brown's distrust of his audience and consciousness of his pioneering role as the first African American author to move openly into the realm of prose fiction. To assert his right of access to fictional authorship, in the 1853 *Narrative* Brown chooses to function as "the editor of his résumé" (Stepto, *From Behind the Veil* 29) by quoting from his own travelogue, abolitionist speeches, and previous *Narrative*. With this decision, however, Brown does not leave his text "bereft of authorship," as Stepto supposes (28). On the contrary, he affirms his own accomplishments as a writer. He treats his own previously published works as primary sources, signaled on a formal level by his shifts from a third-person authorial voice to the first person of the passages he quotes. In the process, he authenticates his ability to elaborate on his personal experiences (instead of simply recounting them) and seizes the authority to make use of an extravagant variety of nonliterary sources to create a "story" (Brown, *Clotel* 245).

In the 1853 edition, this studied debut into fictional authorship does not completely eliminate a "lingering preoccupation with documenting the facts" (Andrews, "The 1850s" 43) that is more pronounced and qualitatively different from conventional nineteenth-century declarations that novels were true to life. In *Clotel*, Brown emerges as both editor and creator of fiction. He selects and compiles stories of American slavery that in keeping with his fictional rather than autobiographical intent he declares to have derived not only from his own experiences but also from such secondary sources as American abolitionist journals, tales from "the lips" of runaways, and other authors' fictional texts (245). The result of this second editorial effort is not only the substantiation of the author's claim that "the various incidents and scenes . . . [are] founded in truth" (*Clotel* 245). Rather, Brown's goal is to insert *Clotel* within a literary tradition of representations of blackness and to give fictional life to a multiplicity of slave voices and experiences often unrelated to the all-but-white title heroine.

Initially Brown does not impose any developmental narrative frame on this material, a fact that, as J. Noel Heermance notes with dismay, continually misleads the reader, who is never given "any idea [of] what characters will or won't be developed" (181). I approach the oft-noted sketchiness that results from this narrative mode not exclusively as an instance of artistic ineptitude (Heermance 181; Andrews, "The 1850s" 45–46) but as a deliberate strategy that succeeds (if we are to judge by the reactions of critics) in making the reader experience the powerlessness, the uncertainty, the absurdities that characterize slave life and are epitomized and thematized both in the "To-Day a Mistress, To-Morrow a Slave" (*Clotel* 149) pattern that governs Brown's sentimental passing plot and in the rebelliousness of his male slaves.[5]

The deliberateness with which Brown advances a realistic, confrontational portrayal of the black community that contaminates and unsettles the more conventional plot of passing can be gauged by examining how the ancillary *Narrative of the Life and Escape* functions to safeguard the seemingly unthreatening sentimentality of his subsequent tale. As Stepto notices, the "personal voice and hardboiled prose" of Brown's 1847 *Narrative* turns into "flat" (*From Behind the Veil* 28) writing in the 1853 version. This change occurs for purposes of validation and authentication but also to disguise Brown's own consummate trickery and to ensure for himself the possibility of double-talk.

The trickery and cunning that characterized Brown's self-presentation in 1847 disappear in the 1853 *Narrative* only to reemerge in the male subplot of his novel, sugarcoated by the romantic, more conventionally moral adventures of his mulatta heroines. In other words, the *Narrative of the Life and Escape* neutralizes the disruptiveness of Brown's authorial persona to mediate the shift from the 1847 defiant autobiographical description of proud acts of slave resistance to the insertion of male defiance within the ostensibly unthreatening, feminine confines of the sentimental novel.

Intertwined but not smoothly integrated with Brown's communal portrayal of slave life is the tale that follows the individual trials and peregrinations of Thomas Jefferson's mulatta offsprings. These characters are sensationalistically emblematic but hardly representative of the community of slaves that populate his novel. In the very first chapter of *Clotel*, Brown explains the choice of all-but-white protagonists by noticing "the fearful increase of half whites" (59) in the Southern states, and he epitomizes the immorality of slavery in the illegality of slave marriages.[6] His acknowledged purpose is "to prepare the reader for the following narrative of slave life" (62) that focuses on the atypical but allegorical and paradigmatic lives and adventures of characters who can pass.

Cognizant of the appeal that "white slaves" had for a white abolitionist audience and concerned with his heroines' gentility and high moral standards, Brown casts their story in the sentimental patterns of female virtue, distress, marriage, or death. In connection with the female passers, trickery as a form of resistance is never glorified for its own sake, even when the author makes clear that deceitfulness would be justified by the immorality of slavery. In contrast with the imaginative trickery of his fictional male characters, Brown's heroines are monotonously engaged in the same strategy of escape from slavery: passing, which relies on physical appearance more than on cunning, on silence more than on verbal skills. Passing proves consistent with feminine ideals of passivity and gentility, and Brown rationalizes the amount of deceit it involves as a minor evil that foils more serious threats to the heroines' fundamental female attributes: chastity or motherhood.

The close connection between passing and traditional notions of true womanhood emerges clearly from the different fates that befall the novel's central passers, Clotel and her daughter Mary. The story of Clotel's flight is based on renowned real-life episodes such as the escape of William and Ellen Craft.[7] It also draws on and radically modifies Harriet Beecher Stowe's best-selling description of Eliza's escape to Canada in *Uncle Tom's Cabin* (1852).[8] In both novels passing secures freedom, but whereas Eliza passes defensively and to emigrate abroad (a decision harmonious with Stowe's procolonization policy), Clotel, once free, continues to disguise and returns to the South in search of her daughter. Clotel's courageous and independent attempt to save Mary eventually fails, and her ensuing public suicide elevates her individual defeat into an exemplum of the evils of slavery. The final powerlessness that makes Clotel choose to plunge into the Potomac rather than return into bondage becomes a more effective abolitionist statement than her living trickery.[9] Her heroism emerges as quintessentially feminine both because it is motivated by motherly self-sacrifice and because it is ineffectual.

The reader familiar with nineteenth-century literary prescriptions of female purity also sees in her death the traditional fate of the seduced woman: However well-meaning and noble-minded Clotel agreed to live with Horatio out of wedlock (84). The poetic justice of seduction novels and Brown's interest in condemning the sexual exploitation of slave women coalesce in requiring the death of the heroine who has been victimized, but also tarnished, by an immoral system larger than herself. Despite his condemnation of white Southern male immorality, Brown does not challenge contemporary prescriptions regarding the sexual behavior of women nearly as radically as Harriet Jacobs, for example. On the contrary, the effectiveness of his passing heroines as tools for antislavery propaganda relies on conventional moral standards.

Mary's escape is less ingenious and more successful than her mother's. Mary's career as a passer starts when she trades places with her jailed fiancé, George, who has been sentenced to death for participating in a bloody slave revolt (227). Her act of self-sacrifice situates her on the same plane as the heroic George, but in a separate sphere: He performs brave deeds, and she supports his activities. Mary's womanly brand of heroism initially worsens her fate, as she is for the first time sold on the auction block, but eventually leads to her freedom. With one of the dramatic reversals of fortune intrinsic to the workings of romantic poetic justice, on the auction block she inspires the love of a Frenchman who is struck by her resemblance to his dead sister and proclaims his determination to marry her if she elopes with him to Europe. Mary shows much more diffidence toward the young Frenchman than Clotel ever did with Horatio and also manages to preserve her chastity, thus qualifying for survival as a legitimate sentimental and abolitionist heroine.[10] Mary recognizes in the Frenchman's offer the danger of a de facto seduction analogous to her mother's, but she also evaluates the presence of a crucial variable because the relocation in Europe makes marriage a legal possibility. Compounding a brilliant stroke of abolitionist propaganda with a critique of American democratic ideals that flattered British liberals, Brown presents exile as Mary's only option to secure freedom and safeguard her chastity.

In the context of nineteenth-century abolitionist fiction, Brown's portrayal of female morality and self-sacrifice proves far less conventional than it may at first seem to a twenty-first-century reader. Brown's revisions of Lydia Maria Child's "The Quadroons" (1842), a short story that highly influenced the plot and language of his novel (Farrison 249–50; Karcher 72),[11] make *Clotel* a radical departure from the tragic mulatta stereotype. Although both authors share an abolitionist intent, and Brown patterns the central mother-daughter relationship on Child's, the destiny of Rosalie and Xarifa, Child's all-but-white counterparts for Clotel and Mary, is remarkably different from that of Brown's protagonists. Abandoned by her "handsome and wealthy . . . Georgian" lover (Child 62), Rosalie wanes in the privacy of her home (70), never attempting to leave the South or creating any public disturbance comparable to Clotel's effort to rescue her daughter. Xarifa is a similarly defenseless, pathetic, and utterly tragic figure. Reduced to slavery and purchased by a "wealthy profligate" (74), she sees her British lover shot to death in the attempt to rescue her and subsequently falls victim to her owner's sexual advances. "In a few months," the author quickly concludes, "poor Xarifa was a raving maniac. That pure temple was desecrated, that loving heart was broken; and that beautiful head fractured against the wall in a frenzy of despair" (76).[12]

Whereas in her abolitionist plea Child capitalizes on utter female defenselessness to condemn those corrupt individuals who have absolute power over a "docile and injured race" (63), Brown expands Child's focus on individual immorality into a direct denunciation of the institutionalized sexual abuse of slave women. In the very first lines of the novel, Brown describes miscegenation as a widespread phenomenon in the South (*Clotel* 59) and capitalizes on popular rumors by attributing the illegitimate paternity of his title heroine to Thomas Jefferson (64).[13] He rewrites Child's tragic mulattas as subversive passers, empowering the offsprings of the sexual violation of black women to become an active menace to the perpetrators of such violence. The female passer emerges as a societal saboteuse because she constitutes a threat both to white property and to the whiteness that legitimizes the ownership of human chattel. Her mixed ancestry calls into question and racializes the very whiteness that marks her body, fragmenting race into a series of somatic and sociocultural signifiers that, though misleading and unreliable, have enormous consequences for "the entire social condition of man" (*Clotel* 62).

Brown takes his all-but-white title heroine out of the privatized space of her "beautiful cottage . . . almost hidden among the trees" (*Clotel* 83) and into the public realm. Even her eventual suicide, which occurs in view of the Capitol, takes on a clearly political and communal significance. The "unvarnished narrative" (210) of Clotel's trials and tribulations may be atypical, but it is emblematic nevertheless. As Brown hastens to clarify, it "tells not only its own story of grief, but speaks of a thousand wrongs and woes beside which never see the light" (210). Unlike Child's, Brown's abolitionist strategy combines emotional appeal with a vision (however genteel) of female resistance and an emphasis (however wishful) on the importance of survival. Although Mary's escape remains singularly successful, even the utter tragedy of her cousin Jane (a secondary character more directly patterned on Child's Xarifa) is described with a concern for her fictional integrity in that she dies before being sexually violated (210). Admittedly, the fate of Brown's characters is as contrived as Child's, but it reveals his reluctance to advance the abolitionist cause at the expense of his female characters.

In *Clotel*, the disruptive potential of passing is foregrounded in still another way. Clotel is aided in her escape by William, "a tall, full-bodied Negro, whose very countenance beamed with intelligence" (171). He pretends to be her servant, does all the talking for her (because her voice could lead to detection), and ends up gaining his freedom when they reach the North. To avoid recognition and also because her escape mate is a dark man, Clotel passes for white and dresses like a man, a double disguise that is replete with irony.[14] On one hand, the idea of disguising as a man originates in her mistress's invidious scheme to turn Clotel into a recognizable slave by cutting off her long hair and making it "as short as any of the full-blooded Negroes in the dwelling" (150). On the other, the need for male attire points to the limited mobility of white women. It implies a sarcastic commentary on the South's paranoid preoccupation with the purity of white womanhood, which complements and sharpens Brown's explicit condemnation of the sexual exploitation of black women that motivated Clotel's decision to escape in the first place.[15]

Brown's attack on the myth of racial purity embodied in the sexual purity of the Southern lady reaches a climax when Clotel returns to the South in search of her daughter. Then, the full disruptiveness of passing and Brown's ironic focus on white misreadings of outward appearances emerge by connection with same-sex attraction. During the stagecoach ride to Richmond, Clotel travels with an older gentleman and his marriageable daughters: "Clotel and they had not only given their opinions as regarded the merits of the discussion, but that sly glance of the eye, which is ever given where the young of both sexes meet, had been freely at work. The American ladies are rather partial to foreigners, and Clotel had the appearance of a fine Italian" (204). In a bold reversal, Brown strikes a blow against slavery by portraying the utter chaos it engenders and the far from clearly defined or decipherable racial and sexual categories on which it is based.

Although passing remains mostly a female prerogative in *Clotel,* and male characters are defined by their oppositional stance, George, who is Mary's lover and looks as white as she, represents the point of contact between the two groups and their respective plots.[16] Like Clotel, he cross-dresses to escape from prison. Wearing Mary's clothes, he has to walk "but a short distance before he felt that a change of his apparel would facilitate his progress" (228). He can afford to do so only when he reaches the free state of Ohio, and his prolonged cross-dressing adds a grotesque twist to the runaway's adventures. Brown confirms his evaluation of passing as unheroic and models George's escape to Canada after the more rugged and heroic pattern of other famous slave fugitives. Like Brown himself (*Narrative* 217), George finds his way to Canada "hiding in the woods during the day, and travelling by the guidance of the North Star at night" (*Clotel* 228). As a participant in a bloody slave revolt and as the "heroic young slave" (225) who risks his life to save valuable deeds belonging to the same city that has sentenced him to death, George provides a fair example of the kinds of confrontational male resistance commended in the novel.[17]

In marked opposition to the innocent sensibility and the genteel individualism of his female passers, Brown's male heroes, many of whom are extolled for being full-blooded or visibly black, engage in violence, act in concert with the slave community, and exhibit a variety of rebellious behaviors that defy and ridicule the power of the slaveholders. The examples of male resistance Brown compiles in *Clotel* are so numerous as to justify impressions of the novel's sketchiness and so explicit as to foreground the novelty, extravagance, and oppositional force of the text. Only twenty-two years after Nat Turner's insurrection (1831), Brown celebrates him as "a full-blooded Negro, who had been born and brought up a slave" and was "distinguished for his eloquence, respected by the whites, and loved and venerated by the Negroes" (213). Turner's example of violent resistance against the outrages of slavery is preceded and followed by the actions of other characters, including Picquilo and George (213–14) and a nameless "Negro man" (109) who stabs the master for having flogged his wife. The description of their deeds notably is not accompanied by condemnations of the un-Christianity of retributive justice. On the contrary, George compounds his participation in a revolt with an eloquent defense of the slaves' right to rebel, which rests on a comparison between the American Revolutionary War and slave insurrections. Concomitantly, Brown reveals and celebrates more covert strategies of resistance that originate in the slaves' knowledge of the peculiar institution. By feigning to be on business for his master, a male slave succeeds in leaving the South with one of his owner's pigs (169); two others attempt to gain their freedom by acting as captured runaway and slave catcher (169). Regardless of the actual percentage of slaves who engaged successfully in such ingenious escapes, Brown's portrayal of these incidents elevates them to the status of exempla, of emblematic instances of slave discontent, intelligence, and love of freedom.

An even more radical affirmation of slave agency, which functions as an important hermeneutic clue to the subversive subtext of the novel and of slave culture as a whole, lies in Brown's revelation of the "unguarded expressions of the feelings of the Negroes" (156), especially of slaves who seem to have fully internalized the value system of their owners and processed it into loyalty. Sam, a self-important house slave of the parson who has bought Clotel's mother, initially is presented as a dialect-speaking, comical folk figure. He rises above his stereotypical status as contented slave after his master's funeral, when he leads other slaves in a song that rejoices at the death of one more slave owner. The first stanza from his song clarifies the slaves' discontent and their awareness of oppression:

> Come, all my brethren, let us take a rest,
>   While the moon shines so brightly and clear;
> Old master is dead, and left us at last,
>   And has gone at the Bar to appear.
> Old master has died, and lying in his grave,
>   And our blood will awhile cease to flow;
> He will no more trample on the neck of the slave;
>   For he's gone where the slaveholders go. (154)

The revisionary depth of Brown's portrayal of Sam emerges also from the author's play with conventional uses of language in the representation of blackness. Sam's song is in standard English, but the response of the slave audience is in dialect: "Dats de song for me" (154). On one hand, Brown may have wanted to prevent superficially quaint readings of his folk song by "translating" it to clarify the seriousness of its revolutionary import to a British audience used to the conventionally high-sounding language of heroic characters. On the other, this seeming inconsistency in Sam's linguistic practices complicates the interpretation of the use of dialect in antebellum African American fiction. Brown does not use dialect solely to distinguish between main and secondary characters but more positively as a linguistic signifier of cultural belonging to the black community and access to its ethos of resistance. In the case of dark-skinned William, for instance, it is the slave himself who deliberately mimics stereotypical linguistic representations of blacks. During his escape, where he performs as the loyal servant of Clotel (who is cross-dressing as white Mr. Johnson), William speaks dialect (172–73), but after reaching the free states he resists discrimination on a train by master-ing standard English (176–78). The powerful strategic bilingualism Brown bestows on some of his folk characters defies the cultural hierarchy implicit in the opposition between black dialect and white standard English and be-comes emblematic of the depth and self-awareness of the black community. From this vantage point, the fact that the female protagonists Clotel and Mary conform to contemporary standards of fictional decorum and speak only in standard English does not elevate them to role models of bourgeois achieve-ment but rather confirms that they skirt the male circle of tricksters.

Because of his attention to the many different contexts and levels at which slave resistance occurs, Brown is able to portray it as (partly) successful and as an instrument of group survival. In this sense, the representation of slave agency in *Clotel* differs in important ways from another text of the 1850s that deals with oppression and revolt: Herman Melville's *Benito Cereno* (1855).[18] Whether we interpret Babo as "everything untamed and demoniac" (Browne 183), as "the most heroic character in Melville's fiction" (James 119), as "monomaniacal" (McCarthy 104), or as "a brilliant trickster" (R. Levine 218), Melville's depic-tion of Babo's manipulation of Captain Delano's delusions of slave content-edness and loyalty is comparable to Brown's celebration of covert slave resis-tance. In *Benito Cereno,* however, the covert rebelliousness that escapes Captain Delano is so completely intertwined with the preceding violent mutiny that the eventual discovery and failure of the latter spells the same fate for the former, as Delano temporarily opens his eyes to the reality behind black servility and faithfulness. Even after the ship has been retaken, however, all is not secure for the whites. The unmanageable immorality of slavery remains unscathed, and the power of blackness survives the death of the mutineers. Don Benito is con-sumed and eventually killed by the "shadow" that "the negro" (Melville, *Be-nito Cereno* 116) has cast upon him, and Captain Delano's only safety is in a retreat within the safe confines of an American "innocence" that proclaims the past to be over (Sundquist, "*Benito Cereno*" 93), insists on Don Benito being saved, and extols the usefulness of forgetting. Black courage results in utter tragedy and group extinction, and white domination eventually is restored. Slavery emerges as a practically manageable institution, a fact that confirms its moral bankruptcy but does not lead Melville to fictionally endorse any aboli-tionist course of action.[19]

In *Clotel,* on the contrary, overt and covert rebellion are not exclusively interdependent, and the admitted failure of Turner's revolt and George's rebellion do not spell the utter defeat of black resistance. Turner's defiant spirit survives and is carried on in the everyday acts of subversion and dis-obedience detailed in the novel. Brown emphasizes resilience and community survival while stressing the unmanageability of slavery on both a moral and a practical level: If rebellions and covert resistance threaten the domination of the slaveholders, passing blurs the most basic racial criteria to distinguish the free from the enslaved. The arbitrariness of caste boundaries in Brown's fictional South contrasts sharply with the isolated and clearly demarcated microcosm of the "San Dominick."[20]

The glimpse of "the acute degree to which some slaves realized they were being exploited" (Stuckey, "Through the Prism" 431), an insight into slave life that historians still debated more than a century later, is compounded by the radicalness of Brown's vision of true Christian humanitarianism. He echoes but sharply revises Stowe's presentation of Little Eva in *Uncle Tom's Cabin*. Sam's aforementioned rebellious lyrics are overheard and fully understood by the defunct slaveholding parson's daughter, Georgiana. A delicate white Southern lady, Georgiana has "been much benefitted by a residence of five years at the North" (94), and her understanding of the slaves' point of view anticipates the character of Camilla in Frances Harper's *Minnie's Sacrifice* (1869). Defined as "the Young Christian" (*Clotel* 118), as Eva was called "the Little Evangelist" (*Uncle Tom's Cabin* 405), Georgiana not only realizes the contradiction between Christianity and slavery but also understands the "lesson" (*Clotel* 156) of her slaves' unguarded expressions. She sympathizes with their longing for freedom and, when she inherits the property and has the power, becomes instrumental to its realization.

Brown's revisions of Stowe's Little Eva aim to create a character who can act on her egalitarian convictions. In the first place, Georgiana is older than Eva. Even so, after inheriting her father's estate, she, as a single eighteen-year-old woman, does not have complete control over her own property. As in the case of the female passer, racial and sexual politics intersect: To seize the power to realize "her most sanguine wishes" (189) and free her slaves, Georgiana deliberately defies gender roles. She overcomes "woman's timid nature" (162) and proposes to the Northern man she loves and has converted to Christianity and abolitionism. Once married, Georgiana enforces a plan of "gradual emancipation" (165), creating a utopian postslavery environment wherein the soon-to-be-freed slaves take their place in a wage labor economy.

Constructing "the Liberator" (161) as a true sentimental heroine, Brown portrays Georgiana as "tall and graceful" (94), loving and deferential, morally superior, and delicate in health. Her untimely death is as pathetic as Little Eva's, but the parallels with Stowe's novel are otherwise only superficial. Whereas Little Eva's sickbed suggestion to "have all slaves made free" (*Uncle Tom's Cabin* 403) quickly shrinks into a more contained plea that "Tom shall have his freedom" (404) and eventually ends in nothing as a result of her father's enervation, Brown keeps Georgiana alive long enough to prove her practical commitment to her antislavery feelings. Doomed to die, characteristically, of consumption, she resolves on the "immediate liberation" (*Clotel* 189) of her slaves and organizes their removal to the North, resisting suggestions for their emigration abroad. Like Eva, the "pale, feeble, emaciated" Georgiana eventually is depicted as "surrounded by the sons and daughters of Africa" (*Clotel* 190), but in her case their grief has a solid base that prevents suspicions of servile docility.[21] Although these evident and significant differences between the two heroines do not undermine their shared status as transparent spokespersons for their authors' ideologies, they do illuminate the dramatically different degrees of agency and self-awareness the two writers bestow on their fictional slaves.

Lost between the genteel female passer and the predominantly male representatives of the slave community is the female slave who cannot pass. She is implicitly subsumed within the plight of the enslaved female passer and the culture of resistance of the black male community without being adequately represented in either. She makes her brief appearance to criticize the religious hypocrisy of "dees white fokes" (103), to blush at Sam's flirtation (132), to voice her jealousy for the title heroine's beauty (150), or to serve as devoted mother in a vision of postslavery harmony (193), but she never gains center stage. Her marginality attests to the inadequacy of the paradigms of true white womanhood and black male resistance to describe her situation. On one hand, Brown proves unable to reconcile confrontational resistance with his fictional ideal of femininity: The verbal skills Harriet Jacobs opposes to Dr. Flint's abuse are nowhere to be found in *Clotel,* for instance. On the other, Brown seems reluctant to describe in detail the plight of black families during slavery because it would involve dealing with the ultimate limitations of covert action and portraying "the degradation to which black men, through their inability to protect and to provide, were forced" (Foster, "Between" 55). Even in the case of the all-but-white protagonists Mary and George, the lovers' reunion is delayed for ten years. This deferment of the happy ending, which characterizes the novels of post-Reconstruction African American women writers such as Frances Harper and Pauline Hopkins, indicates Brown's determination to defy the complacency of easy solutions to the familial disruption engendered by slavery.

* * *

The extravagant wealth of documentation and the proliferation of episodes and subplots that enriched the British edition of *Clotel* are notably missing from the second book-form edition of Brown's novel, which was published in the United States in 1864 under the title *Clotelle: A Tale of the Southern States*. This difference often is interpreted positively as an indication of Brown's increased artistry and greater attention to narrative form (Heermance 195), but it can be read in other ways also. On one hand, it reveals the difficulties (which the limited success of *Clotel* in England made clear to Brown) of trying to adapt novelistic conventions to the presentation of indigenous, nonstereotypical, nontragic portrayals of African American life. On the other, it demonstrates the self-awareness with which from the beginning black novelists geared their texts to an internally divided black and white American audience with diametrically opposed interests and points of view.

Brown's maneuverings to face these difficulties become unequivocally clear when we compare the second book-form edition of *Clotelle* with the earlier and lesser-known serialized version, which appeared under a completely different title, *Miralda; or, The Beautiful Quadroon: A Romance of American Slavery, Founded on Fact*. *Miralda* was published at the outbreak of the Civil War (from December 1, 1860, to March 16, 1861) in *The Weekly Anglo-African*, the same African American journal that a few months later serialized Martin Delany's *Blake*.[22] As a sign of Brown's increasing fame and his achieved freedom from the need to authenticate his status as author of fiction, *Miralda*, like the two subsequent book-form American editions of *Clotelle*, is not preceded by any autobiographical narrative. Although the first two installments are missing, the text of *Miralda* that is available differs only slightly from the 1864 *Clotelle* in the ways Brown revised the plot and narrative structure of the British edition.[23] However, Brown tried to offset these changes with the greater outspokenness that characterizes his critique of slavery and race prejudice in *Miralda* by comparison with the two subsequent American editions of *Clotelle*. Although he decimates the chorus of secondary black characters, in *Miralda* he retains the sensationalism of an all-but-white protagonist who is "a descendant of Thomas Jefferson" (*Miralda*, January 19, 1861, 1). Also, Brown's use of the trope of passing to dissect race as a sociocultural construct takes a more literal and morbid turn in *Miralda* as he inserts the minor episode of a trial in which a woman is subjected to medical experiments to determine whether she "showed any signs of African descent" (*Miralda*, December 22, 1860, 1).

Addressing the readership of a black weekly that presented on the front page the confrontational motto "Man must be Free!—if not through Law, why then above the Law," in *Miralda* Brown involves his protagonists (both black and white) in long speeches denouncing Southern slavery, religious hypocrisy, the hollowness of American egalitarian ideals, and "that revolting prejudice against the negro which has long characterized the people of the nominally free States" (*Miralda*, February 16, 1861, 1).[24] In keeping with the sentiments expressed in these speeches, Brown does not close *Miralda* on the optimistic note of father-daughter, master–escaped slave reconciliation that characterizes the 1864 *Clotelle*. Rather, in the last lines of *Miralda* Brown apologizes to the audience of *The Weekly Anglo-African* for having "sometimes seemed to favour the slaveholder" (*Miralda*, March 16, 1861, 1) and claims to "have tried to do justice to both master and slave," thereby indirectly affirming the objectivity of his "true tale of American slavery" and his awareness of the unrepresentative but emblematic value of his subversive passers (*Miralda*, March 16, 1861, 1).

Not only are these closing lines eliminated from all subsequent American editions of *Clotelle*, but also the controversial speeches against slavery and race prejudice are dramatically curtailed in the 1864 *Clotelle: A Tale of the Southern States*. While the Civil War was raging, *Clotelle* was reissued in James Redpath's dime novels series of "Books for the Camp Fires." The novel's professed goals of relieving "the monotony of camp life to the soldiers of the Union" and of kindling "their zeal in the cause of universal emancipation" (*Clotelle: A Tale* 104) result in extensive revisions of the original 1853 text. What used to be "A Narrative of Slave Life in the United States" becomes "A Tale of the Southern States." In keeping with the more expressedly fictional and more geographically circumscribed subtitle, Brown preserves the denunciation of the immorality of Southern slaveholders that characterizes *Clotel* but voices his criticism of Northern prejudice more mildly.[25] Also, for the comfort of Union soldiers and of a country at war, he edits out the most documentary evidence of Southern brutality against blacks and whites, emphasizing instead the domestic crises engendered by slavery within Southern white homes and the familial disruption and de facto homelessness characteristic of slave life. More specifically, Brown eliminates Sam's song of discontent together with several other important episodes that share common features: They are only remotely connected with the heroine's story, they reach a level of naturalistic directness that remains undisguised by the superimposed sentimental plot and even in striking contrast with it, and they are dominated by male figures and by death.[26]

As a result of these cuts, which in *Miralda* are substituted with outspoken antislavery speeches, Brown's portrayal of the life of the black folk and his naturalistic depiction of white violence become increasingly subordinated to the sentimental tale that follows the individual trials and peregrinations of his passers. Even in their case, however, Brown quells the sensationalism of the British edition and of *Miralda* by substituting the miscegenous President Jefferson with a senator. The ostensibly more conciliatory thrust of his revisions is both a cause and a result of his greater attention to narrative conventions, which leads him to heighten the importance of the female-dominated sentimental plot and to emphasize the plight of emblematic individual males rather than the multifaceted portrayal of the slave community.

However, the greater importance of his female characters is not complemented by a new conceptualization of their relational role. On the contrary, Brown eliminates some of the most controversial implications of his heroines' passing (e.g., the same-sex attraction Clotel inspired during the stagecoach ride in the 1853 edition) and reduces Georgiana to the conventionally sentimental proportions of a "Virginia Maid" (57). The communal impact that her abolitionist commitment had in the British edition shrinks into ineffective attempts to protect two individuals (Clotelle and Jerome), and her role as "The Liberator" (*Clotel* 161) is implicitly taken over by the Union soldiers to whom the book is addressed. Cognizant of the diminished oppositional import of the 1864 volume, Brown comments on it using one of the hermeneutic clues that enriched the first edition and are less common in the second. He explicitly illustrates the monitory impact of passing for his white readers through a new minor episode inserted in 1864 in which he describes the sensation produced by Lizzie, "the white slave-mother" (*Clotelle: A Tale* 16), aboard a ship that is carrying slaves to the market: "Every one that saw her felt that slavery in the Southern States was not confined to the negro. ... Those who were not opposed to the institution before, now felt that if whites were to become its victims, it was time at least that some security should be thrown around the Anglo-Saxon to save him from this servile and degraded position" (16).

As Brown curtails the episodes of resistance involving a chorus of members of the slave community, he also dramatically reduces the depth of folk figures such as Sam, whose tricksterism and cunning now emerge only in his attending a ball without his master's permission.[27] This is true also in the case of Uncle Tony, a character included in *Miralda*, but in a much longer episode in which Brown sharpens his depiction of the violence of slave life and the unchecked power of slaveowners with a tragicomic tone that anticipates Charles Chesnutt's *The Conjure Woman* (1899). In the shorter episode in *Clotelle*, instead, Uncle Tony's denunciation of his mistress's Christian hypocrisy is reduced to a sketch whose comic effect derives from the superstitious fears of the old slave.

In the absence of an emphasis on the culture of resistance of the slave community, Brown compensates by focusing on individual heroic manhood. George, now renamed Jerome, is imprisoned not for participating in a slave revolt, but, à la Frederick Douglass, for striking the master who intended to

flog him. Although the scope of Jerome's resistance is reduced and his eloquent speech in favor of violent self-defense is remarkably shortened, he
becomes more representative of the slave community. First, whereas in 1853
George was described as looking "as white as most white persons" (224), in
1864 Brown proclaims Jerome to be "of pure African origin" and "perfectly
black" (57). Second, his escape is presented in greater detail as more dangerous, and it comes to incorporate episodes of cunning and bravery attributed to nameless slaves in the British edition.[28] Through such changes Brown
inserts in the sentimental plot a sustained discussion of the societal impact
of skin color. Both in Canada and in Britain, Jerome prospers as a free black
man because he is given a chance to prove his skills, and his courageous "self-
forgetfulness" (90) gains him admission into high British society. As a clerk
in a British manufacturing house, however, Jerome does not become as rich
as the white-skinned George in the 1853 edition or as the successful passer
Clotelle. Although he is not the one to ensure that the title heroine's rags-
to-riches movement becomes permanent, Jerome's successful fight against
an American nation "in which his right to manhood had been denied him"
(87)[29] elevates him to a heroic stature unparalleled by the more glamorous
but less self-reliant success of Clotelle's deceased French husband or of the
passer George in the British edition.[30]

Brown's glorification of the real-life plight of black men is integral to the
main sentimental plot, but it remains submerged beneath a series of romantic
coincidences and happy meetings. In an attempt to improve "the work as art,
if not as argument" (Farrison 328) by unifying the plot around a few protagonists and to prove inspirational to his predominantly white intended
audience of Union soldiers (whose potential racial conservatism he would
neither discuss nor underestimate), Brown's greater focus on the sentimental plot results in a new closure that underscores the possibility of future reconciliation while insisting on the present necessity of war. Brown emphasizes
survival by renaming the protagonists and shifting the focus from the defeated to the successfully subversive passer. The brave heroine who tries to rescue her daughter and eventually prefers death to bondage is renamed Isabella,
and the new Clotelle who succeeds in escaping to France is Isabella's daughter.[31] Although the ending still takes place abroad, the final reconciliation
comes to include not only Clotelle's long-lost lover, Jerome, but also her slaveholding father. After she forgives him for his earlier desertion and for his
initial disapproval of Clotelle's marriage with dark-skinned Jerome, she converts him into freeing his slaves and escaping the perverse influence of slavery by relocating in France (104).[32] The passer thus develops from a genteel
saboteuse into the agent of moral suasion, and she continues to complement

more active male abolitionist activities such as Jerome's short but eloquent defense of the slaves' "right to be free" (103). As a result of their efforts, Clotelle and Jerome's forced homelessness is compounded by the aristocratic slaveholder's voluntary exile, which expands the impact of abolitionism and grounds it in a discourse of future sectional reconciliation. Union soldiers (black and white, as Brown makes clear in the third edition of the novel) thus emerge as the rescuers not only of blacks in bondage but also of a white South that has fallen victim to the wickedness of its own institutions.

* * *

The scope of this fictional reconciliation, the variety of uses of the trope of passing, and the emphasis on the sentimental plot expand even further in the third and last edition of *Clotelle; or, The Colored Heroine: A Tale of the Southern States* (1867), in response to the momentous legal changes that were taking place in the country: Slavery had been abolished, and the Fourteenth Amendment guaranteeing citizenship for ex-slaves was being ratified. Although Brown does not substantially revise the text of his previous American editions, he adds four more chapters that follow Clotelle's story up to the present of his writing, "June, 1867" (114). The new closure enhances the artistic unity of his work by intensifying the focus on the title heroine, but it also seems to alter the overall political thrust of the novel, leaving the author shackled to the obligation of a happy ending.

In keeping with their unquenchable patriotic feelings, feelings not even hinted at in the British *Clotel* or in *Miralda*, Brown hastens the exiles "home to take part in the [Civil War] struggle" (105).[33] In the South, Jerome dies heroically while attempting to rescue the body of a Union officer, and Clotelle resumes passing, this time for the patriotic and womanly purpose of "alleviating the hardships of . . . sick and imprisoned soldiers" (107). After her husband's death, Clotelle becomes more daring in her role as the "Angel of Mercy" of the Union Army and gains access to confederate prisons by passing as a "rebel lady" (107). Her experiences with the "brutal treatment and daily murders" committed in confederate prisons (107) enable Brown to reiterate in relation with Northern troops his earlier condemnation of Southern violence against the slaves. Similarly, black participation in the Civil War remains as multifaceted as antebellum resistance in the 1853 edition, varying from the "noble daring" of the colored battalion (105) to the practical help of black servants who save Clotelle from capture and the cunning duplicity of "a negro man named Pete" (107), a confederate prison employee who, "having the entire confidence of the commandant, was in a position to do much good without being suspected" (107). Potentially a Melvillian

Babo, Pete now emerges as patriotic because the slave's struggle for liberation is compounded by a similar commitment on the part of the country.

Postemancipation excitement seems to dominate the ending. That Clotelle survives her return to the South signals the difference between the Civil War era and the prewar period, when such return cost her mother's life. Clotelle's postwar purchase of the farm where she used to live as a slave further underscores this sense of change. Yet in opposition to the sweeping progressive movement of the plot, the most striking features of the novel's new ending are its openness and its far-from-triumphant tone. After all, Jerome's act of heroism contains a strong critique of Northern troops because the dead body of a white officer is deemed more important than the lives of the black soldiers who are asked to rescue it. Brown himself explicitly singles out this episode as one that, "while it reflects undying credit upon the bravery of the negro, pays but a sorry tribute to the humanity of the white general who brought the scene into existence" (105–6).

Brown's sobering vision of his heroine's postwar life and the silence that surrounds Clotelle's son after her return to the United States also qualify optimistic assessments of the societal impact of Emancipation. Clotelle's landed independence stems from a wealth that originated in her passing for a white European and does not imply any collective change in the economic power of African Americans. On the contrary, the author reminds his audience that "everywhere the condition of the freedmen attracted the attention of the friends of humanity" (114). Through Clotelle's postbellum decision to put her privilege to the service of the community by opening a freedmen's school on her own property, Brown insists on the continued need for national activism on behalf of the ex-slaves. He argues for the duty of restitution that should be felt by all those who have enjoyed the societal privileges of whiteness and also problematizes any easy complacency in the millennium of Emancipation. Clotelle's plantation haven is not idealized, and even the defiant act of owning the place where she used to be owned does not eliminate the sense of defensive enclosure in a space that is temporarily safe mostly because it is privately owned. From this vantage point, Clotelle's devotion to the freedmen appears to be informed by the same protonationalist self-help philosophy that dominated the post-Reconstruction period.[34]

With the end of the war and the final acquisition of a home, the ex-exiled passer can exercise her genteel supportive role in favor of the larger black community rather than solely of individual enslaved men. At the moment when Clotelle forsakes passing, the black folk whose fictional presence had been curtailed by the needs for "narrative order and character solidity" (Heermance 183) become thematized and reenter the text through Clotelle's individual commitment to their welfare. Foreshadowing the role that will be played by a host of post-Reconstruction genteel Angels of Mercy such as Iola Leroy, Clotelle the ex-passer becomes a tool for solidarity building within the black community. Once the elimination of slavery makes the United States a home, however inhospitable, the principal significance of Clotelle's passing resides no longer in its subversive use but in its relinquishment, in her statement of preference for the values of black culture, in her free, voluntary choice of belonging to the African American community.

Frank J. Webb

> Great sacrifices never will be made, great objects never will be accomplished, except under the influence of strong emotions: and strong emotions are not always exactly observant of drawing-room decencies. Complaints and reproaches are ugly and disagreeable things; as such, they are excluded, by common consent, from polite society. But did polite society and soft speeches ever yet make a revolution? (Hildreth, "Complaint" 57)

A revolution does not seem to be what free black Philadelphian Frank J. Webb had in mind when he wrote *The Garies and Their Friends,* but he certainly did put "drawing-room decencies" to new and bellicose fictional uses. Published in London in 1857, four years after the first edition of Brown's novel, *The Garies* contrasts sharply with *Clotel,* most obviously because it does not possess the sustained abolitionist thrust of its antecedent. Less obvious are the continuities between the two novels, especially their shared focus on the life of the black community and the use of the trope of passing to illuminate it. Although Webb treats these themes in ways that differ significantly from Brown's, their presence highlights some of the constitutive features of the emerging African American novel. These continuities point to the conscious craft that characterizes the African American literary tradition from the beginning and reveal the writers' awareness that fiction, by widening and legitimating the gap between author, narrator, and characters, enabled the African American novelist to play by a different set of rules than those governing the required autobiographical authenticity of the slave narratives, however fictionalized.

As the second known novel in the African American tradition, *The Garies* is of great literary historical significance.[35] Nevertheless, Webb's avoidance of direct abolitionist propaganda, his focus on Northern free blacks rather than Southern slaves, his own nonslave status, the dearth of biographical information about him, and his decision to make passing an important theme in his novel have had crippling repercussions on his reception among scholars of African American literature to this day. Very little criticism has been devoted to *The Garies,* despite the oft-voiced critical conviction that Webb is a "more conscious artist than William Wells Brown" (Whitlow 47).[36] Critical lamentations on the lack of information about Webb's life and work have often resulted in a reiteration of the few biographical comments Harriet Beecher Stowe made in her introduction (Stowe, Preface v–vi) or in speculation about Webb's own racial identity.[37] Such speculations are an instance of the critical bias that assumes early African American fiction to be highly autobiographical and documentary, but they remain unsubstantiated, as scholar Rosemary F. Crockett has conclusively demonstrated. Though far from complete, the biographical information currently available on Webb dispels doubts about his racial background and documents his continued involvement with black communities throughout the United States.[38] Such insider knowledge dominates Webb's representation of black life in *The Garies.* His dual focus on the free blacks' happy domesticity and on their matter-of-fact responses to the quotidian injustices of segregation emerge as complementary elements of Webb's narrative strategy of celebratory protest.

* * *

The chorus of visibly black characters that Brown surreptitiously inserted in *Clotel* gains center stage in *The Garies* and displaces the centrality of the more conventional tale of miscegenation to which Webb's title refers. Grounding his celebratory protest in the tensions between blacks as the subjects of their own lives and the objects of racial discrimination, Webb disrupts the representational violence both of a racist discourse that saw blacks as deserving of victimization and of the "romantic racialism" (Fredrickson 101) that imagined them as helplessly docile figures. He challenges the discourse of racial segregation in the North by devoting his primary attention to the domestic life of black families, decentering the experiences and ideological perspective of white characters. He locates whites mainly in a public sphere that, from the familial standpoint of his novel, provides a background against which his African American characters stand out in their full individuality.[39]

Homelessness, intended as the lack of both home ownership and control over one's family, dominates early African American fiction as the paradigm of the utter social dispossession of blacks in bondage (e.g., Brown's *Clotel*) or of their de facto servitude in a "free" but prejudiced North (e.g., Harriet Wilson's *Our Nig*). *The Garies,* instead, represents the first unabashedly domestic African American novel.[40] Families constitute the basic units of Webb's fiction, and the few free-floating individuals who appear in *The Garies* enter the family orbit at first informally and eventually in a permanent way through marriage. As he shifts the focus of the domestic novel from gender to racial concerns, however, Webb's positive portrayal of black women comes to coincide with the erasure of female issues, and the idealized harmony of his fictional families relies on the suppression of all tensions in the gendered dynamics at play within the home. The subordinated and restricted role women play in Webb's fiction is confirmed by his treatment of the theme of passing. In contrast with Brown, Webb bestows this kind of racial mobility only on male characters because his focus on middle-class families and his interest in portraying free black patriarchs does not make it necessary to introduce subversive mulattas.

To approach the home settings, the quaint humor, and the moralistic character types that dominate *The Garies* as typical of the domestic genre, rather than as personal artistic weaknesses of Webb's,[41] provides an important framework to appreciate his unprecedented portrayal of the life of free blacks in the segregated North. Webb's focus on happy bourgeois families emerges not solely as a symptom of his class bias (Gayle, *The Way* xv) but also as a strategy to illustrate and celebrate African American communal survival. Centering his attention on the more privileged strata of the Philadelphia black community,[42] Webb foregrounds the mechanics of discrimination rather than the resulting evil of black poverty that, for instance, dominates Wilson's *Our Nig* as the Northern equivalent of Southern slavery.

Pointing out the mistake of seeing slavery as the only racial problem in the United States, Webb focuses on the paradoxes of free black life in the North. To quote the terse assessment of a minor Southern character in *The Garies,* "Well, I must say you Northern people are perfectly incompwehensible [*sic*]. You pay taxes to have niggers educated, and made fit for such places—and then you won't let them fill them when they are pwepared [*sic*] to do so" (292). Despite these obstacles, his black bourgeoisie is able to survive and respond by developing parallel institutions and support networks. Webb celebrates the viability of free black life in the North against prevalent stereotypes of black dependence, contemporary proposals for the deportation of the free blacks, and uninformed bleak assessments of their socioeconomic situation that Webb sees as a proslavery ploy (*The Garies* 49). *The Garies* thus articulates not only a straightforward indictment of Northern prejudice but also a critique of the stereotypes of black unfitness for freedom that provided a rationale for slavery.

The domestic context and the bourgeois setting of *The Garies* shape the political import of Webb's commentary on Northern racism. Paralleling what

Brown did with the sentimental romance and the antislavery novel in *Clotel*, Webb appropriates a popular genre in his time used mostly by white women and infuses it with his own thematic interest in the life of the free blacks and with a new angle of seeing. Notwithstanding the presence of white characters and of black characters who enter white circles by passing, the novel centers on and is told from the point of view of a Northern black community whose material and spiritual life looms much larger than their dealings with whites seem to indicate. Very early in the *The Garies* (chapters 2 and 3) Webb makes it unmistakably clear that his domestic novel is not a novel about domestics. The many pages dedicated to young Charlie Ellis's disruption of the household where he has been sent to serve for a few months decry the discriminatory hiring practices that relegate African Americans to service jobs and also preempt stereotypical literary expectations of monodimensional, obedient, contented black characters. Later in the text, Webb advances a more direct critique of the politics of representation of blackness, which works retroactively as a hermeneutic tool similar to those Brown inserted in *Clotel*. One of the main black characters, Mr. Walters, denounces racist disfigurements of African American history and heroism by describing a portrait he owns of Haitian revolutionary Toussaint l'Ouverture: "That . . . looks like a man of intelligence. It is entirely different from any likeness I ever saw of him. The portraits generally represent him as a monkey-faced person, with a handkerchief about his head" (123).

In his depiction of Northern segregation, Webb systematically infuses the domestic novel with racial concerns and with an emphasis on the ethos of resistance of the black community. The life of his characters is brutally disrupted by Northern racial violence, as the story line of *The Garies* evidences. Mr. Garie, a white Georgia planter, leaves the South with his family and relocates in Philadelphia, hoping to secure the permanent freedom of his ex-slave wife-to-be and their all-but-white children, Clarence and Emily. In Philadelphia, the Garies enjoy the society of the Ellises (a black family Mrs. Garie knew in the South) and Mr. Walters, a wealthy black self-made man. After experiencing in various instances the race prejudice pervasive in the "free" North, the Garies eventually fall victim to the greediness of a long-lost relative (Mr. Stevens) who instigates a riotous mob against the free blacks of Philadelphia.[43] During the riot, Mr. Garie is shot to death, Mrs. Garie dies after giving premature birth to a stillborn child in the cold shed where she has taken refuge, and Mr. Ellis is made an invalid for life. Also as a consequence of the riot, the two orphaned Garie children are separated: Clarence leaves Philadelphia and passes to enter a white boys' school, and Emily is raised by the Ellises.

Racial hatred leaves his characters "almost overpowered" (*The Garies* 237), yet Webb insists that their lives are not completely overdetermined by it. The author imbues the plot of violence with an emphasis on survival, life within the black community, and the comforts of domesticity. He deals with the representational tensions between protest and celebration, violence and resistance, victimization and agency, by portraying segregation from the two different points of view of sympathetic white outsiders and of the black community itself. Webb recounts in detail the public indignities to which his black characters (especially the men, because the women remain mostly confined within the home) are subjected in transportation, education, and hiring. On these occasions, anger and indignation are verbalized chiefly by sympathetic white characters who suffer by reflex and for the first time the consequences of discrimination. This strategy of "indirect depiction . . . of anger" (Hedin 35) contains the public voicing of black emotions but temporarily transposes the burden of resenting racial bigotry onto white characters. Discrimination itself thus provides a fictional bridge that links the experiences of black and white characters and serves propagandistic functions. The vocal indignation of sympathetic whites underscores the importance of opposing segregationist practices, while the dignified silence of the principal black victims of discrimination elevates them to heroic stature and turns experiences of public debasement into feats of proud male stoicism.

However, such stoicism is only a temporary and circumstantial phenomenon. Silence turns into a keen analysis of and self-reliant resistance to segregation when Webb's gaze moves from white-dominated public spaces to the black-dominated private sphere of the home. As a micro-unit of the separate but industrious, cultured, thriving black world that remains for the most part beyond the gaze even of sympathetic whites, the home becomes the place where the point of view of blacks comes out uncensored. There, the oppositional uses of Webb's celebratory protest and his politics of domesticity become clear: Scenes of familial bliss reveal the presence of parallel black institutions and support networks, confidential talks incorporate outspoken political comments, filial love leads to stark condemnations of white violence, and youthful disappointment cannot be separated from the denunciation of occupational discrimination.

As a result of Webb's dual intent to condemn the evils of segregation and celebrate the happier aspects of life within a black community, the most violently outraged comments against white racism are voiced by Caddy Ellis, a secondary character who is a caricature of the overzealous housewife. Caddy verbalizes repeatedly her hatred for the "white devils" (267) as a group, but the emotional tone of her outbursts connotes her as an unauthoritative speaker who is often reprimanded for her "sweeping . . . remarks" (300). Despite these authorial strategies of containment, Caddy vents her anger repeatedly, and her extremism serves a crucial function in the novel. It represents an African American appropriation of the dominant logic of racial hatred, which shifts the angle of seeing from whites to blacks and creates a context for presenting other forms of race consciousness.

The occasional indignation of sympathetic whites and Caddy's persistent hatred constitute the opposite ends of the spectrum of reactions to discrimination in *The Garies.* Unlike Caddy, most of the central characters abstain from condemning whites en masse and prove cautiously ready to recognize individual acts of kindness. However, such acts are so rare that they do not undermine more general assessments of white bigotry. All the central African American characters share an awareness of how systematic institutionalized race prejudice is, and although their knowledge is voiced infrequently precisely because it is shared, at some point in the novel Esther, Charlie, Mr. Walters, and Mr. and Mrs. Ellis express their anger and frustration. On such occasions, the directness of their outbursts contrasts with their usually controlled reactions and brings to the surface the culture of everyday resistance that informs Webb's fictional African American community. The keen race consciousness they reveal emerges as one of the community's political responses to racial discrimination and constitutes the rationale for its cohesiveness, resilience, and protonationalist self-reliance.

That these denunciations are made within a domestic context does not undermine their political significance. Though ostensibly confidential and privatized, those utterances of discontent become dialogized by the very fact of their inclusion in the novel. Webb locates his "propagandizing impulse" (Bakhtin 283) in the contrast between public (white) discourse and domestic (black) discourse, and the realities of segregation remain implicitly present even in the most private conversations between black characters. This racially polarized internal dialogization that dominates *The Garies* shapes and politicizes the style of the novel. It highlights both the presence of "socially alien languages within the boundaries of one and the same national language" (Bakhtin 285) and the dialectical tensions between agency and victimization in Webb's representation of African American life in the segregated North.

These tensions take center stage also in Webb's sophisticated handling of language for purposes of characterization. On one hand, Webb thematizes and defamiliarizes stereotyped literary assumptions of dialect-speaking blacks. For instance, he portrays two ostensibly servile black waiters who pretend to support slavery. They speak in black dialect to extract money and information from visiting Southerners, but in reality they are agents of the Underground

Railroad who normally talk "as correct English, and with as pure Northern an accent as anyone could boast" (40). On the other hand, Webb complicates the supposedly linear bourgeois progression from dialect to standard English by extending the deliberate manipulation of linguistic codes to most of his black characters, whose choice of a more or less formal English is contextual and reveals varying degrees of familiarity with the interlocutors.[44] He also makes sure to show linguistic and other individual differences between ostensibly faithful house servants such as Aunt Rachel and Robberts. For instance, he discourages hurried evaluations of the former's obedience to her mistress by depicting how, when she has the opportunity, Aunt Rachel makes "the most of the injury inflicted on her toe" (81) by the resistant Charlie. Having "declared herself unfit for service," Aunt Rachel is last seen "ensconced in a large easy-chair, listening to the music of her favourite smoke-jack" (81).

Linguistic variations substantiate the self-awareness and internal differentiation of the black community while confirming the political valence of familial life. In *The Garies,* the home represents a privileged space of communal resistance where dramatic scenes of self-defense are played out. Webb epitomizes the strength of the race in the solidity of black families, and countering negative stereotypes of black womanhood thus becomes indispensable to the celebration of the free black community and to the indictment of racial discrimination. As he appropriates the traditionally female-dominated domestic sphere to accommodate his presentation of the black community as a whole, however, Webb reduces women characters to contentedly relational figures. Their all-consuming devotion to their fathers, brothers, and husbands effectively masculinizes Webb's otherwise overly domestic portrayal of black male heroism.

The intersections between discourses of race and gender in *The Garies* emerge vividly from the characterization of the two Ellis sisters. Both Esther and Caddy are morally unblemished and emphatically industrious, but the latter is described as "plain in person . . . [and] of rather shrewish disposition" (16). Equally distant from the "mammy" as from the "loose woman" stereotypes (Christian, *Black Women* 11, 13), Caddy often becomes an object of ridicule, but only for qualities that shed positive light on her community, such as her excessive efficiency on behalf of her own family and friends. As in the case of her antiwhite hatred, Caddy's extremism shifts the frame of evaluation away from prevalent negative stereotypes and creates the context for appreciating Esther's true black womanhood. "Coloured," "of considerable beauty," and "lady-like" (Webb, *The Garies* 16, 307), Esther possesses a quiet dignity, passionate race pride, and nurturing disposition that qualify her as the ideal woman of *The Garies.*

This contrastive portrayal of the two sisters illuminates Webb's conceptualization of womanly strength in relation to black manhood. Caddy is chastised because she is headstrong to the point of disciplining and even endangering black men.[45] Esther instead is praised because she is selfless and utterly supportive of black male figures. Interested in not reproducing stereotypes of "unwomanly" strong black women, Webb extols Esther's presence of mind when she averts an explosion in Mr. Walters's house but reaffirms her feminine delicacy by adding that she was "so overcome with excitement and terror, that she fainted outright" (209). Similarly, a secondary character such as Aunt Comfort, a domestic of "ebony countenance" (251) who revises the popular figure of the unfeminine Mammy, collaborates in Charlie's successful participation in a church meeting by speaking out for the first time but then sinks down "completely extinguished" (251). The temporary entrance of women characters into the male realm is counterbalanced by their quick return to more "feminine" activities such as fainting. Despite these attempts at containment, Webb's celebration of the true womanhood of the race leads him into extravagant territories of black women's heroism whose implications he is not willing to explore. When beautiful Esther insists on learning how to load guns to help defend the hearth from a riotous mob, she exceeds the boundaries of female piety and enters the realm of violent self-defense that Webb has coded as masculine. This vision of active female resistance unsettles the rigid gender dichotomies that dominate the novel and foregrounds the representational tensions that result from Webb's attempt to separate the politicization of race from that of gender.[46]

Webb's celebration of middle-class domesticity liberates his heroines from the need to work as domestics, but insofar as it predicates their contentment and confinement within the home, it proves empowering chiefly for African American men and functional to the depiction of an established free black patriarchy. In addition to the much-written-about Mr. Walters, an imposing self-made millionaire real estate investor "of jet-black complexion" (121), Webb introduces several bourgeois breadwinners who achieve varying degrees of success. Mr. Ellis, for instance, is an enterprising carpenter who earns the bulk of his family's income, although his wife and daughters also work as seamstresses. Even after being made an invalid for life during a riot, he maintains a crucial role in the novel. He becomes a living memento of white hatred against courageous black manhood, and his tragedy occasions the description of the trials and discriminations faced by his son Charlie, a patriarch in the making. In his depiction of enterprising black men Webb echoes the rhetoric of the American dream. As the riot makes clear, however, the bourgeois status of his protagonists remains precarious because of racism, and Webb emphasizes it to extol black self-reliance in the face of overwhelming prejudice rather than America as the land of opportunities. Even in the case of Mr. Walters, the principal spokesperson for bourgeois values, his most optimistic espousal of the American success ethic is linked to a critique of occupational discrimination and is intended to save Charlie from becoming a domestic worker (62–63). Analogously, his most bitter and "sneering" (275) evaluation of white privileges rests on a condemnation of the racial prejudice that creates them.[47]

* * *

With respect to Webb's enterprising black male characters, George Winston and Clarence Garie, the two passers of the novel, occupy a position of marginality. Although they are important characters, they never emerge as major actors in *The Garies,* nor do they represent the future of the African American community, as Mr. Winston emigrates to South America and Clarence Garie dies prematurely. Because they do not build families, they skirt the domestic economy of the novel and remain at the community's periphery because of their unwillingness and incapacity, respectively, to make a positive choice to belong to it. Their experiences frame the novel, gaining center stage only at its beginning and end, and their unheroic status enables a contrastive reaffirmation both of powerful dark-skinned patriarchal figures and of the desirability of belonging to the African American community.

Like Brown, Webb reveals a significant uneasiness about the invisibility of the passer's blackness, an uneasiness that comes to the surface in the description of the Garie siblings. To "the casual observer," Webb writes, Emily and Clarence show "no trace whatever of African origin," but the "critically learned in such matters, *knowing* [*their*] *parentage*" might find telltale clues in the "slightly mezzo-tinto expression of his [Clarence's] eyes, and the rather African fullness of his lips" (2, emphasis mine) or in the "slight kink" of Emily's chestnut hair (337). These racial signifiers, whose readability relies on a knowledge of the passers' genealogy, delimit the outer boundary of the visibly black community. Together with essentialized notions of blackness, Webb undermines equally essentialized notions of whiteness in defiantly extravagant ways. For instance, after the villainous Mr. Stevens takes off his nice suit to avoid recognition, Webb notices how by the "change in his attire he seemed completely robbed of all appearance of respectability" (184). This leads to his being tarred by mistake, then taken for black and further abused, in an ironic reversal that turns the ridiculing force of blackface against the white impersonator. In another instance, Webb capitalizes on the precariousness of white identity and describes both the passer Mr. Winston and the Southerner Mr. Western as gentlemen of "dark complexion" (3, 289), suggesting once again how "whiteness" might rest on nothing more than unawareness of one's mixed genealogy.

As a result of their marginality and peculiar life stories, George Winston and Clarence Garie acquire a narrative authority that complements and reinforces that of the principal black characters who do not or cannot pass. Having passed as insiders qualifies them as knowledgeable critics of white society, and their exposé corroborates the portrayal of race discrimination as suffered by the black community. Mr. Winston and Clarence serve, respectively, important structural and interpretive functions in the novel. On one hand, as a relative of Mrs. Garie and a friend of the Ellises, Mr. Winston is highly instrumental to the family's removal to Philadelphia. He mediates their transition with comments on Northern prejudice that he has gathered both from his black friends and from the confidential comments of a wealthy white family among whom he passes for white. On the other, unlike Mr. Winston, Clarence starts passing as a child and becomes an exemplum of the evils of internalizing the discriminatory value system of white northerners. He becomes a touchstone to interpret and celebrate, by contrast, the content of black manhood, the positive role of the black community, and the uses of black culture.

In Webb's novel of segregation, the passers stand out as crossover figures whose peculiar experiences confirm the artificial but nevertheless operative racial boundaries that separate black and white society. Far from involving a trope of conciliation, Mr. Winston's and Clarence's ability to pass for white and become temporary insiders in two worlds ultimately results in a powerful demonstration of the virulence of racial prejudice. Whether it is lived as a subversive trick by Mr. Winston or expiated as a fatal seduction by Clarence Garie, passing does not provide a means to break free from the perverse dynamics of segregation. Webb's passers may be able to cross racial boundaries, but in the process they experience the pervasiveness of prejudice.

The marginality of Mr. Winston's life starts during his childhood as a slave in Virginia. Webb's brief portrayal of Winston's early years indicates a concern with refuting stereotypes of black inferiority, but his description of the industriousness and economic success of which blacks in bondage could be capable if they were free necessitates a contrived and problematic circumvention of the institution of slavery. In fact, George Winston is able to become a slave entrepreneur because Mr. Moyese, his master, does not treat him as chattel; furthermore, he can act effectively on behalf of his owner because, like him, he does not look black. Despite Webb's brief but broad condemnation of "the blighting influences" of slavery, his final portrayal of the "warmhearted, kind old man" (8) who owns George Winston directs attention away from the institutionalized immorality of slavery and into the private office where Mr. Moyese spontaneously gives the manumission papers to "his favourite" (12). Webb's clear condemnation of slavery places his text outside the tradition of apologetic plantation fiction. Yet his focus on a completely positive master–slave relationship reveals how *The Garies* is also outside the contemporary abolitionist discourse on slavery, which insisted on contextualizing individual white benevolence within the larger structural inhumanity of the peculiar institution. George Winston maintains his strong attachment to Mr. Moyese even after becoming free. He waits six years, until the death of his ex-owner, before going in search of his long-lost mother, and the pathos of discovering that she had died a few miles from where her son lived is diluted by George's lengthy deferment of his filial concern.

Only when he goes North does Mr. Winston's story take on explicitly polemic overtones. In the North, the loyal George emerges defiantly as the subversive mulatto saboteur Mr. Winston and becomes the first African American character to "treat ironically . . . the problem of the color line" (Davis, Introduction ii). His lightness and wealth enable him to tour the North, infiltrate the society of the upper classes, and become confidentially acquainted with the depths of racial prejudice in the free states. Mr. Winston's narration of his Northern adventures during a dinner at the Garies' plantation opens the novel and constitutes a fitting example of the oppositional ways in which Webb uses domestic conventions. In the unthreatening familial context of a dinner table conversation, readers become privy to Mr. Winston's secret and to the ironic situations in which he has found himself. The passer's ability to become an insider in racially different domestic contexts becomes an effective narrative tool to expose from within the absurdity of racist stereotypes. A case in point occurs when Mr. Winston recounts how the same man (sarcastically named Mr. Priestly) who prides himself on "being able to detect evidences of the least drop of African blood in any one" (4) also begs the amused passer to escort his daughter, a "Fifth-avenue belle" (3), to a ball.

A living mockery of the credo espoused by Mr. Priestly that "a 'gentleman' with African blood . . . is a moral and physical impossibility" (4), Mr. Winston connects his own peculiarly unrepresentative experiences to the more general situation of the free colored people in the North. The fierce discrimination they experience there is based on the same dichotomized color consciousness that enabled him to pass and be welcomed in exclusive white circles. Mr. Winston functions as a narrative device of mediation between blacks and whites that proves both its own precariousness and shows how racial prejudice makes a permanent communal mediation impossible. Far from con-

sidering passing an "ethnic jeu" (Boelhower 135), a privileged situation of liminality that enables him to function to his best interest in both worlds, Mr.
Winston refuses to continue to hide his racial heritage. He eventually decides
to emigrate abroad because he is determined to leave the South but also reluctant to move North because "whilst . . . he would have found sufficiently
refined associations amongst the people of color to satisfy his social wants,
he felt that he could not bear the isolation and contumely to which they were
subjected" (14). It is revealing of the peculiarly American construction of
whiteness that Mr. Winston moves to South America, one of the non-Anglo-
Saxon places, like Italy and France, that are considered ethnically fit to inte-
grate the Mediterranean-looking passer.

The Webb analyzes the systematic nature of racial oppression in the United
States and the political and economic interests behind acts of racial violence,
which are exemplified in the description of Mr. Stevens's careful planning
of a riot, a clear antecedent of Charles Chesnutt's better-known episode in
The Marrow of Tradition (1901). His analysis leaves no room for individual
solutions, as the fate of Webb's second passer makes clear. Contrary to nineteenth-century racist discourses on the mulatto, in *The Garies* Clarence's
tragedy stems not so much from his mixed heritage per se as from the debilitating prejudice he experiences in the process of passing. Rather than a means
of escape, as in *Clotel,* or a subversive trick, as in the case of Mr. Winston,
Clarence's passing is an externally imposed lifelong necessity that emerges
as one more form of racial oppression. In a state of shock caused by the riot
that has disrupted his happy familial environment, young Clarence falls victim to the white family lawyer's conviction that as a white person he "will be
better off" (275). Though well meaning, Mr. Balch reasons and acts in un-
questioning compliance with his society's racial hierarchy that devalues black
life. He underestimates the psychological strains of passing, disregards Mr.
Walters's objections to the plan, and impresses on young Clarence the need
for permanent racial concealment (279).

The passer's difficulties in operating even an individual mediation between
blacks and whites in a segregationist society become dramatically clear after
Clarence's removal to a different city to attend a preparatory school for white
boys. The poetic justice characteristic of the domestic novel shapes the passer's fate, and Clarence's adoption of white supremacist values leads to the evil
of familial alienation. Initially, Clarence is separated from his sister and his
friends in the black community of Philadelphia only by distance and by the
need for secrecy that characterizes the passer. As an adult, however, he consciously distances himself from them and expresses feelings of fear and re-
vulsion for the "degradations" blacks have to bear (323). This deepening alien-

ation and his internalization of the dominant white supremacist ideology culminate in Clarence's objections to Emily's marriage with "coloured" (6) Charles Ellis. Even when he curses his fate and wishes he had not passed, his comments reveal no memory of the closeness he experienced with his family and the Ellises. On the contrary, they disclose his outsider's understanding of black life as unending suffering and sound as condescending as they are superficial: "It is a pity . . . that I was not suffered to grow up with them, then I should have learnt to bear their burthens, and in the course of time might have walked over my path of life, bearing the load almost unconsciously. Now it would crush me, I know" (323). The overwhelming self-pity that undermines his credibility and the contradictory insincerity that makes him curse passing but also insist that his sister should pass identify Clarence as a direct precursor of James Weldon Johnson's Ex-Coloured Man, another figure of cultural alienation whose simplistic comments on black culture shed ironic light on societal stereotypes.

That the somatic mark of whiteness rather than blackness is the load that eventually crushes Clarence is the irony that governs his fate and explains the narrative function of his passing. In his resolve to remain white he becomes paranoid of discovery, and his fears undermine his mental and physical strength to the point of feminizing him. Though "strikingly handsome" (322), he is not described in terms of powerful manhood: "Thin," "pale," and "feverish" (321), the adult Clarence emerges as enervated and hysterical. After his racial heritage is revealed by a white villain from his hometown and he is forced to leave his worshiped fiancée, Miss Bates, Clarence slowly wastes away and dies of debilitation. The mode of his death and the retributive justice at work in *The Garies* further feminize Clarence by aligning him with the fallen heroines of nineteenth-century popular fiction.

Because it originates in his seduction by the white values and prejudices embodied in Miss Bates and her family, Clarence's death says more against the evils of segregation, which made passing seem expedient, than against the supposedly inherent tragedy of mulatto life. On one hand, unlike him, Clarence's chestnut-haired and blue-eyed sister, Emily, is smoothly incorporated within the free black community. Her eventual domestic happiness contrasts starkly with Clarence's dire assessments of the tragedy of black life and his eventual loneliness. On the other hand, in the novel there is a double pattern of seduction, abandonment, and death whereby prejudice destroys not only the passer but also the white woman it purported to protect. Webb is daring in portraying black male sexuality and defying interracial sexual taboos. Although the union of Clarence and Miss Bates is not consummated on earth, they do not disavow the exclusivity and consensuality of their relationship even after Clarence's mixed racial background becomes known.[48] Melodramatically, but significantly nonetheless, after Clarence's death Miss Bates "walked about mournfully for a few years, pressing her hand upon her heart; and then passed away to join her lover, where distinctions in race or colour are unknown, and where the prejudice of earth cannot mar their happiness" (391). The end of Clarence's plans for permanent passing drama- tizes the virulence of race prejudice, and Webb reincorporates Clarence with- in the black community after his death as an emblematic "poor victim of prejudice to . . . color" who lost his battle "with that malignant sentiment that . . . has crushed energy, hope, and life from many stronger hearts" (391).

Clarence's death confirms the importance of the race pride, solidarity, and industriousness that characterize those protagonists who do not pass. Con- sistently, the happy ending of the novel takes place entirely within the black (mulatto included) community. In accord with the conventions of the do- mestic novel, at the end of *The Garies* all the central protagonists find suit- able spouses and are blessed by economic prosperity and by the elimination of dangerous white villains. However, this optimistic closure does not efface the racial tensions that inform Webb's strategy of celebratory protest. The domestic happiness of the novel's denouement is possible because of the less conventional ending of an episode that occurs earlier in the novel. In a fiction- al rendition of a race riot, inspired by the real-life ones that broke out in Philadelphia in the 1830s and 1840s,[49] Webb takes a daring step and portrays Mr. Walters, the Ellises, and some other members of the community as they organize an armed resistance and succeed in pushing back the lynching mob.

The actual description of collective black male violence should be credit- ed as another significant first of Webb's novel by comparison with other works of this period. William Wells Brown, for example, tells of violent slave rebellions in *Clotel* but does not depict them *in fieri,* and Martin R. Delany details a bold plan for a general insurrection of the slaves that does not take place in the available chapters of his novel *Blake; or, The Huts of America* (1859). In *The Garies,* even before Mr. Walters converts his house "into a tem- porary fortress" (203), anonymous black characters have been fighting back during racial skirmishes. As the Irish McCloskey reports to the man who is paying him to foment the riot, "They're not so aisily bate out—they fight like sevin divils. One o' 'em . . . split Mikey Dolan's head clane open, and it's a small chance of his life he's got to comfort himself wid" (176).

Webb provides graphic details of black self-defense but also diffuses the radicalness of his depiction of collective black violence. He admits that few made "every exertion for a vigorous defence" (203), he intercalates the mounting tension with quaintly humorous scenes, and he connotes the whole process as domestic. What ultimately succeeds in repelling the mob and saving the house under siege are Caddy's and Kinch's kettles of scalding water and cayenne pepper. Despite this domestic context and Mr. Walter's declaration, "I want to be strictly on the defensive—but at the same time we must defend ourselves fully and energetically" (211), the violence of the scene emerges with full force when the two groups fire at each other, and the guns of the besieged make "fearful execution amidst the throng of ruffians. Two or three fell on the spot, and were carried off by their comrades with fearful execrations" (213–14).

It is revealing of Webb's intention to portray black self-defense as a successful and viable option that Mr. Ellis falls victim to white brutality only outside the domestic space he has helped to defend. Volunteering to traverse the city to warn the Garies of the mob's impending attack, Mr. Ellis is overtaken by a group of white rioters. Despite his dramatic escape and valiant self-defense, he is eventually thrown off a roof. Webb describes in detail the "fierceness and energy" (218) with which Mr. Ellis attacks his persecutors but maintains the moral balance on his side by placing black violent self-defense within a context of wanton white cruelty. In keeping with the author's concern to portray a spectrum of racial attitudes among nonblacks, the mangled and mutilated body of Mr. Ellis is subsequently rescued by a "gentleman and some of his friends" (219), whose appalled surprise betrays them as white. Most of Webb's fictional white sympathizers share a kind of naiveté that is reminiscent of Captain Delano's forgetfulness in Melville's *Benito Cereno*. In their propensity to underestimate the systematic nature of race prejudice, they are continually taken aback by new instances of its virulence.[50]

Together with the successful collective attempt to repel the riotous mob, Webb extols more generally the tenacious everyday resistance of his fictional black community. However, the incomplete efficacy of minority resistance in a segregated society is epitomized both by Mr. Ellis's invalidism and by the ultimate failure of the individualistic mediations Webb's passers operate. Webb's indictment of racial hatred thus exceeds the boundaries of the novel by qualifying the happiness of its ending, and from this vantage point *The Garies* highlights new thematic and formal continuities in the African American narrative tradition. First, in light of its pioneering focus on segregation and on the dialectic of agency and victimization in an ostensibly free society, *The Garies* may indeed be considered "the novel that defined the central themes of African American literature for the next one hundred years" (Crockett 122). Second, the author's extravagantly unrealistic close-up, in the last two pages of the novel, on the happy domestic future of his protagonists within a vague societal context from which all racial tensions seem to have miraculously disappeared, adds to Webb's happy ending a voluntaristic utopian quality not unlike that which is prominent in the turn-of-the-century African American novels I discuss in chapter 2. Third, Webb's strategy of celebratory protest, his success at dialogizing the discourse of segregation and expressing the indigenous viewpoint of the free blacks, and his dual use of passing as a trope of subversion and a way to illuminate the value of belonging to the black community provided the next generation of African American authors with an arsenal of fictional strategies for the counterhegemonic representation of African American life and culture.

2. Race Travel in Turn-of-the-Century African American Utopian Fiction

> We believe in the Negro, in the majesty of his patient soul, in the
> brilliancy of the future that awaits him as a distinct branch of the
> human family. . . . Who knows but that he is being evolved as the
> special guide of the host of the dark millions across the waters?
> (Griggs, *Wisdom's Call* 125–26)

IT IS SURPRISING that despite the great scholarly interest in nineteenth-century African American literature that has characterized the past three decades, so little attention has been paid to African American contributions to the extraordinary outpouring of utopian fiction in the last two decades of the 1800s.[1] Especially after the 1888 publication of Edward Bellamy's best-selling *Looking Backward, 2000–1887,* the popularity and relevance of this genre were such that "even established and distinguished authors like William Dean Howells turned to stories of Utopia" (Hart 172).

And so did African American authors such as Frances E. W. Harper, Sutton E. Griggs, Pauline E. Hopkins, and Edward A. Johnson, although the eugenic tendencies, totalitarian overtones, and later unpopularity of turn-of-the-century white utopias have directed scholars' attention away from the significance of this genre for interpreting post-Reconstruction black fiction. On one hand, specialists of African American literature have eschewed the term *utopian* to describe such novels, even as they consistently use related terms such as "prophetic" (Bell 62; Fleming, "Sutton E. Griggs" 76), "fantastic" (Gloster, "Sutton E. Griggs" 337; Watson 144), "visionary" (Elder 73), and "wildly unbelievable" (Ammons 84).[2] On the other hand, among utopian scholars the assumption of the absence of a significant body of late nineteenth-century African American utopian texts can be regarded as a critical commonplace.[3] In comparing African American works with better-known white American utopias such as Bellamy's *Looking Backward,* critics remark that "Afro-American literature has never had any significant utopian dimension" (Nichols and Henry 39) or that the African American utopian impulse

as it emerges from the spirituals has not resulted in formal literary utopias
(P. Williams 47). Others have explained that supposed absence or the "failure" (Reilly 62) of the African American utopias that have appeared in print
by reference to the incredible oppressiveness of African American historical
circumstances and the consequent difficulty of imagining a perfect future.
From this perspective, even in the African American utopian texts we do
know, the imagination of the author remains "constrained" (Shor 49) and
stops short of articulating a "full-fledged" utopian vision (Reilly 62).

That an oppressed people could be reduced to such a state of abjection as to
lose the power to imagine a better future seems hard to believe. It is especially
hard in the case of African Americans, a nation within the nation with a long
history of political and cultural resistance and with a narrative tradition that
has characteristically thrived on the subversive revision of popular literary
modes. And because the utopian novel was popular at the turn of the century,
it is also hard to believe that African American authors would not have engaged
with this genre, notably because it had become an important playground for
the racialist, eugenicist, and segregationist discourse of white writers.

In this chapter I focus on the trope of passing to propose a pioneering taxonomy of turn-of-the-century African American utopian novels, making references to Pauline E. Hopkins's *Of One Blood* (1902–1903) and discussing more
extensively Sutton E. Griggs's *Imperium in Imperio* (1899), Frances E. W. Harper's *Iola Leroy* (1892), and Edward A. Johnson's lesser-known *Light Ahead for
the Negro* (1904). I interpret these texts not as isolated, idiosyncratic, maybe
"brilliant, even if not totally realized" (Ammons 84) attempts at experimentation but rather as literary appropriations of the conventions of an established
genre that dates back to Thomas More's 1516 *Utopia*. This generic contextualization foregrounds the originality and formal awareness that post-Reconstruction black writers demonstrated in crafting their novels. They articulated a
tradition that belongs to utopia as a genre and is also distinctively African
American. The recovery and reinterpretation of their neglected texts alters profoundly the literary critical approach to late-nineteenth-century utopias as a
whole.

Toward a Taxonomy of Turn-of-the-Century
African American Utopian Fiction

> The utopian function is the unimpaired reason of a militant optimism.
> (Bloch 107)

The uses of fiction to create "alternative worlds" (Peterson, "Capitalism" 563)
were already clear to African American authors of the antebellum period, but

utopian fiction as a genre sanctioned the political import of imagining alternative societies. Grounded in a "play between a design that is not yet real and the reality which the design contests" (Fortunati 22), the imaginative creation of an ideal polity that is characteristic of utopias implies a detailed sociopolitical critique. This critique emerges by force of the contrast between the society in which the author and his or her first readers live and the alternative, supposedly better world described in the text. In their utopian novels, African American writers transformed a contemporary dystopian historical reality of racial violence, segregation, and disfranchisement into an "anticipatory" (Bloch 110)[4] vision of liberation and empowerment that acquired inspirational value by expanding the "horizon of expectations" (Jauss 25) of the readers. Insofar as these novels were intended to bring about the desired social change, they can be described with Ernst Bloch's "apparently paradoxical term of concrete utopia" (107), which indicates "the unfinished dream forward, the *docta spes*" (119), the "known hope" (120).

Characterized by rather "stereotyped" fictional conventions, as Robert C. Elliott notes, the "prescriptive pattern" of the utopian genre requires a "central character [who] embarks on a voyage, lands alone in a strange country, makes contact with the inhabitants, learns about the customs and institutions of their land, makes certain comparisons with Europe, returns home" (108). Operating "by example and demonstration" (Suvin 37), the utopian novel relies on dialogue to bridge the cognitive gap between the known present and the ideal world. And because "the utopia is designed to describe a unified society, not individual varieties of existence" (Frye 122), the detailed description of utopian life tends to deflect the author's attention from the rounded portrayal of his or her characters. A similar "lack of interest in psychological realism" (Gates and McKay, *The Norton Anthology* 907) has been traditionally noted also with regard to the somewhat wooden quality of Griggs's and Harper's characters, but in the absence of a generic contextualization of their novels as utopias, it has often led to doubts about the authors' abilities as fiction writers.

African American authors adopted but also adapted in important ways the prescriptive pattern of the utopian genre to their fictional needs. Less convinced of the liberatory potential of technological progress than their white counterparts, African American utopian writers focused on the process of individual and collective ideological change that would lead to utopia rather than on the accomplished perfection of utopia itself.[5] Thus, African American utopias are characterized by a "radical *this*-worldliness" (Spillers, "Moving" 94) that emerges from the centrality of the tropes of passing and miscegenation as well as from the prominence of what I call race travel as the distinctive literary device that structures these texts. Whereas in classic European and white American works the journey to utopia entails an "extraordinary dislocation of someone's consciousness in time" or space (B. Franklin 364), African American texts propose instead an extraordinary dislocation of point of view. Their utopias are situated roughly in their own time and place, in a transitional limbo between an "old South" that is passing away and a "new South" that is "yet to be" (Griggs, *Imperium* 52). African American writers thus defamiliarize contemporary white-dominated reality by presenting American society from the displaced, marginalized perspective of segregated black Americans. It is indeed an eloquent comment on late-nineteenth-century politics of literary representation of blackness that the "distortion" of reality (Andrews et al., *The Oxford Companion* 683), the estrangement effect of race travel should stem from the unusually direct depiction of the life experiences and point of view of rebellious African American characters. These characters do not inhabit some future never-never land but express their rebelliousness in the author's present or, as in Iola's case, recent past.

The primacy and distinctiveness of race travel as structuring principle remains clear even in a formally traditional utopian novel such as Hopkins's *Of One Blood*. The space travel that takes Reuel, the protagonist, to Africa and leads to his discovery of the hidden city of Telassar soon turns into race travel as the voluntary passer frees himself from the cultural hegemony of white America, develops greater pride in his black heritage, acquires the ability to read the signs of this powerful heritage even in the United States (in Mira's visionary powers, for instance), and ultimately arrives at a new understanding of the inextricable connections between blacks and whites. At the same time, Reuel's movement in and out of utopia (i.e., between Africa and the United States) and the threat that European colonialism poses to the city of Telassar situate historically Hopkins's utopian city and differentiate it from the traditional *ou-topoi* (nonplaces) of utopian fiction.

The adventures of Southern belles who suddenly discover that their mothers were slaves (e.g., *Iola Leroy*), the secessionist plans of a secret African American government headed by a mulatto (e.g., *Imperium in Imperio*), or the aforementioned revelation that an American ex-passer is the long-lost descendant of an ancient dynasty of Ethiopian rulers (e.g., *Of One Blood*) are instances of race travel. They foreground and defamiliarize the existence of parallel black and white worlds that are societally differentiated by race, class, gender, and caste. And as they defamiliarize contemporary society for both their black and white readers by foregrounding and revealing the power of blackness, respectively, they also insist that these ostensibly separate worlds are inextricably linked at a more profound level. The marked body of the all-but-white mulatto provides a narrative frame for that link. The biblical notion "of one blood" is central to the turn-of-the-century African American utopian vision. "Know ye not that ye are parents and children?" asks Griggs in *Imperium* (45). And in *Of One Blood,* the most thorough articulation of this theme, Hopkins foregrounds the issue of intermingling as she describes the descendants of an ancient African civilization as "rang[ing] in complexion from a creamy tint to purest ebony" (545). She moves beyond the pathological connotations miscegenation had in the United States and provides a utopian vision of peaceful cohabitation of people of different colors in the hidden city of Telassar.

Both on a formal and on a thematic level, the African American utopian texts under consideration are informed by the intersections between the tropes of miscegenation and passing. On one hand, miscegenation and passing are symptoms of a dystopian contemporary world where whiteness as normative utopia makes the rejection of blackness a tempting option. On the other, race travel operates on a fictional level as an ideological reversal of racial hierarchies that is eventually epitomized in the passer's choice to forsake passing and belong to the African American community. In keeping with the authors' awareness of the double audience they were addressing, turn-of-the-century African American utopias thus emerge both as a defensive tool to combat the discourses of segregation and white supremacy and as an aggressive fictional means of community building. In *Iola Leroy,* for instance, the protagonist's choice in favor of the African American community turns blackness from a mark of inferiority into the emblem of heroism, both for the ex-passer and for all the unmistakably black characters that populate Harper's novel. From this vantage point, African American utopian novels emerge as "resocialization" texts (Tate, *Domestic Allegories* 140) not only because they teach middle-class values. They also shape their fictional black communities out of a common historical condition of enslavement and segregation as well as out of the liberational consciousness of cultural distinctiveness and the inspirational vision of a brighter common future.

Sutton E. Griggs's *Imperium in Imperio*

For one thing, Negro American consciousness is . . . a product of our memory, sustained and constantly reinforced by events, by our watchful waiting, and by our hopeful suspension of final judgement as to the meaning of our grievances. For another, most Negroes recognize themselves as themselves despite what others might believe them to be. Thus, although the sociologists tell us that thousands of light-skinned

> Negroes become white each year undetected, most Negroes can spot a
> paper-thin "white Negro" every time simply because those who
> masquerade missed what others were forced to pick up along the way:
> discipline." (Ellison, *Shadow and Act* 124)

The celebration of the African American consciousness of cultural distinctiveness takes center stage in Griggs's *Imperium in Imperio* (1899). *Imperium*
is one of the few black utopias to have been recognized as such and one of
the few nineteenth-century African American novels (together with Delany's
Blake) to have been consistently praised by critics for its modern-sounding,
outspoken assertion of black power. Despite this exceptional status among
nineteenth-century texts, it is by analyzing the aspects *Imperium* shares with
other African American utopias (i.e., the focus on miscegenation and the use
of race travel as structuring device) that it becomes possible to explain the
puzzling quality that even admirers cannot help noticing in this text without invoking Griggs's ideological ambivalence or supposed artistic ineptitude:
In *Imperium,* the author's defiant rhetoric remains in unresolved contrast
with his ultimate neutralization of the rebellious organization he portrays.

Griggs's novel follows the life and adventures of Belton Piedmont and, less
closely, Bernard Belgrave. The two protagonists eventually become leaders of
a secret African American organization that is based in Waco, Texas. Founded
in the early days of the American Republic, the "Imperium in Imperio" ("the
empire within the empire") has institutional and military powers parallel to
those of the United States government and functions to protect the lives and
property of "over seven million five hundred thousand" black Americans (*Imperium* 189). The novel reaches its climax when, in the face of widespread lynchings and the institutionalization of segregation, the Imperium leaders disagree
on how they should defend the rights of black Americans. To Bernard's proposal of an immediate, violent rebellion, Belton opposes a more gradual plan
that includes the formation of an independent black state in Texas. Bernard
manipulates the congress of the Imperium into approving his plan, and Belton is executed as a traitor. Eventually, Bernard's war plans are exposed and the
Imperium is dismantled, but the novel ends with the fictional narrator reiter-
ating the possibility of realizing at any time a new social order based on black
self-determination, should America fail to live up to its egalitarian ideals.

The boldness of Griggs's utopian plan emerges fully by foregrounding the
historical context of violence and discrimination in which African Americans lived at the turn of the century. This intense racial dichotomization
entered contemporary fiction not only in the obvious racism of Thomas
Nelson Page's or Thomas Dixon's infamous novels but also in the ostensibly bloodless, "natural" erasure of racial differences that characterizes Bel-

lamy's best-selling *Looking Backward*.[6] Within this sociocultural context, Griggs's decision to title his novel *Imperium in Imperio* evokes and overturns the ideological paradigms of his time. The title is polysemic, and its bellicose valence emerges from the interplay between the historical and literary referents it evokes. On one hand, Griggs asserts African American agency by presenting his black empire in terms that would at once echo and subvert the logic of what used to be called "invisible empire," the Ku Klux Klan, a notorious white supremacist organization very active after the Civil War. On the other hand, the phrase *"imperium in imperio"* comes from Bellamy's *Looking Backward, 2000–1887*. Protagonist Julian West comments that "womanhood seems to be organized as a sort of *imperium in imperio* in your system," but, as utopian host Dr. Leete hastens to clarify, it is an empire from which "there is not likely to be much danger to the nation" (143). In conspicuous contrast with Bellamy, Griggs capitalizes on the potential danger posed by the Imperium to reinsert blacks in utopia. He portrays them as important, albeit unrecognized historical agents whose activism in "solidifying the race for the momentous conflict of securing all the rights due them according to the will of the heavenly Father" goes "unnoticed and in fact unseen" by whites (*Imperium* 133–34).

Griggs thus explicitly places his own text within the contemporary tradition of utopian fiction, adopting and adapting thematic and formal conventions of the genre. In classic utopian style, for instance, Griggs presents the Imperium through the eyes of Bernard, who is being initiated into its mysteries and whose function as participant observer overwhelms the author's interest in his psychology. At the same time, Griggs describes the headquarters of the secret black government in ways that recall Thomas More's 1516 prototypical description of Utopia.[7] He also provides characteristically detailed explanations of the sociopolitical inequalities of white America and of the institutions of the Imperium, which he defines as "well-nigh perfect in every part" and "present[ing] a form of government unexcelled by that of any other nation" (*Imperium* 199).

In adapting these conventions to his representation of black life, Griggs revises them profoundly. The intense and distinctive sense of estrangement elicited by Griggs's utopian novel derives not only from the discovery of a secret black government, literally a nation within the nation, but mostly from his vision of black power, which emerges from the race travels on which his protagonists embark. Far from proposing a dislocation in time or space, in his note "To the Public" Griggs's authorial persona supports the veracity and contemporaneity of his text. He declares to have personally known the late Berl Trout, the fictional narrator, and to have received directly from him the papers on which *Imperium* is based. Bellamy uses a similarly authenticating device in *Looking Backward* but presents it as a document from the year 2000. To anchor his fiction in contemporary reality he has to argue the short-term feasibility of his utopian plan in the postscript, which is dated 1888. The deployment of race travel, on the contrary, enables Griggs to present his vision of black power as a fact of the present, or rather of the very recent past, because the novel ends with the dismantling of the Imperium.

Griggs's insistence on the here and now of the Imperium results in an extraordinary dislocation of point of view that rearticulates the power relations between the races and turns a segregated American minority into a self-sufficient and secessionist nation within the nation. This is not simply a raced version of the "sex-role reversal" Daphne Patai analyzes in the context of women's utopias (56). By placing his utopia in his own time and place, Griggs has foreclosed the possibility of a complete reversal of power. He dramatizes instead a process of individual and communal black empowerment that survives even the dismantling of the Imperium. It is precisely in the protagonist's ability to differentiate between power and empowerment that Griggs locates the means for realizing a new, utopian, and egalitarian social order.[8]

Griggs's distinction between power and empowerment structures the novel and provides a crucial interpretive key to the otherwise puzzling ending of *Imperium* and to the relationship between Belton and Bernard. The expectation of an important secret and the solemnity, grandeur, and suspense of the opening pages reverberate throughout the text. However, the author's actual depiction of the Imperium starts in chapter 15 and dominates only the last third of the novel. This last section follows utopian conventions most closely as the secret African American organization is shown and described to an outsider, Bernard, who is the privileged, albeit unacknowledged mulatto son of a powerful white senator. Bernard's race travel to the utopia of Imperium sees his initiation into the spiritual and material life of the black folk. He has always been marginal to that life. His mother, like many of her kept mulatta fictional antecedents, used to live in "isolation" (*Imperium* 83), and he enjoys all-but-white privileges thanks to the protecting influence of his white father. Griggs's description of Bernard draws on previous and foreshadows later African American depictions of the mulatto: Whereas his family background of miscegenation and female self-sacrifice recalls *Clotel*, his deep-seated admiration for the power of whites places Bernard on the continuum that links Webb's Clarence with Charles Chesnutt's John Walden and James Weldon Johnson's Ex-Colored Man.

Bernard's initiation into utopia is mediated by Belton, who can play utopian host because of the far more dangerous and painful race travel he has undertaken in the first fourteen chapters of the novel. Tracing the "small be-ginning" (3) of his race leader back to a poor cabin and an "ignorant" (3) but intelligent and caring mother, Griggs details the education and *Bildung* of a "new Negro, self-respecting, fearless, and determined in the assertion of his rights" (62). Belton is an exceptional man of the future who nevertheless hap-pens to live and function in a society that has room only for Old Negroes. The *Bildung* of this New Negro moves along through a proliferation of anecdotes and episodes that in terms of quantity and extravagance fall clearly in the tra-dition of Brown's *Clotel*. They also serve a similar function by introducing as wide as possible a variety of situations and contexts that present to the reader the absurd workings of blackness in a white-dominated society.[9]

The transgressive extravagance of Griggs's description of Belton's *Bildung* emerges with particular force in two episodes that involve passing. In the first, Belton decides to cross-dress as a woman and work in a leading white family "to find out just what view the white people were taking of the Negro" (131–32) and analyze the unprotected status of the black woman. As with George in *Clotel* and Kinch in *The Garies,* Belton's experiment of passing as a wom-an is short lived, in his case because it is too dangerous. Harassed by the young men of the family he works for, Belton turns down their sexual advances very forcefully. He is nevertheless "kidnapp[ed] and overpower[ed]" (134) by them and subsequently leaves his job and returns home. This "very remarkable and novel" (131) first-hand investigation of prevailing negative stereotypes of Af-rican American women is immediately followed by another episode of extrav-agant passing. Belton's beloved and noble-minded wife, Antoinette, gives birth to a baby boy who, unlike his parents, looks white. Wild with desperation, assuming that "his failure to properly support her [Antoinette] had tempted her to ruin" (137), Belton leaves his family and embarks on a series of adven-tures that lead him to the Imperium. Initially ostracized by the community, Griggs's blameless African American version of Hester Prynne eventually is vindicated: her child "grow[s] darker" (256) as he gets older, and Belton's pride as father and husband ultimately is restored, albeit a few weeks before his execution. In this second episode of passing, Griggs reverses the more tradi-tional plot of stories such as Kate Chopin's "Désirée's Baby" by foreground-ing the shock of begetting a visibly white child and by featuring what might be considered the first all-but-black character in African American literature.

Belton's dramatic *Bildung* epitomizes Griggs's reflection on masculinity, power, and the distinctiveness of black American culture. Belton's utopian qualities derive not only from his "precociousness" (15), superior intelligence, self-respect, and combativeness, but also from his almost superhuman ability to survive his obvious misplacement in a white-dominated world that is at a more primitive stage of development. *Imperium* thus emerges as a deliberate and significant revision of Bellamy's better-known utopia. At the end of *Looking Backward,* Bellamy describes protagonist Julian West's return to the nineteenth century as an unbearable nightmare that in less than twenty-four hours drives him almost insane. In *Imperium* instead, Griggs portrays Belton's life in the late 1800s as a nightmare that lasts more than twenty-four years and from which there is no permanent waking up. Indeed, Belton's utopian qualities, which shed positive light on the extraordinary struggle of the more "ordinary" African Americans who surround him, rest precisely in the strength he reveals in facing the ordeal of surviving that nightmare. And he survives whole, retaining a sense of humanity and justice that confirms his superior wisdom and transcends his own hard-won knowledge of the world he happens to live in. In *Imperium,* Belton's world ultimately emerges as upside-down. It is a world where (black) intelligence, courage, and self-respect are not only not rewarded but also continually met with cruelty, violence, discrimination. Rather than presenting them simply as an unavoidable reality, Griggs defamiliarizes his violent, segregationist times by describing them in a tone that betrays the same quality of wonder at unnecessary injustice that generally characterizes the utopian traveler's reflections on his preutopian past.

The sense of estrangement that dominates the first fourteen chapters of the novel derives precisely from the author's adoption of utopian conventions to describe Belton's race travel, a race travel that differs from those of passers such as Iola Leroy or of privileged mulattos such as Bernard. Belton's is the race travel of a (black) person who has to undergo compulsory societal training to become a specific kind of black (person), that is, a white person's stereotyped version of the thriftless, obedient, cowardly Negro. And from the point of view of his New Negro protagonist, a point of view that is normative within the novel, Griggs shows us in detail that the training is systematic and societally enforced. It implies making no job opportunities available to black graduates, threatening to lynch outspoken black activists, and subduing resistance by opposing a mob to an individual. It is in light of his *Bildung* in a dystopian world and of his heroic resistance to it that one can interpret Belton's fast-paced journey through the United States of the late 1800s and the climactic series of misadventures that in chapter 12 see him survive a hanging and a dissecting board until he is finally catapulted into the utopian world of Imperium.

Even the moment of respite Belton enjoys after he becomes one of the leaders of Imperium is short-lived. Bernard's election as president leads to a disagreement over the means to expand the influence of the organization. Through long digressions of sociopolitical analysis, which are characteris-

tic of utopian fiction, Griggs contrasts Belton's utopia of black empowerment with Bernard's dystopian thirst for power. Griggs relishes Bernard's
rhetoric of violence but nevertheless indicts his desire for uncompromising revolt and revenge against white oppression, as well as his irresponsible
disregard for the dangers of "internecine war" (242). The author scatters
throughout the novel numerous hermeneutic clues to condemn the venge-
ful use of violence when not in self-defense (68, 76–77, 111, 241–42, 247). The
violent tendencies of his leadership epitomize Bernard's lack of the self-dis-
cipline that Belton has painfully had to acquire in his life as a lower-class,
visibly black person (262). Bernard's desire for revenge is also a symptom
of his seduction by the power of whites. Although they reject him because
of his mixed genealogy, he has enjoyed the privileges of whiteness through
the secret support of his powerful white father, and Griggs provides several
clear hermeneutic clues to interpret the incompleteness and ultimate failure of Bernard's race travel as the result of his being ideologically colonized
by acquisitive white values. A case in point are the color-coded images Bernard uses to convince the Imperium members to "strike a blow for freedom": "If we die on the mountain-side, we shall be shrouded in sheets of
whitest snow, and all generations of men yet to come upon the earth will
have to gaze upward in order to see our whitened forms" (221).

In contrast with Bernard's suicidal war plan, Belton proposes a solution
that "courts a peaceable adjustment, yet it does not shirk war, if war is forced"
(246).[10] Griggs presents this strategy, which contemplates a four-year trial
period to educate whites and the eventual emigration of all blacks to Texas,
as rooted in and consistent with the distinctive history and culture of African Americans. It is a utopian vision of empowerment that implies a complex notion of self-assertion and self-determination that moves beyond retributive and suicidal retaliation. If "transforming the individual" can be
considered "the most difficult step on the road to utopia" (Roemer 58), Griggs
presents us a New Negro who remembers the scars he has "received at the
hands of the South" (229) but can still declare that the South "cannot drive
truth from my bosom" (229) or drive the logic of survival from his quest for
black self-determination.

Belton's superior humanity and vision of a truly better society explain his
death and the dismantlement of Imperium not as symptomatic of Griggs's
inability to sustain his own revolutionary vision but rather as the inspirational
martyrdom of a Christlike figure. Belton confirms his stature as an African
American leader by resigning himself without further fighting only to a black-
inflicted death. His courage in accepting death affirms the values that informed his proposal for advancing the Imperium, including the importance

of violent self-defense, if necessary. Similarly, Berl Trout's patriotic betrayal of the Imperium is a seeming oxymoron that foregrounds the fictional narrator's Du Boisian "twoness" (Du Bois, *The Souls* 17) and the antagonistic subject positions of blacks and whites in American society.[11] His betrayal forestalls the power fantasies of Bernard, "reared in luxury, gratified as to every whim, . . . deeming nothing impossible of achievement," a person who does not possess the "restraining" (262) control of Belton and who has embarked on a personal mission of suicidal revenge that would lead to "a universal groan," where even "those who had not been killed [would be] too badly wounded to cry out" (264).

It would be simplistic to interpret Griggs's novel simply as a dated plea to white America to change its ways or as just a literary tool to "force an acknowledgement of equality from the proud lips of the fierce . . . Anglo-Saxon" (*Imperium* 247). *Imperium* is certainly all that, as Griggs himself makes clear metanarratively. But *Imperium* is also a complex and very modern reflection on the pitfalls of nationalism, the complexities of lasting social change, and the dangers of being co-opted by the oppressor's ideology of power in the very process of fighting against it. Griggs succeeds in keeping his vision of black power alive as a utopia, as *docta spes* (Bloch 119), exactly because he (like Delany in *Blake*) does not give fictional reality to the "awful carnage" (*Imperium* 43) and race suicide that would be necessary for its immediate realization. However, he gives fictional reality to the readiness "to buckle on our swords and go forth to win our freedom with the sword just as has been done by all other nations of men" (247), should other means fail. This spirit of self-determination and self-reliance, which gave birth to the Imperium in the first place, survives and is even kindled by Belton's death and the dismantlement of the organization. The possibility and explicit threat of constructing an even "more powerful" (265) organization are reiterated at the very end of the novel and sustain the utopian vision of unstoppable black empowerment and liberation Griggs projects.

Frances E. W. Harper's *Iola Leroy*

> We stand then, it seems to me, in this last decade of the nineteenth
> century, just in the portals of a new and untried movement on a
> higher plane and in a grander strain than any the past has called forth.
> It does not require a prophet's eye to divine its trend and image its
> possibilities from the forces we see already at work around us; nor is it
> hard to guess what must be the status of woman's work under the new
> regime. . . . She stands now at the gateway of this new era of American
> civilization. In her hands must be moulded the strength, the wit, the

statesmanship, the morality, all the psychic force, the social and
economic intercourse of that era. To be alive at such an epoch is a
privilege, to be a woman then is sublime. (Cooper 132, 143)

Whereas Griggs's masculinist bias is so pervasive and un–self-conscious as
to add an unintended dimension to the estrangement a contemporary reader
may feel when approaching *Imperium*,[12] seven years earlier Frances E. W.
Harper had foregrounded in *Iola Leroy* the impact of race *and* gender on the
formal conventions, thematic concerns, and ideological content of utopian
fiction. Reading *Iola Leroy* (1892) as a feminist utopian text foregrounds the
"liberational discourses" (Tate, *Domestic Allegories* 123) underlying a novel
that has traditionally been read as a melodramatic and nonexperimental
romance. Building on Tate's distinction between the romantic cover story and
its deeper significance as an allegory of political desires, I argue that in *Iola
Leroy* the cover story itself is explicitly shaped by the "desire for an ideal
polity" (Tate, *Domestic Allegories* 107) and by a complementary critique of
contemporary racist practices.[13] As a result, Harper's novel is not only allegorical, in the sense that it points to a more radical hidden story, but truly
utopian, because it is thematically and formally structured by Harper's anticipatory vision and depiction of an alternative, better social system. Harper follows classic utopian models far less closely than Griggs or Hopkins,
and her novel is more influenced by other genres such as the *Bildungsroman*
and romantic fiction, which enable her to devote greater attention to psychological processes. However, *Iola Leroy* qualifies as a utopian text both because
it is pervaded by a consistent strain of "utopianism" (Kumar, *Utopia* 81) and
because Harper's utopianism culminates in the articulation of the institutions and principles that will inform the new ideal social order she envisions.

Harper's novel is structured around the literal and metaphoric race travels of the title character. Iola grows up as a privileged, proslavery Southern
belle. After the death of her aristocratic white father, she learns that her
mother was a mulatta slave, albeit so light skinned that she could pass for
white. Her mother had never officially gained her freedom, and because in
the antebellum South children inherited the mother's condition, Iola discovers that she and her siblings, Harry and Gracie, are legally slaves. Whereas
Gracie does not survive the shock of this revelation and dies prematurely,
Iola, though "wild with agony" (*Iola Leroy* 105), lives and is sold as a slave.
Soon thereafter the Civil War breaks out and she is rescued by Northern
troops. The rest of the novel, which represents the longest and most important part of *Iola Leroy*, follows the protagonist's adventures after she decides
to cast her lot with the black race.

Suddenly and dramatically Iola's world is turned upside down. She used to be a person of property and becomes someone's property; as a privileged white woman she was treated as a "lady," but as a slave she is legally beyond the pale of honorable womanhood; whereas formerly blacks were the objects of her pity, blackness becomes a constitutive element of her identity. Iola's condition undergoes a process of change that dramatizes the tensions between the representation of blacks as the objects of racial discrimination and the subjects of their own lives. This metanarrative reflection builds on Harper's opening depiction of the "mystery of market speech," the secret code of communication and resistance among slaves (7), and it becomes even more explicit at the end of the novel, where the obvious similarities between Iola's and Harper's comments on the interventionist uses of writing emerge as hermeneutic clues similar to those Brown and Webb intersperse in their novels.

As in the case of other utopian travelers who suffer psychologically from their change of context, Iola's racial displacement is neither easy nor painless, although it does not prove fatal, as in her sister Gracie's case. It is "a fiery ordeal of suffering" that changes Iola's personality, undermines her health, and exposes her to the risk of madness (*Iola Leroy* 195, 200, 105–6, 274). It is an ordeal that Harper has Iola recount over and over again (*Iola Leroy* 97–108, 113–15, 142, 273) to avoid the easy linearity of the traditional "riches-to-rags" and "rags-to-riches" plots (Baym 35). However, this ordeal also starts Iola on her journey from passing to utopia. As Iola travels beyond the privileges of whiteness into the reality of chattel slavery first and segregation later, she has to "learn to see anew" (Roemer 60), and it is not surprising that even in a novel as centered on dialogue as *Iola Leroy* conversations often are excuses for the long, didactic explanations that are so characteristic of utopian fiction.

In Harper's novel the emphasis on learning is more than a fictional strategy that enables the author to critique her society while envisioning a new one. Rather, it is a process that creates the very possibility of a utopian vision of social change. After having experienced some of the indignities perpetrated by her ex-peers on slaves, and more specifically on female slaves,[14] Iola acquires a different consciousness both of the violence and injustice that underlie her old (white) world of privilege and of the more humane values of her new (black) world.[15] This consciousness is gendered and politicized as Iola reevaluates the disjunction caused by slavery between (black) female virtue and standard notions of (white) female propriety: "I was sold from State to State as an article of merchandise. I had outrages heaped upon me which might well crimson the cheek of honest womanhood with shame, but I never fell into the clutches of an owner for whom I did not feel the utmost loathing and intensest horror. I have heard men talk glibly of the degradation of the negro, but *there is a vast difference between abasement of condition and degradation of character. I was abased, but the men who trampled on me were the degraded ones*" (*Iola Leroy* 115, emphasis mine).

Critics have noted that within the economy of the romantic plot Iola's growing race consciousness and understanding of the connections between patriarchal power, sexism, and racial discrimination are signaled by her rejection of white Dr. Gresham's marriage proposal. Accepting his offer would ensure her reintegration into the privileges of whiteness but at the cost of accepting a situation of racial invisibility, disavowing her genealogy and surviving family ties. In this utopian novel that crosses "the generic boundary between romance and essay" (Donawerth and Kolmerten 5), however, Iola's romantic choices are only one outcome of her race travel. Her critical awareness of her new subject position as a black woman is at once the cause and the result of the journeys she embarks on after her fall from whiteness. These travels are an integral part of Iola's process of learning. They take her through places and experiences that are central to the history of blacks in America and that have been elaborated into fundamental tropes of the African American literary tradition: the black church, Southern folk cultures, the trip South in search of her mother and her ancestral cultural roots, the migration North and the experience of discrimination even there, and the closing "immersion" (Stepto, *From Behind the Veil* x) in the South to uplift the freed blacks and contribute to realizing the utopia of civil equality Harper has argued to be in the making.

Harper's construction of *Iola Leroy* as a utopia emerges clearly by comparison with the recently rediscovered *Minnie's Sacrifice*, a novel she serialized in 1869 in *The Christian Recorder*, a newspaper published by the African Methodist Episcopal Church. Twenty-three years before *Iola Leroy*, Harper conceived the story of Minnie and Louis, unwitting passers who learn about their African American ancestry on the eve of the Civil War. In the post-Emancipation period, after having reunited with their long-lost families, they marry and move South to uplift the freed blacks. The similarities between the plots of *Minnie's Sacrifice* and *Iola Leroy* are obvious, and the earlier novel is even quoted verbatim in the later one. However, in *Minnie's Sacrifice* Harper follows her ideal social workers' lives in the South a little longer, and the tragic outcome of their story is stunningly revealing for us today. In the postbellum South, where "violence and murder were rampant" (Harper, *Minnie's* 85), Minnie's and Louis's lives beyond the happy marriage see the disruption of traditional narrative expectations of heterosexual bliss. Whereas Louis voices very openly his forebodings about the difficulties of Reconstruction in terms that predict the institutionalization of segregation a few years later, the author realizes such forebodings in the plot as Minnie loses her life for the cause she has embraced. Within the economy of the novel, Minnie's untimely death emerges as the celebration of a heroine whose martyrdom acquires mythic status and becomes part of the community's lore a few hours after her death.

Minnie's tragic end lends new and important insight into the utopian features of the happy ending of *Iola Leroy* and into the voluntaristic qualities of the "optimism" that Harper is supposed to have "so readily expressed" in her turn-of-the-century fiction (Tate, *Domestic Allegories* 161). It is by stubbornly and "passionately pursu[ing] the formula of happy endings" (Spillers, Introduction xxvii) that in the later novel Harper tries to bridge the gap (imposed by contemporary racist social practices and re-presented in her novels) between the long-term goal of utopian social change and the short-term need to endure oppressive conditions. In *Iola Leroy*, the brief final portrayal of romantic happiness coexists with an explicit, sustained critique of the "savage elements in our civilization" (*Iola Leroy* 259) and of the discriminatory practices Harper indicts in *Minnie's Sacrifice*.[16] Having portrayed in detail the gender and race limitations imposed on her characters, Harper deploys obtrusively romantic conventions to enable her protagonists to overcome, if only temporarily, the societal obstacles that stand in the way of their self-realization. Invested with the function of saving the heroines from the relentless demands of necessity by opening a space beyond contemporary social realities, the romantic happy ending emerges as self-consciously utopian.

The closing marriages signal the eventual success of self-reliant practices of survival and self-empowerment and emerge metonymically as an inspirational microcosm where social change is successfully realized. The marital happy ending makes the reader experience a veritable utopian moment. A taste of the long-term ideal society is already contained in the ideally egalitarian heterosexual relationship between heroines who have succeeded in achieving an independent sense of self and enlightened heroes of the future who have moved beyond the restricted patriarchal notions of their age, including "complexional prejudices" (*Iola Leroy* 278). Although the romantic aspect remains the most prominent and the most commented upon, Harper's feminist utopia does not simply propose a more perfect or idealized version of traditional ideals of women's self-realization through marriage. Rather, Harper explicitly redefines and expands women's role in ways that rearticulate the representational politics of blackness and result in a detailed project for the utopian restructuring of American society and the American South in particular. Harper's consistent focus on Iola's point of view and on her singular privilege to choose her racial affiliation enables the author to foreground explicitly both the distinctiveness of black culture and the possibility of female heroism.

Although Iola remains largely marginal to the internal dynamics of the slave community (which are described in the first four chapters, whereas the heroine is mentioned for the first time in chapter 5), the representation of post-Emancipation black culture is largely connected with Iola's peregrinations, with her courage and decision-making power. On one hand, Harper emphasizes Iola's duty to choose to be either black or white because there is no societal middle ground between the races. On the other, by portraying Iola's preference for blackness and her subsequent experiences as a member of the African American community, Harper succeeds in moving beyond the tragic mulatta trope that was so popular among contemporary white writers. She reconstructs black cultural distinctiveness on different grounds, foregrounding the specific history of African Americans, the culture of resistance that resulted from the experience of slavery, their truer religious faith, and the group solidarity and self-help philosophy that continue to characterize the black community in the postslavery period.

Iola's repeated and explicit statements of preference for the more humanistic values of black culture and her choice of belonging to the African American community succeed in transforming the narrative significance of blackness. From a visible, ostensibly unambiguous signifier of inferiority and oppression, blackness becomes a cultural force of social change, a grand social mission to construct a new, more egalitarian civilization. Harper represents Iola's shift to a black subject position as paradigmatic of the ideological change that has to occur if utopia is to be realized. It is a process of acquiring a knowledge of the black community and black history that goes beyond the derogatory or condescending stereotypes Iola grew up with and never had any interest in problematizing before the revelation of her own mixed ancestry. In turn, Iola's acquisition of knowledge gives greater fictional visibility and relevance to the black communities she encounters. For the heroine those communities acquire a vitality and complexity that contrast sharply with her initial views on the ineluctable tragedy of black life (*Iola Leroy* 91). Iola's choice of blackness thus opens up the possibility of literary heroism and of a new fictional role beyond contemporary stereotypes to the many unmistakably black characters who surround her. Those characters cannot choose their racial affiliation because of their unambiguous skin color, but they can proudly decide to devote their lives to the advancement of their race.

The chorus of visibly black and often dialect-speaking characters comprises the utopian guides who accompany Iola the race traveler into the new world of blackness. They open the novel with comments on the impending Civil War and on Iola's situation at a time when the newly enslaved heroine is conspicuously absent from the scene. They gain further prominence in their postbellum dialogues with her as they emerge as the repositories of a cultural and historical knowledge that Iola does not possess but wants to learn and share. On a narrative level the difference between them and Iola is marked most obviously by language. The contrast between dialect and standard English functions as a literary marker of the differences between blacks that are determined not only by education but also by age and its implications (i.e., the number of years one has spent in slavery and the amount of black cultural knowledge one possesses). As already noted in the case of *The Garies*, in *Iola Leroy* the contrast between standard English and black dialect is further complicated by the various registers adopted by different characters as well as by instances of strategic bilingualism. For instance, Iola's uncle Robert speaks standard English because he was the "favorite slave" of a mistress who "had fondled him as a pet animal, and even taught him to read," as the reader is told in the very first page of the novel (7). However, Robert also knows dialect (136) and the secret codes of communication among the slaves. Robert's standard English is more informal than Iola's, whose participation in conversations with witty but illiterate ex-slaves such as Aunt Linda remains well-meaning but remarkably wooden until the end, in recognition that as a latecomer into the African American community she does not yet possess enough black cultural knowledge to master a variety of linguistic registers with ease. The professionally successful Lucille Delany, who does not "show the least hint of blood admixture" (199), also speaks standard English, and in ways that can be less stiff than Iola's. Harper describes but does not really show her ability to "banter" (278), which links Lucille's use of standard English with the verbal skills and humor of the dialect-speaking characters, undermining traditional readings that see the acquisition of standard English in itself as progress.

The novelty and complexity of Harper's black characters emerge with great force by comparison with a nineteenth-century text that is often cited as a precursor of *Iola Leroy*: William Dean Howells's *An Imperative Duty* (1891). *An Imperative Duty* resembles *Iola Leroy* for its focus on an unwitting female passer, but otherwise the authors' representations of passing and blackness differ remarkably and significantly. Howells is courageous and "undeniably progressive" (Wonham, "Writing" 720) in his treatment of a controversial issue such as miscegenation because he attempts to undermine through irony prevalent contemporary notions of the tragic mulatto and atavism. Nevertheless, Howells's potentially disruptive deconstruction of race into such sociocultural components as class, education, and beauty is mostly finalized to minimizing the controversial quality of the closing interracial union. He demonstrates that qualitatively (because she is educated and upper-class and looks white) and quantitatively (because she is only one-sixteenth black) his heroine, Rhoda, is not really, or at least not very, black. To the extent that Howells's strategy to undermine the racist stereotype of the tragic mulatta is to question the degree of Rhoda's blackness, his deconstruction of race leaves untouched both negative and condescendingly positive notions of blackness that compare "the remote taint of her [Rhoda's] servile and savage origin" to the "grace of a limp, the occult, indefinable lovableness of a deformity" (*Imperative Duty* 133). Rhoda, unlike Iola, never undergoes a process of learning. Her conviction that the revelation of her mixed ancestry has "murder[ed]" (*Imperative Duty* 88) her remains unshaken throughout the novel, nor does it seem to be questioned by her husband-to-be, Dr. Olney, or by the narrator. In *An Imperative Duty* whiteness remains the normative utopia and passing the best of all possible endings.

As Howells's dissection of race to ensure a happier ending for his heroine leaves intact traditional stereotypes of visibly black African Americans who are supposedly blessed by "natural gayety and lightness of heart" (91), it is not surprising that for Rhoda blacks continue to be interchangeable because they are unknown entities who possess either "no discernible features" (92) or "sad, repulsive visages" (93). Rhoda's prejudiced conviction of the absence of a viable black community has a strong impact on the level of characterization in that it dramatically flattens the heroine. Inserted within a pathological framework of "dutiolatry" (132), "hypochondria of the soul" (149), and shrill nerves, Rhoda's remarkably short-lived desire to "go down there and help [the freed blacks]" (142) can be dismissed easily as a "whimsical suggestion" (106) or an "aimless act of self-sacrifice" (149). The cancellation of black culture thus comes to coincide with the elimination of female autonomous decision making, and Rhoda's self-determination is reduced to the confession of her secret to Olney, who is already privy to it anyway (*Imperative Duty* 135).

It is by contrast with this novel, which some contemporary reviewers already considered excessively liberal ("More Novels" 154), that the thematic and formal novelty of Harper's fiction becomes more evident. In her process of growth, Iola moves beyond Rhoda's "hysterical weakness" (*Imperative Duty* 129) toward heroic decision making, and likewise Harper's novel moves beyond the pitfalls of aimless self-sacrifice and beyond Howells's realism toward the inspirational uses of the utopian. Iola travels beyond the privileges of whiteness, which she discovers to be based on dystopian inequality, into the realities of blackness, whose resilience and humanistic values hold the promise of a better future. Her increasingly sophisticated knowledge of African American culture eventually culminates in the articulation of the social, economic, legal, and Christian principles on which a utopian, egalitarian social order should be based.

Harper's utopian project involves both the private and the public sphere as it grows by a process of expansion. Harper acknowledges the birth of new black women "radiant in beauty and gifted in intellect" (*Iola Leroy* 214), such as Iola and Miss Delany, whose independent sense of self is strengthened by a hard-won understanding of the jeopardies of race and gender.[17] Then she connects self-empowerment to self-fulfillment by conceptualizing "utopian relations" of equality between black women and black men who "do not engage in the patriarchal exchange of women" (Carby, Introduction xxiv). Although she portrays the violent reality of racism through such episodes as the burning of Iola's school and her experiences of discrimination in the North, as well as through her characters' repeated discussions and condemnations of Southern lynchings, Harper's utopia finally achieves societal three-dimensionality as she envisions the cooperation of these new African American individuals and family units in creating a new South that will be a land of freedom for all.

In the last chapter of *Iola Leroy*, Harper details some of the socioeconomic features of her ideal polity, and to give them greater fictional reality she suddenly moves from the narrative past to the present tense in the closing pages of her novel (278–81). Iola's community work to educate children and mothers; Dr. Latimer's activism as "a successful doctor . . . a true patriot and a good citizen" (279) and his involvement in reform movements that valorize the "influence [of the Negro] upon the South" (279); Harry and Lucille's "large and flourishing school" (280); Lucille's defiance of contemporary dictates that married women should not teach (280); Robert Anderson's distribution of land to "poor but thrifty laborers" (280), a belated and black-sponsored realization of the unfulfilled postwar promise of forty acres and a mule; and the possibility for the ex-slaves to live productively and peacefully in the South are some of the features of the utopian social order Harper envisions as a viable, rational, Christian alternative to the dystopian post-Reconstruction reality of segregation and violence she describes in her novel.

The first utopian, truly freed inhabitant of this new world is Lucille Delany, even more than Iola. "Is she young and handsome, brilliant and witty?" Iola asks her brother, and in Harry's answer Harper describes her ideal "new Negro" (Griggs, *Imperium* 62) woman: "She . . . is more than handsome, she is lovely; more than witty, she is wise; more than brilliant, she is excellent" (198).[18] As a successful professional woman "of unmixed blood" (199), Lucille is a harbinger and a promoter of the utopian social system Harper envisions. Through her "school to train future wives and mothers" (199), Lucille is the spokesperson for a rational reordering of society that, in keeping with nineteenth-century feminist notions, starts from the private sphere and expands to "social housekeeping" (Hewitt 301). In portraying Lucille's own successful determination to continue her professional life even after marriage, Harper bridges the gap between private and public sphere, giving fictional reality to a utopian enlargement of woman's sphere that goes beyond the separate but supposedly equal status of female laborers her contemporary Edward Bellamy describes in *Looking Backward*.

Yet in Harper's final vision of utopian bliss, the references to the postmarriage life of the happy couples remain tellingly brief. Harper defies the tendency to closure that Angelika Bammer describes as "the particular paradox" of the utopian genre, in that the "transformative potential [of utopias] is undermined by the apparatus of their self-containment" (18). The ending of *Iola Leroy* stubbornly retains a dual valence. On one hand, it emerges as an inspirational and voluntaristic moment of imaginatively enforced respite where the author, her genteel heroines, and her audience entertain the anticipatory vision of a successful struggle for social change. On the other, in her novel Harper takes us only "on the threshold of a new era" (*Iola Leroy* 271), an era that Harper and her first readers knew had not been realized.[19] It is through the open-endedness of her utopia-in-the-making that Harper effectively injects a sense of estrangement into the extratextual reality of the audience, in the attempt to pass on the tension to fulfill the "concrete" utopian vision she projects (Bloch 107).

To ensure that the consciousness-raising message of her utopian novel would not be swept away by the readers' fulfilled romantic expectations, Harper, like other utopian authors who want "to anchor [their] fiction in reality" (Elliott 112), closes *Iola Leroy* with direct nonfictional statements that function as hermeneutic tools to interpret the novel: "From threads of fact and fiction I have woven a story whose mission will not be in vain if it awaken in the hearts of our countrymen a stronger sense of justice and a more Christlike humanity in behalf of those whom the fortunes of war threw, homeless, ignorant and poor, upon the threshold of a new era" (*Iola Leroy* 282). Distrusting the ability of her white compatriots to appreciate the revisionary import of her story of "uplifted shadows" and wanting to inspire her black readers to "use every power God has given them" (282), Harper clarifies that her own text participates in the project of social change she thematizes in her protagonists' lives and provides metanarrative comments that unequivocally spell out the intended social function of her feminist utopian romance.

Edward A. Johnson's *Light Ahead for the Negro* (1904) and the Politics of Racial Indeterminacy

> But there is a difference between looking on a man as an object of pity and protecting him as such, and being identified with him and forced to share his lot. (Harper, *Iola Leroy* 126)

In his 1988 annotated bibliography of British and American utopian fiction, Lyman T. Sargent briefly describes *Light Ahead for the Negro* as "one hundred years from now a segregated South as eutopia" (132). Although it is not clear whether he recognizes Johnson as a black author, Sargent's brief summary is emblematic of the interpretive difficulties of Johnson's work. Edward A. Johnson's lesser-known and largely neglected utopian novel, *Light Ahead for the Negro* (1904), sheds important light on the distinctiveness of the African American utopian tradition mostly because of its anomalous status within it. As we have seen, the African American utopian novels that deploy race travel as structuring device feature a diversified chorus of black characters and foreground explicitly the epistemological and experiential impact of being black in the United States. In those novels passing, or rather its relinquishment, is a crucial component of race travel because it dramatizes with great immediacy the differences between a normative white and a subaltern black subject position.

Unlike the writers already discussed in this chapter, however, Johnson does not deploy race travel. He presents a new and more enlightened attitude toward African Americans as a measure of the social change that has taken place in his utopian society of the twenty-first century, but his novel is not structured around the dramatic dislocation of point of view that is characteristic of race travel. Instead of thematizing and foregrounding passing in his fiction, Johnson engages in it by choosing to tell his story from the point of view of a racially indeterminate protagonist. As Johnson surely knew, and as Barbara Christian notes, in a societal context of normative whiteness a racially indeterminate character would "generally [be] translated as white" (Introduction xxvii). Readers may also surmise that Johnson's protagonist is not or at least does not look black because his utopian hosts talk to him about "Negroes" in a way that reveals their conviction that he is white (or is he an undetected passer?).

Johnson's choice of racial indeterminacy was far from unique at the turn of the century. Amelia E. Johnson, Paul L. Dunbar, and Emma D. Kelley, for instance, deploy racially indeterminate characters in the hope of reaching and influencing a wider, mixed audience. E. A. Johnson has a similar purpose in mind, as becomes clear from his "Preface" to *Light Ahead for the Negro*. In a context of sharp racial polarization and of scarce interest, as Chesnutt laments, "for books in which the principal characters are colored people, or written with a striking sympathy with that race as contrasted to the white race" (qtd. in Andrews, *Literary Career* 127), Johnson explicitly addresses his only utopian novel to a white audience, and more specifically "to the thousands of sympathetic and well-wishing friends of the Negro race" (v). He constructs a narrative that passes for white, insofar as it presents itself as a novel on the race issue written by an enlightened white time traveler.

By contrast with the novels by Amelia E. Johnson and Emma D. Kelley, the race issue is explicitly addressed in and dominates *Light Ahead for the Negro*. In the very first pages of the novel the protagonist and first-person narrator, Gilbert Twitchell, describes his father as "an abolitionist before the war and afterward an ardent supporter of missionary efforts in the South" (1). Twitchell himself, after completing his degree at Yale in 1906, decides to go south to work as a teacher in a "Negro school" (2) and help "to fit them [the Negroes] for the new citizenship that had developed as a result of the war" (1). At the beginning of the novel Twitchell tells us of how, before going South to start teaching, he boarded a friend's airship for a brief vacation and of how its engine exploded in midair. Twitchell gets lost in the atmosphere, survives in suspended animation, and wakes up 100 years later, in 2006, in a strange room. He then spends the greatest part of this short novel describing the contrast between his past and new society and courting Irene, the niece of his utopian host, Dr. Newell. The marital happy ending ensures his integration in utopia.

When compared with contemporaneous African American utopias by Hopkins, Griggs, and Harper, Johnson's novel provides very clear insight into the different degrees of formal experimentation and thematic subsersiveness that pertain to thematized versus unthematized passing. In the absence of the dramatic foregrounding of a marginalized black subject position that is characteristic of race travel, Johnson's narrative passing results in his greater formal adherence to the conventions of the utopian genre. The novel is structured around the protagonist's time travel, by his dialogues with his utopian hosts, and by his characteristically lengthy digressions on the differences between the utopian present and the preutopian past, especially with regard to the status of African Americans. On a thematic level Johnson's novel seems to confirm the aforementioned lamentations on the limited imagination of African American utopian authors. In *Light Ahead for the Negro,* in fact, segregation has not been eliminated completely, a fact that makes the author's vision of the future appear disappointingly mild. Johnson's text also seems to exemplify the accommodationist aspects of successful passing. When it is not thematized, passing leads to invisibility, to absorption and disappearance into normative whiteness, and to rhetorical inefficacy. Even if one interprets Johnson's choice of engaging in narrative passing as a strategy to reach a larger white audience by circumventing the dichotomized racial discourse and audiences of his time, the fact remains that the price of his choice was a dramatic decrease in the oppositional force of his text, a decrease that emerges clearly by contrast with contemporaneous African American utopias.

Only by exposing Johnson's narrative passing and by contextualizing *Light Ahead for the Negro* within its author's lifelong commitment to advancing his race does it become possible to appreciate the interventionist aims and the significance of Johnson's literary project. Although this contextualization does not necessarily increase its effectiveness for twenty-first-century readers, it does enable us to interpret *Light Ahead for the Negro* in ways other than as an aberration in the career of an otherwise militant spokesperson for black culture and black rights.[20] Johnson's life reveals the utopian impulse and commitment to a better future that also inform his utopian novel. Born a slave in 1860 in North Carolina, after Emancipation Johnson received a formal education and eventually graduated from Atlanta University. He began his career as high school teacher and principal in North Carolina. While teaching he studied law, and in 1907, because of the harsh racial discrimination he faced in the South, he moved to New York, where he practiced law and entered politics. In 1917 he became the first African American elected to the New York State legislature, where he promoted civil rights legislation banning discrimination in public accommodations, hospitals, and employment.[21] He died in 1944 at age eighty-three.

Throughout his long life Johnson was also active in preserving and promoting black history and culture. His published nonfiction works are informed by the same strain of utopianism that inspired the full-fledged utopian vision he articulated in *Light Ahead for the Negro.* In 1893, for instance, he published *A School History of the Negro Race in America from 1619 to 1890,* which became popular as a school text in North Carolina and Virginia and went through several editions. Johnson wrote it at the risk of his own teaching position, to overcome what he describes in the Preface as "the sin of omission . . . on the part of white authors, most of whom seem to have written exclusively for white children, and studiously left out the many creditable deeds of the Negro" (iii). *A School History of the Negro Race* ends on a hopeful note, spelling out the promise of a better day: "Time is yet to bring forth better things for the race. Let there be patience, and an honest, persistent endeavor to do the very best in everything, and ere long we shall 'reap if we faint not'" (190).

A similar faith in the possibility of bringing about social change characterizes his later volume, *Adam vs. Ape-Man and Ethiopia*, which he published in 1931, in the midst of the Depression, at the venerable age of seventy-one. In this scholarly work, which draws on archaeology, scientific theories of evolution, and classical texts to establish the historical importance of ancient African civilizations for the creation of Western culture, Johnson recuperates the central elements of the utopian vision he articulated some thirty years earlier in *Light Ahead for the Negro*. In the introduction Johnson reiterates his lifelong conviction that "The golden rule, 'whatsoever you would that men should do unto you, do ye even so unto them,' seems to be the highest criterion of human conduct coupled with the legal maxim '*sic utere tuo ut alienam non laedas*,' meaning we should so use our own as not to injure others" (vi).[22] In the conclusion, however, which he significantly titled "Looking Ahead," Johnson notes, "Just what the American civilization will bring out in the next hundred or thousand years is difficult to predict, but civilization has existed longer than America, then vanished as mist before the merciless rays of the sun" (283). Threatening America, in Griggs-like fashion, with the possibility of fall and destruction if it falls prey to "injustice and greed" (283), Johnson concludes his last published volume with an exhortation: "America claims to be a Christian nation; it can vindicate this claim only by just and tolerant treatment of the various groups within her borders" (284).

Johnson's lifework sheds important light on his novel, which he must have planned as a *feasible* utopia, an inspirational vision of a realizable and not too distant future. Keeping in mind his intended white audience and the attending "distrust of the reader" (Stepto, "Distrust" 300), one is not surprised to realize that the potential feasibility of Johnson's proposal rests precisely on its incomplete novelty. In describing the twenty-first century, Johnson does not express much faith or interest in the liberatory potential of technological progress in itself. He focuses instead on a collective ideological transformation whereby "many changes considered well nigh impossible one hundred years ago have taken place in almost all phases of the so-called Negro problem" (21).

The most basic ideological transformation is from racial antagonism to racial cooperation, a change that, as Dr. Newell explains, initially resulted "more from a sense of necessity than of justice to the Negro" (71). This trans-

formation becomes the foundation of what could be called a civil rights utopia of affirmative action. It is a utopia based on the recognition, as the female
protagonist puts it, that the "chances [of African Americans] have not been
as favourable as ours" (16) and that positive efforts should be made to assist
those who are "worthy" and "competent" "to fill many places that they otherwise could not" (17). The surprised hero finds out that in the year 2006
"Negroes in the South [were] allowed the use of the books, and . . . were encouraged to read by various prizes" (20), and it becomes easier for a twenty-
first-century reader to share his surprise when one thinks that many years after
the publication of *Light Ahead for the Negro,* in his 1945 autobiographical
volume *Black Boy,* Richard Wright recounted that he still had to lie to get books
out of a Southern library. From an economic point of view, this newly coop-
erative attitude sees the government parcel out the cotton lands "to young
Negroes at a small price, accompanied with means and assistance for the production of the crop" (96). This belated fulfillment of the post-Emancipation
promise of forty acres and a mule is finally described in 2006 as "an act of
the highest statesmanship" (96).

Whereas Bellamy, with whom Johnson has been unfavorably compared
(Reilly 61–62), pushes the race issue out of the picture to imagine a perfect
future, Johnson reinserts blacks in utopia by presenting the solution of the
"so-called Negro problem" (54) as the epitome of utopian social change. He
goes through every possible aspect of it and emphasizes how the new attitude toward the issue of race was accompanied by a more general "triumph
of reason over partisanship and demagoguery" (103). This change benefited
all races and invested all other aspects of the social and political life of the
nation because "the American people had resolved . . . to have the government run according to the original design of its founders, upon the principle of the greatest good to the greatest number" (103–4). The extent of the
"wonderful transformation" (118) that has taken place in the South of the
twenty-first century can be gauged by the fact that blacks stand "on the same
footing legally as other people" (105) and that affirmative action programs
are systematically bridging the socioeconomic gap that centuries of slavery
and segregation created between blacks and whites.

Far from being the result of a stifled life and a stifled imagination, Johnson's
utopian vision of "a 'better' rather than a 'best' life" (Reilly 61) can be rein-
terpreted as a coherent proposal for social change that relies on a plan that is
feasible exactly because it is incomplete. The deliberate quality of this incompleteness is openly admitted in the novel, as Dr. Newell describes his own
world as a utopia in progress: "The end is not yet, the hey-day of our glory is
not reached and will not be until the principles of the Golden Rule have be-

come an actuality in this land" (101). Johnson's South is not a eutopia of segregation but rather a eutopia where civil equality is being systematically realized. The author does not describe a fixed state of perfection but rather the
utopia of a collective desire and commitment to strive toward social justice.

Foregrounding the politics of racial indeterminacy and exposing Johnson's
narrative passing brings to light his use of narrative strategies characteristic
of African American fiction and especially the formal choices he makes to
negotiate his distrust of an intended white readership that he knew to be
complicitous with segregation. The long, central chapter of *Light Ahead for
the Negro*, which comprises more than half the novel, is titled "Now and
Then" and provides a detailed description of the differences between the
utopian present of civil equality and the past of segregation. This chapter
presents an intermingling of fiction and nonfiction that cannot be explained
solely by reference to the utopian writer's preoccupation with the "imaginative reality" (Elliott 104) of his novel. Rather, such intermingling emerges also
as a strategy to anticipate the skepticism of potentially hostile readers through
documentary evidence and can be traced back to the first African American
novel.[23]

Johnson's longest chapter is a patchwork of different fictional "historical"
documents from the preutopian past, loosely tied together by conversations
between the time traveler and his utopian host. For instance, the tirade in
favor of black voting rights is quoted from one of Dr. Newell's history books
(82) that summarizes the opinions of various turn-of-the-century leaders.
This strategy may not be so new in utopian novels, but Johnson, like his
antecedent Brown, self-consciously substantiates the authenticity of these
"documents" by providing numerous footnotes where he quotes extensively and verbatim from a variety of nonfictional historical (without quotation
marks) sources such as newspaper articles, published letters by such figures
as Booker T. Washington (44), and other historical novels such as Albion
Tourgee's 1879 *A Fool's Errand* (53). He articulates a doubly oblique, carefully documented critique of turn-of-the-century white supremacist arguments.

Toward the end of the novel, after having established by such documentary means both the utopian quality of the year 2006 and the irrational, prejudiced, unjust views prevalent a century before, Johnson introduces the trope
of passing in surreptitious and reticent ways so as not to draw too much attention to it or to the ambiguous racelessness of his first-person narrator. In
chapter 7 Johnson touches briefly on one of the most controversial and taboo issues at the turn of the century: miscegenation and the continuing practices of sexual harassment perpetrated by white men on black women. He
does so by telling a "real" story that evokes and blandly revises the most

popular protagonist of nineteenth-century white sentimental fiction: the tragic mulatta. His utopian version of the typical triangle of white husband, white wife, and black mistress may have been intended as paradigmatic of how the new spirit of racial cooperation has come to influence the private sphere of sexuality and the family. As it is told by Irene, however, this story of miscegenation does not escape the conventions of traditional, white-authored tragic mulatta fictions, despite Johnson's attempt to give it a happier ending. The cheated octoroon, who does not know that her supposed husband already has a white wife, falls characteristically and conveniently out of the picture by dying. Supposedly, she dies happily, "never knowing but that she was the true wife of her deceiver" (115). "Her children," Johnson writes, "were adopted by the Guilfords as their own, grew up and entered society under the Guilford name and no-one today will charge them with their father's sin" (115).

By comparison with the other utopian novels discussed in this chapter, Johnson's puzzling portrayal of miscegenation, though clearly intended as a happy overcoming of race prejudice and the one-drop rule, reveals with great clarity the limitations of the author's strategy of narrative passing. The ending of this brief story strongly resembles that of Howells's *An Imperative Duty* because it does not destabilize the racial hierarchies that make passing the happiest possible ending. No ironic or parodic intent seems to be at work here, and this episode emerges as a most obvious indication of the dramatic curtailment of oppositional force that results from Johnson's decision to engage in, instead of thematizing, narrative passing. For a sustained parodic treatment of the representational politics of passing and a dissection of passing as normative utopia, one has to turn to another first-person narrator, James Weldon Johnson's Ex-Colored Man.

3. "New People" and Invisible Men in Charles W. Chesnutt's *The House Behind the Cedars*

One finds appreciation from those who *know,* a very agreeable thing. I think you understand how difficult it is to write race problem books so that white people will read them,—and it is white people they are primarily aimed at. Mine are doing as well as could be expected. (Chesnutt, *"To Be an Author"* 156)

CHARLES W. CHESNUTT's first published novel, *The House Behind the Cedars* (1900) shares with Johnson's *Light Ahead for the Negro* the choice of whites as primary intended readers. As in Johnson's case, Chesnutt's privileged focus on a white readership and his determination to achieve success as an author by publishing with "high class" white publishing houses (Chesnutt, letter to Houghton Mifflin, September 8, 1891, *"To Be an Author"* 75) had a strong impact on his fictional choices. In contrast with Harper and Griggs and with his own earlier unpublished experiments at novel writing (e.g., "Rena Walden" and *Mandy Oxendine*), in *The House Behind the Cedars* Chesnutt foregrounds the white community, while African American life remains in the background, largely beyond the pale even of the light-skinned "old issue free negroes" (*The House* 156) who seem to share many of the caste prejudices and materialistic spirit of the white townspeople. The tone of *The House Behind the Cedars* is remarkably milder and more subtly ironic than that of *Mandy Oxendine* or of Chesnutt's "Future American" essays, which appeared in the Boston *Evening Transcript* in August and September 1900, only a couple of months before the publication of his first novel. Some of the realism of *Mandy Oxendine* and sarcasm of the essays also made its way into *The House Behind the Cedars,* especially through the character of John Walden. Yet Chesnutt's ostensible capitulation, in the second half of the novel especially, under the oppressive weight of a melodramatic plot that consigns the female passer to a tragic mulatta ending notably absent from *Mandy*

Oxendine seems to reveal a compromise with prejudiced white audiences similar to the one Johnson made in his treatment of the interracial love triangle in *Light Ahead for the Negro*.

However, the innovative quality and oppositional force of Chesnutt's fiction are not as curtailed as in Johnson's novel for several important reasons. On one hand, whereas in *Light Ahead for the Negro* the issue of passing receives little and ambiguous thematic attention from the author, it becomes the central topic of *The House Behind the Cedars*, a novel that, "bluntly stated," recounts "the story of a colored girl who passed for white" (Chesnutt, letter to H. D. Robins, September 27, 1900, *"To Be an Author"* 149). On the other hand, Chesnutt devised strategies of narrative passing that represent more complex, sustained, radical, and sophisticated versions of the one used by Johnson. As discussed in chapter 2, Johnson engaged in passing by telling his story from the point of view of a racially indeterminate and presumably white first-person narrator. Chesnutt starts his novel in a similar way by foregrounding the limited point of view of John Walden, whose racial identity is not specified and who is perceived as white by other characters in the novel, and initially by the reader as well. However, Chesnutt undermines slowly and systematically, through indirect circumstantial clues, the impression he has created of the protagonist's whiteness and also reveals explicitly his mixed-race background halfway through the novel. In so doing, Chesnutt unequivocally undermines the reader's assumptions of the legibility of race and foregrounds the narrative shift in point of view from a presumed white to a legally black character. He structures the story of John Walden and his sister Rena around a series of dramatic reversals that recall the "To-Day a Mistress, To-Morrow a Slave" pattern of Brown's *Clotel* or Harper's *Iola Leroy*.

Even after the identity of the passer has been disclosed to the reader, Chesnutt continues to use and to call attention to other strategies of narrative passing.[1] Ironically double-voiced discourse, the "textual miscegenation" (Hattenhauer 28) of literary styles such as realism and melodrama, revisionary intertextuality, and an unreliable third-person narrator—these devices enable Chesnutt to camouflage his unorthodox approach to passing and his insider's perspective on the workings of the color line and to assume a more detached and seemingly unthreatening narrative pose to undermine the "subtle almost indefinable feeling of repulsion toward the negro" (Chesnutt, May 29, 1880, *Journals* 140) of his intended mainstream white readers. Chesnutt's decision to deploy passing both as theme and as narrative strategy in *The House Behind the Cedars* is the source of the stratified, treacherous, and at times puzzling and seemingly contradictory qualities of a text whose literary complexity has not been fully acknowledged and explored.[2]

* * *

Desirous of bringing about a "moral revolution" and "obtaining success" (Chesnutt, May 29, 1880, *Journals* 140), Chesnutt had long been used to strategies of indirect intervention that aimed at covertly influencing his intended white readers without threatening them or pushing them into a defensive posture. His "soft-sell" strategies (McElrath and Leitz 19), which he deployed in the conjure stories that appeared in prestigious magazines such as *The Atlantic Monthly* and eventually were collected in a volume published by Houghton Mifflin, had made him well known and opened a promising literary career for him. His appropriation of a plantation tradition genre such as the local color short story in the black vernacular also granted Chesnutt a forum for his revisionist representation of slavery and its aftermath. Chesnutt succeeded in adding new depth to a popular genre and complicating stereotypical representations of contented and nostalgic ex-slaves. Like Uncle Julius's negotiations with the power of Northern capitalism embodied in John, however, his attempts to subvert a mainstream genre while continuing to address mainstream readers suffered from severe limitations, as Richard Brodhead's critical reconstruction of the publishing history of *The Conjure Woman* confirms.

To a certain extent, however, Chesnutt counted on his message being missed or rather received at an almost subliminal level. Covert intervention had long been part of his poetics, and he had theorized its uses in his journals as early as 1880, when he was twenty-one years old. In a famous passage, Chesnutt writes,

> If I do write, I shall write for a purpose, a high, holy purpose, and this will inspire me to greater effort. The object of my writings would not be so much the elevation of the colored people as the elevation of the whites,—for I consider the unjust spirit of caste . . . a barrier to the moral progress of the American people; and I would be one of the first to head a determined, organized crusade against it. Not a fierce indiscriminate onslaught; not an appeal to force, for this is something that force can but slightly affect; but a moral revolution which must be brought about in a different manner. . . . The subtle almost indefinable feeling of repulsion toward the negro, which is common to most Americans—and easily enough accounted for—, cannot be stormed and taken by assault; the garrison will not capitulate: so their position must be mined, and we will find ourselves in their midst before they think of it. . . . It is the province of literature . . . to accustom the public mind to the idea; and . . . while amusing them to . . . lead them on imperceptibly, unconsciously step by step to the desired state of feeling. (Chesnutt, May 29, 1880, *Journals* 139–40)

These terroristic tactics, which Chesnutt had already deployed with success in *The Conjure Woman,* must have seemed to him even more necessary in *The House Behind the Cedars,* a novel where he aimed to expand commonly held notions on the controversial topic of miscegenation and to give greater psychological depth to one of the most popular, stereotyped, and abused characters in white American fiction: the tragic mulatta.[3] The need to use oblique strategies of narrative passing to circumvent the resistance of the literary establishment to a novel treatment of a taboo issue was felt all the more strongly because Chesnutt had already been working on this story, originally titled "Rena Walden," for many years with little positive response from critics and publishers.[4] Chesnutt's repeated failures to find a publisher for "Rena Walden" in the early 1890s introduced him to "the problem of white editorial resistance to new departures in literary realism dealing with Afro-Americans" (Andrews, *Literary Career* 24). This was a problem he encountered throughout his career. It spelled a fate similar to that of "Rena Walden" for *Mandy Oxendine,* a novelette that, after being rejected in 1897 by Houghton Mifflin "as both an *Atlantic Monthly* serial and a book" (Chesnutt, *"To Be an Author"* 98), eventually merged with "Rena Walden" to produce *The House Behind the Cedars* (Andrews, *Literary Career* 144–50). Chesnutt may have chosen early on to adopt a strategy of indirect intervention, but these experiences made it painfully clear to him exactly how profoundly indirect and imperceptible he had to be to reach the mainstream white audiences he was interested in.

The comparative analysis of *Mandy Oxendine* and *The House Behind the Cedars* is in this respect particularly fruitful, both because Mandy is "the first girl who passes for white in Chesnutt's fiction" (Andrews, *Literary Career* 146) and because of the striking differences in tone between these two books. Chesnutt's rewriting of his original story of passing aims at containing its novelty and realism in ways that recall Brown's revisions of *Clotel* and therefore sheds important retrospective light both on the artistry of the earlier author and on Chesnutt's debt to that tradition of novels of passing, in which he was "well read" (Andrews, Foreword xi).[5] By comparison with *The House Behind the Cedars, Mandy Oxendine* is remarkable for the realistic directness with which it addresses controversial issues such as sexual harassment, lynching, and the legitimacy of passing as a response to white prejudice. In this novelette the opportunities for status and wealth available to whites remain the object of desire, especially for the all-but-white title character, but Chesnutt's primary focus is on the black and mulatto community. In contrast with *The House Behind the Cedars,* in *Mandy Oxendine* Chesnutt reveals the racial identity of his two potential passers early and therefore does not engage the readers themselves but only the other characters in the novel in the play with racially indeterminate characters that characterizes the first half of *The House Behind the Cedars*.

Determined to move beyond the Uncle Julius type of black character toward a more innovative and realistic literary depiction of blackness, in *Mandy Oxendine* Chesnutt foregrounds a large chorus of visibly black secondary characters, following a strategy that can be traced back, through Harper and Griggs, to Brown. He also grants unprecedented visibility and dramatic force to the character of "a little negro girl" (*Mandy Oxendine* 8): Rose Amelia. Though at times giving in to the more traditional comic characterization of lower-class, poorly educated blacks, Chesnutt's portrayal of the psychology of the curious, intelligent, but unattractive black girl who falls precociously in love with her professor, resents dominant standards of white beauty, attempts to secure the object of her desire, and eventually succumbs to a tragic ending reaches dramatic tones of psychological realism that foreshadow the character Pecola in Morrison's *The Bluest Eye*. In its depiction of black characters *Mandy Oxendine* shows clearer connections than *The House Behind the Cedars* with the tradition of novels of passing I have outlined in the previous chapters. All-but-white Tom Lowrey, who unlike Mandy does not pass and is a committed teacher in a black school, also is in line with the race heroes of other turn-of-the-century African American novels, although Chesnutt in the end plays with the disruptive possibilities of passing in ways that, for instance, were ruled out of *Iola Leroy*.[6]

Chesnutt's revisions of his treatment of passing in *The House Behind the Cedars* are enlightening of the ways in which he planned to reach and influence his white audience imperceptibly. By comparison with *Mandy Oxendine*, in fact, *The House Behind the Cedars* possesses a pervasive romancelike quality. The main characters are more idealized: The scheming and determined Mandy is substituted by naive Rena, her lecherous white suitor Utley by a more sincerely passionate Tryon, the possessive and vindictive Amelia by noble-hearted Frank.[7] The most controversial themes, such as lynching, disappear and illicit sexual desire and harassment are foregrounded most explicitly in connection with the secondary character Jeff Wain. In romancelike fashion, the allegorical qualities of these characters are emphasized by their names (e.g., Judge Straight) and their fairy-tale valence through intertextual references to characters from such novels as Edward Bulwer-Lytton's 1843 *The Last of the Barons* (e.g., Warwick the Kingmaker, George Duke of Clarence) and Sir Walter Scott's 1819 *Ivanhoe* (e.g., Rowena), references that were very familiar to Chesnutt's readers. This initial aura of romance of *The House Behind the Cedars* eventually becomes so overshadowed by the strong melodramatic tones of the second half of the novel, where allegory also degenerates into caricature, as to make the first half seem realistic by comparison, but not by comparison with *Mandy Oxendine.*

In *The House Behind the Cedars* Chesnutt also makes greater compromises with traditional gender roles and sacrifices the originality of his earlier heroine to further the career of his male hero. As Andrews notes, "John Walden [takes] on many of the characteristics of Mandy Oxendine" (*Literary Career* 148) and voices her determination and entrepreneurial spirit. Chesnutt cross-dresses Mandy, so to speak, and makes her pass as a man in his new novel, playing with gender identities in ways that recall Brown's *Clotel.* But whereas Brown thematizes such cross-dressing to his heroine's benefit, to grant her greater freedom of movement, Chesnutt engages in it to enhance his own freedom of movement as an author and circumvent the resistance of publishers and audience alike to his irreverent treatment of miscegenation by reassuring them at least of his more traditional gender politics.

This instance of narrative cross-dressing points to the most significant change Chesnutt made in revising *Mandy Oxendine* for inclusion in *The House Behind the Cedars:* the different role and increased unreliability of the narrator. The omniscient narrator of *Mandy Oxendine,* the realistic recorder of mulatto life, acquires a more crucial and at the same time more covert and insidious role in *The House Behind the Cedars* as he hides behind and manipulates the limited point of view of his characters. In *The House Behind the Cedars* the narrator, though at times outspoken in defending his protagonists' right to pass or in philosophizing about the relativity of right and wrong, for the most part acts incisively behind the scenes, manipulating the structure of his tale to lead the reader on, proving his unreliability by withdrawing crucial information (such as his characters' racial background) for half the novel, intervening in the narrative most forcefully and effectively through oblique metanarrative clues. The narrator himself deploys strategies of passing that parallel those he describes in the adventures of his protagonists.

This strategy of narrative passing strongly influences the structure of *The House Behind the Cedars,* especially the aforementioned contrast between the first half of the novel, which foregrounds the pragmatic point of view and success story of John Walden (alias Mandy Oxendine, alias John Warwick, as he renames himself after passing), and the second half, which recuperates the melodramatic sweep and tragic ending of the earlier manuscript of "Rena Walden." The contrast between the two halves is so obvious and jarring as to call attention to itself in ways that reverberate with intertextual resonances. An immediate intertextual referent is Howells's 1891 race novel, *An Imperative Duty,* where the thematized contrast between realism and melodrama is central to the happy resolution of the all-but-white heroine's dilemma. Unlike Howells, Chesnutt does not resolve the contrast between the "practical point of view" (*The House* 79) of John Walden and his heroine's melodramatic qualities by ridiculing her as whimsical or portraying her scruples as ultimately groundless. Rather, Chesnutt emphasizes the contrast by taking melodrama to its predictably tragic conclusion and leaving it in unresolved opposition with the wonderful prospects that were so reasonably outlined in the first half of the novel. Chesnutt's strategy is once again reminiscent of Brown's dual plot device in *Clotel,* a continuity that is indirectly substantiated by the similarly critical judgments of scholars who, also in Chesnutt's case, have noted the "strained" credibility of the plot (Andrews, *Literary Career* 171).[8]

As I have already argued in Brown's case, assuming that Chesnutt simply made a mistake would not do justice to the artistry with which he constructed his novel or to the fact that, because he had been working on this story for years, *The House Behind the Cedars* was not really a "novice effort" (Andrews, *Literary Career* 171). Rather, the very obviousness of the contrast between the first and the second half of the novel and the author's critically acknowledged "concern with the architectonics of fiction" (Andrews, *Literary Career* 171) reveal Chesnutt in the process of destabilizing the new literary hierarchy that opposed experimental (white) realism to the old-fashioned melodrama of race. As Chesnutt knew, this opposition reverberated with broader, far-from-novel implications of black inferiority and was on a continuum with the "feeling of repulsion toward the negro" (Chesnutt, May 29, 1880, *Journals* 140) that Howells himself voices even in the process of ridiculing race prejudice.

This deliberately jarring and unresolved contrast between realism and melodrama in the novel is anticipated by the similarly jarring contrast between "affection" and "bitterness" (*The House* 2) that dominates the memories of the mysterious "stranger from South Carolina" (*The House* 1) who walks around Patesville at the very beginning of the novel. Flashes of the violence of slavery stubbornly intrude into the description of a small Southern town "with which Time had dealt . . . tenderly" (4).[9] These flashbacks have a surprising, unsettling effect in a novel that seems to start off as a plantation tradition–style reminiscence of the good days before the war as experienced by a character who is perceived to be one "of the South Ca'lina bigbugs" (2). As the first part of the novel draws to its close and the secret of John Walden's identity is unequivocally disclosed, the reader can account for that contrast retrospectively as a result of Walden's mixed heritage, but its unsettling effect lingers, undermining any unexamined tendency to nostalgic reverie. It also provides a hermeneutic clue that reverberates through the rest of the novel as an expectation of ambiguity, as a distrust of a potentially treacherous text.

The text is indeed treacherous. In the first half of the novel, slavery works as a subtle but potent undercurrent at another level as well. This undercurrent qualifies John Walden's rhetoric of heroic self-making, revealing the nefarious, posthumous impact of the peculiar institution on American society in ways that add a structurally ironic echo to the initial paean on the American dream and to Walden's rationalizations of the pleasures of passing. The clues are indirect but not too subtle. In the second chapter, for instance, Walden's plans to "save" his sister from the continuing stigma of caste exact a high price from Molly. Chesnutt points out exactly how high it is by casting the scene in the classic terms of a slave mother who begs the slaveowner not to sell her children away from her: "The mother looked from son to daughter with a dawning apprehension and a sudden pallor. When she saw the yearning in Rena's eyes, she threw herself at her son's feet. 'Oh, John,' she cried despairingly, 'don't take her away from me! Don't take her, John, darlin', for it'd break my heart to lose her! . . . Don't take Rena, John; for if you do, I'll never see her again, an' I can't bear to think of it. How would you like to lose yo'r one child?'" (24–25). To make the clue harder to miss and foreshadow the heavy costs of the American dream for some American citizens, Chesnutt titles chapter 4, where Rena leaves with her brother to enter his world of white privilege, "Down the River." This is an ominous beginning for the career of a potential self-made woman, one that links the first half of the novel with the closing chapters where the once–Queen of Love and Beauty will turn into a fugitive slave pursued by obtrusive suitors turned slave catchers.

The sense of impending doom is created almost imperceptibly by these underlying references to slavery even before the reader learns of the Waldens' mixed racial background. It is confirmed on a more overt level by Chesnutt's ominous intertextual references to historical romances that were popular among his readers. Admirers of Edward Bulwer-Lytton's historical novel *The Last of the Barons* would have recognized the names and connected Chesnutt's male protagonists with the historical figures of Warwick the Kingmaker and George Duke of Clarence. They may have been taken aback, if only subliminally, by the discrepancy between the bourgeois, "practical point of view" (*The House* 179) of John Walden (alias Warwick) and Bulwer-Lytton's more idealized portrayal of the Kingmaker as "the symbol of the feudal state" fighting against "the new commercialism" (Campbell, *Edward Bulwer-Lytton* 83). They may have also recalled that in Bulwer-Lytton's novel George of Clarence is an evil, vain, and "perjured" (*The Last* 602) traitor. Similarly, fans of Sir Walter Scott would have enjoyed Chesnutt's play with the scene of the coronation of the Queen of Love and Beauty in *Ivanhoe*, but they may also have recognized the ill-boding difference between the "stately beauty" of Rena, with her Rebecca-like "dark and glossy brown" hair, "ivory" skin (7), and "large dark eyes" (86) and the Saxon beauty of Scott's Rowena, with hair "of a colour betwixt brown and flaxen," an "exquisitely fair complexion," and "clear blue eyes" (*Ivanhoe* 56).[10]

Only halfway through the novel, after Rena's secret has been disclosed to the reader, does Chesnutt have a minor character "well up in her Scott" comment explicitly on the fact that Tryon's dark beauty "should have been named Rebecca instead of Rowena" (*The House* 137).[11] By then, Chesnutt's strategic misquotation of the original texts has served its functions: First, it has intensified the ominous subtext that runs through the first half of the novel, foreshadowing and building up to the explosion of melodrama in the second; second, it has elicited "human interest" (Chesnutt, letter to H. D. Robins, September 27, 1900, *"To Be an Author"* 150) for his protagonists by inserting them in a literary and historical tradition of established heroes and heroines. By first playing with the readers' expectations and then explicitly drawing their attention to his own misquotation of those popular texts, Chesnutt makes his white audience experience "the ironic and somewhat treacherous relationship between the black reader and white western" literature (Herron 291), which Chesnutt knew very well from his own experience as a black writer trying to appropriate and revise white literary genres. Chesnutt thus provides a metanarrative clue to the unreliability of his own novel and its deceiving subtexts, offering a veritable Ariadne's thread to guide the reader through the melodramatic maze of the second half of the novel.

The real master of treachery in the first half of *The House Behind the Cedars* is John Walden. He dexterously controls the ironies of his secret identity through a detached, carefully two-toned discourse that mirrors the narrator's own. In a conversation between "white" men on "the subject of negroes," for instance, the "lofty and impersonal manner that gave his [Walden's] words greater weight than if he had seemed warped by a personal grievance" (*The House* 42) represents a hermeneutic clue à la Brown. It alerts the reader to the treacherousness of the narrator's own assumed "traditional narrative pose of the detached, somewhat condescending observer of 'the southern Negro'" (Andrews, *Literary Career* 25), the very pose that had ensured the success of *The Conjure Woman* and that Chesnutt now parodies through John Walden. As Chesnutt aspires to lead his readers on imperceptibly, Walden manipulates people and situations with an intelligence and ability the reader is compelled to admire. His use of his mother's ambitions to convince her to let go of Rena, the light irony with which he ridicules Southern feudal plantation nostalgia and dissects contemporary notions of Southern chivalry as nothing more than a "masquerade" (62), and the argumentative skill with which he leads Rena "to regard silence [about her racial heritage] in the light of self-sacrifice" (82) all substantiate the sense of his enterprising spirit and "power of attraction" (68).

Walden's power is reinforced on a less overt structural level as well. The author makes him enter the text surrounded by an aura of mystery on his identity that enables him to pass for white "on the reader before [he does] so in the novel," as Andrews insightfully notes (*Literary Career* 159). This strategy of narrative passing, whereby the reader is as ready as the characters in the novel to assume that Walden is white, serves several important uses. As it is initially told, Walden's success story is quintessentially American. A "bright" (165), "stout-hearted" (166) lad convinced that he "need not be black" (172), he has "taken a man's chance in life" (18) and has proven able to make the most of it. When he explains in vague terms to his unsuspecting, blue-blood friend Tryon (and to the reader) that he and his sister are "new people" (83), Walden's American dream has already been realized; he has risen from his original circumstances thanks to his luck and pluck. Tryon predictably responds by applauding American individualism and making a proud nativist comparison between Europe as the land of oppressive social hierarchies and the United States as the land of opportunity: "I will tell you a family secret, John, to prove how little I care for ancestors. My maternal great-great-grandfather, a hundred and fifty years ago, was hanged, drawn, and quartered for stealing cattle across the Scottish border. How is that for a pedigree? Behold in me the lineal descendant of a felon!" (84).

By the time the secret of Walden's identity is unequivocally disclosed to the reader, though not yet to Tryon, and passing becomes a theme in the novel, Chesnutt's strategy of narrative passing has already undermined traditionally negative responses to mulattos and created the kind of human interest for his characters that Chesnutt wanted to inspire in his readers. The readers who took Walden's whiteness for granted feel tricked but have to continue admiring the trickster or become aware of the inconsistency that would make them withdraw their admiration. Like them, the white characters in the novel who share the passer's secret (i.e., Judge Straight and Tryon) develop a kind of double consciousness similar to his as they are compelled to realize the discrepancy between Walden's quintessentially American success story and the equally American tradition of racial prejudice that makes his success an aberration and a threat.[12] Following a long-standing tradition in African American fiction, Chesnutt thus dramatizes through his white characters the kind of reaction he wanted to elicit in his white readers.

Distrustful of his white readers' willingness to sustain the weight of this double consciousness, Chesnutt devotes the central chapter, "Under the Old Regime," to discussing the making of his "new people" (83).[13] The author traces the Waldens' family history back to "the misty colonial period" (156). He places miscegenation at the very origin of America's new people as a whole, as one of the country's "ancient landmarks" (164), and explains its continuance as a result of the economic exploitation and marginality to which blacks, whether in slavery or in freedom, have been condemned for the economic benefit of whites. The gospel of acquisitiveness at the heart of the American dream makes it "convenient" and "profitable" (*The House* 170) to keep blacks in subjection, but it also turns against itself because it provides the rationale for social climbing by any means possible, including passing.

In this retrospective chapter, the conversation between Judge Straight and young Walden shows the depth of this contradiction by foregrounding the double consciousness of a lawyer of high social standing and ancient lineage who represents the best and rarest qualities of the Old South. The judge is caught between the "immemorial tradition" of white prejudice (*The House* 120), the equally immemorial but unacknowledged tradition of miscegenation, and the evidence of his senses, which proclaims young Walden's blackness to be a social fiction. The judge "look[s] in vain for any sign of negro blood" (171) in the young man. He notices only "the lad's resemblance to an old friend and companion and client" (167), the wealthy white man who had had a long-lasting affair with Walden's mother and had died without making any of his intended financial provisions for his illegitimate mixed-blood children. Capitalizing on his protagonist's white looks and counting on the fact that his white readers would share young Walden's conviction that white is right, Chesnutt turns racial hierarchies against themselves and makes them a commonsense rationale to justify the expediency of passing.[14] As the mental processes of the judge unfold in chapter 18, his decision to help young Walden acquire a profession and further his plan of passing emerges less as racial treachery than as a deed inspired by respect for a dead friend and by the quintessentially American notion of giving a chance to an obviously exceptionally motivated young man who happens to have been born a social outcast.

In *The House Behind the Cedars*, then, the double consciousness that results from the contrast between ideals and customs, between American individualism and racial discrimination, is not exclusive property of the passer. Rather, Chesnutt portrays it as almost contagious. At some level it is obvious even to those, such as Dr. Green, who are stolidly impervious to its broader implications (*The House* 112–13). This troubling double consciousness affects more deeply the whites who know the passer's secret and reaches the status of a destructive obsession in the case of characters who have a personal stake in the passer's fate. On Tryon, for instance, the Waldens' secret seems to have a debilitating effect like the one Webb describes in his passer Clarence. In the second half of the novel especially, Tryon becomes moody, doubt-ridden, given to violent oscillations between despondency and rashness, between nightmares of Rena turning into "a hideous black hag" (147) and his love dream with Rena as Queen of Love and Beauty.

Chesnutt's sustained and conspicuous emphasis on the double consciousness that unsettles the white characters who know the passer's secret represents a hermeneutic clue to the broader contrast between the first and the second part of the novel. Like Tryon, after the revelation of Rena's ancestry the reader is thrust into the dramatic contrasts, exasperated feelings, and nightmarishly Manichean descriptions of good and evil that characterize the "unwholesome vapors" (Howells, *"Editor's Study"* 76) of melodramatic fiction. That they are unwholesome the reader is also warned. The dramatic change of narrative tone does not come unannounced because the second half of the novel opens with a conversation between the two Walden siblings in which the pragmatic logic of John's argument in favor of passing is for the first time not so much defeated as submerged by the flood of Rena's commonplace arguments "of divine foreordination" (182) and the separation of the races. John Walden, who until now has been the hero of the novel and whose judgment has been established as powerful, "attach[es] no weight whatever" (182) to that argument. He easily undermines it with the usual force of his irony and influences the reader to do the same. Chesnutt's intended white readers may well have shared Rena's belief in divine foreordination and the need for the races to remain separate, but their conviction would be unsettled by the context in which that argument is abruptly put forth (i.e., by the fact that its spokesperson is a powerless and superstitious heroine who also believes in dreams) and by the contrast between the "excited" (*The House* 94) tone of Rena and her brother's masterful irony.

Chesnutt calls attention to the stereotypical melodramatic sweep into which the novel has plunged through other means. The allegorical valence that names such as Straight and Frank have in the first part of the novel turns into blatant caricature in the second half of *The House Behind the Cedars*. In the case of Jeff Wain, for instance, the stereotyped wickedness of this mulatto is so emphasized as to call attention to itself, especially because Chesnutt has already commented on, and dismissed, the prototype of "the sneaking, cringing, treacherous character *traditionally ascribed* to people of mixed blood" (128, emphasis mine) in the first part of the novel. The grotesque description of Wain certainly was familiar to Chesnutt's white readers, and some of them may even have thought it founded in truth, but, as with Rena's arguments on divine foreordination, by the time Chesnutt introduces him, this stereotyped figure is connected with such a sharp change of narrative tone as to seem strange.

The ominous intertextual references to white novels that characterize Chesnutt's initial portrayal of George Tryon and Rena Walden become clearer in the second part of the novel, where they function as another way to foreground the artificiality of melodrama and the dichotomized notions of race that traditionally informed it. To portray Tryon's transformation from Prince Charming into the Bulwer-Lytton-like villain who is partly responsible for Rena's death, Chesnutt evokes once again *An Imperative Duty* and attributes to Tryon much of the hysterical weakness that characterizes Howells's Rhoda Aldgate. Although at the tournament he gives an impression of "coolness and steadiness" (53), after learning the Waldens' secret Tryon shows his true colors, so to speak, and falls prey to confusion and indecisiveness. His nightmares of Rena becoming "black" parallel Rhoda's disgusted reactions in the black church, and his uncontrolled oscillations between love and disgust for blacks and for himself echo hers. To ensure that they would not be missed, Chesnutt provides an explicit clue to these intertextual references. He titles "Imperative Business" the chapter in which Tryon expresses a self-sacrificing readiness to pay "whatever . . . price must be paid for her [Rena's] salvation" (208), a readiness that proves as short-lived as Rhoda's imperative duty to devote her life to her mother's people. As a matter of fact, even before he discovers his beloved's secret, the "magnanimity" (*The House* 84) with which Tryon initially treats the subject of the Waldens being new people vanishes quickly as he talks with prejudiced Dr. Green and feels, as Chesnutt ironically phrases it, "a certain strong illumination upon the value of birth and blood" (137). Like John and Rena, Tryon has been masquerading, camouflaging his true identity and deep-seated prejudices.

The effect of Chesnutt's revision of Howells's novel on Rena is to endow her with authentically tragic stature and to save her story from being stereotypical. Initially portrayed as passive, then as illogical, and finally as naively idealistic, Rena eventually acquires greater self-awareness and determination as a result of her experiences as an unprotected working woman, and she also starts defending herself actively from her importunate suitors. By that time, however, she is already caught in an oppressive web of circumstances whose deterministic sweep dramatizes the lack of a safe space for women like Rena both in society and in fiction. Her story seems to be finally channeled into a tragic mulatta plot, but with an important difference. Rena's death results not from some Howellsian aimless self-sacrifice but from an effort of self-preservation. As all her systematic, cautionary maneuvers to discourage her unwanted suitors are undermined by the ill judgment of one of her pupils, Rena escapes from her persecutors and goes through a dramatic ordeal that breaks open the melodrama of the second half of the novel and endows Rena's story with some of the heroic overtones of the slave narrative. Rena's ill-fated flight for freedom has a direct antecedent in Harper's *Minnie's Sacrifice*, in the character of the fugitive slave Moses who dies after reaching the North. Rena does not die like the stereotypical tragic mulatta as a result of "the painfully acquired knowledge which prevents her from being white and her own inner being which will not allow her to be anything else" (Payne 19). Neither is "the plot of return" (Posnock 348) romanticized in *The House Behind the Cedars*. On the contrary, she dies because the conditions of racial subordination that would have made her beauty "her greatest curse" (Jacobs 27) during slavery are still powerfully at work in an unregenerate post-Reconstruction South.

The depth of Rena's character emerges clearly by contrast with Tryon's. Chesnutt takes pains to make Tryon more likable than the "loud, blustering bigot" (Sedlack 131) he was in a version of "Rena Walden" and less negative a character than Utley in *Mandy Oxendine*. Nevertheless, after his love dream falls through, Tryon is overwhelmed by confusion, self-pity, and nervous excitement, and he does not seem able to come to a manly decision about Rena. By contrasting him with such a grotesque villain as Wain, Chesnutt maintains the readers' sympathies on Tryon's side. Yet this "impressionable and impulsive young man['s]" gentlemanliness (*The House* 225) is tarnished by his uncontrolled mood swings, a self-commiseration that makes him feel "raped",[15] and less than honorable, albeit temporary, intentions that he does not even have the courage to acknowledge to himself.[16] Tryon's final readiness to lose the world for love does not emerge as anything more serious than the fixation of a spoiled child whose toy has acquired value only because it has been taken away from him,[17] and his psychological ordeal does not seem more profound or authentic than his earlier gilt paper and cardboard disguise as a knight. Tryon turns into an exasperated and parodic imitation of the romantic hero, and his selfish disregard for Rena's wishes ultimately is as instrumental in precipitating her death as Wain's meanness. He also becomes the object of the structural irony of the author, who dooms to failure all his hectic efforts to find Rena.

Chesnutt not only reveals Tryon to be but a poor, hysterical, and ineffective imitation of a knight in shining armor but also finally gives increased visibility to the real chivalric spirit of a seemingly secondary character: Frank

Fowler. In *The House Behind the Cedars* a crowd of visibly black secondary characters surround the protagonists and make cameo appearances in the novel. Workers, clerks, servants, "negro boys" (*The House* 121), and school-children play an important but, in contrast with other African American novels of passing, unwitting role in moving the plot forward. Dark-skinned, dialect-speaking, working-class Frank Fowler initially stands out in this crowd mostly because of his selfless and hopeless love for Rena. A decade before the publication of *The House Behind the Cedars,* in a letter to George Washing-ton Cable in which he laments the rejection of the "Rena Walden" manu-script by *Century* editor Richard Watson Gilder, Chesnutt notes that "all the good negroes . . . whose virtues have been given to the world through the columns of the *Century,* have been blacks, full-blooded, and their chief vir-tues have been their dog-like fidelity and devotion to their old masters," and he adds, "I don't care to write about these people" (June 13, 1890, *"To Be an Author"* 65). Frank seems to be exactly one such person (in fact, he was one of the few characters Gilder liked in Chesnutt's rejected manuscript), but in *The House Behind the Cedars* he comes back with a vengeance. It is in his depiction of Frank that Chesnutt articulates a sustained metanarrative reflec-tion on the politics of representation of blacks in fiction and on the invisi-ble but crucial presence of what Morrison almost a century later called the "Africanist presence" in nineteenth-century American fiction (Morrison, *Playing* 6).

To do that in ways that would elude the censorship of the mainstream publishing houses he wanted to infiltrate, Chesnutt once again resorts to narrative passing. Just as John Walden passes for several chapters in *The House Behind the Cedars* before the reader realizes that he is of mixed ancestry, so does Frank Fowler make his invisible presence felt long before the reader be-comes acquainted with him enough to realize that he is going to be an im-portant actor in the novel. From the very beginning, as we discover later on, Frank has been present in all the crucial scenes of the novel: He has been looked at, but not seen, although he manages to see everyone and everything. In the first chapter, an unnamed man sees John Walden look furtively at the house behind the cedars, and the latter "scarcely noticed" him (12). Again in chapter 2, Walden is not able to see clearly the man whose figure is "outlined in the yellow light streaming from the open door of a small house between Front Street and the cooper shop" (14). Like John Walden, readers see only the outline of the unnamed character whom we discover to be Frank only in chapter 4. Though described in positive and far-from-stereotypical terms as "a dark-brown young man, small in stature, but with a well-shaped head, an expressive forehead, and features indicative of kindness, intelligence, humour, and imagination" (37), Frank is scarcely noticed because he does not possess any of the traditional requirements for a hero, being neither beautiful nor rich, neither powerful nor highly educated. It is briefly mentioned that "he had saved her [Rena's] life once" (38), but he is described as "not proud" (38), "humble" (38), and "faithful" (39), and his marginal role as a visibly black working-class character seems confirmed when Rena goes with her mother to the boat that will take her to a new life of privilege while "Frank follow[s] with the valise" (40).

Chesnutt's play with Frank's invisibility and with traditional representations of black characters in fiction becomes more conspicuous in the chapters that take place in Clarence. In chapter 5, "The Tournament," in which Rena triumphs in white society and starts her love story with Tryon, a long and conspicuously digressive paragraph is dedicated to a small event: A piece of one of the riders' lances strikes "the head of a colored man . . . who stood watching . . . with an eager and curious gaze" (49) and who later follows the passers home, although "no one of the party noticed" him (57). The reader does not notice him either for the next nine chapters, until in chapter 14 the narrator reveals that the protagonist of that minor episode was Rena's "loyal friend" (124) Frank, who had followed her to Clarence, contented to see her happy in her new life and choosing not to reveal his presence in order not to "sow the seeds of doubt or distrust in the garden of her happiness" (127).

This revelation of Frank's unseen presence even in Rena's white life occurs at the same time as the other major revelations of Rena's mixed genealogy and Tryon's own reversion to racist white type. Nobody is what he or she seemed anymore, and this is true for Frank as well, who acquires greater depth and relevance in the novel. By deciding not to reveal his presence to Rena, Frank emerges not only as a "natural," because dark-skinned and working-class, invisible man but also as someone who has nobly chosen to remain invisible to protect the woman he loves. Remarking explicitly on his generosity and "fine delicacy" (127), the narrator slowly revises Frank's status within the novel and prepares the ground for the role reversal that takes place in the second part of *The House Behind the Cedars*. There, Tryon the would-be knight gives in to his selfish desires in ways that fatally endanger Rena. He emerges on a moral level as the specular image of Jeff Wain, although he is richer, more beautiful, and more polished than the manipulative mulatto. Frank instead proves to be the only knightly character in the novel because he is governed by impulses that are not blindly selfish and is also the only one who actually helps Rena. Frank's capacity to see while remaining unseen by whites enables him to find the fugitive heroine and take her back to her mother, eluding Tryon's search.

Chesnutt's emphasis on Frank's invisibility in the white world is too systematic and conspicuous not to have been deliberate. It constitutes a strategy to complicate and destabilize traditional literary representations of race that in many respects anticipates, for instance, Ralph Ellison's *Invisible Man.* However, its effectiveness in *The House Behind the Cedars* remains limited because the author, unlike Ellison, never explicitly thematizes the trope of invisibility he uses in his characterization of Frank. Although the practice of passing for white is discussed in the novel by both the Walden siblings and the narrator, Frank's invisibility is not. It functions mostly at a metanarrative level, a fact that may explain the relative success of *The House Behind the Cedars* by comparison with *The Marrow of Tradition,* in which Chesnutt portrays black resistance in more overt ways.[18] Analogously, Frank's awareness and strategic use of his invisibility can be surmised but are not explicitly stated. The plot makes clear that he possesses survival skills, but the only time Frank shows his potential for tricksterism occurs at the end of the novel when, to draw the attention of some white men away from the unconscious Rena he is taking home on his cart, he pretends to believe that she may have a contagious disease.

In *The House Behind the Cedars* the greater visibility and relevance of Frank at the end of the novel still fall short of resulting in the kind of unequivocally revisionary, oppositional portrayal that characterizes some of the visibly black characters in Harper's and Griggs's novels or even in the earlier ones by Brown and Webb. Frank's status as a secondary character is never fully revised, and his invisibility, although it gives him some advantages over white characters, leaves him powerless to save Rena from discovery and later from death. He remains "a godmother without a wand" (Harris, "Chesnutt's Frank Fowler" 21). The ending sees him join Rena briefly as protagonist of the closing melodramatic scene, but he is not closer to being a potentially suitable partner for her.

The really new and invisible man in *The House Behind the Cedars,* the one who escapes the unwholesome vapors of melodrama by disregarding both his own responsibilities toward his sister and the serious dilemmas of Rena's life as an ex-passer, is John Walden. Halfway through the novel, he returns to the invisibility from which he had suddenly emerged at its beginning. When he leaves for the first time to make his fortune as a white lawyer, Walden gives Rena "a silver dime with a hole in it for a keepsake" (174), but during the next ten years he does not help her or her mother in more concrete ways, even after becoming wealthy. As he goes away for the second time, he leaves the women to pick up the pieces of his initial, seemingly generous intervention. He can return then to the happy selfishness that enabled him to prosper, but to the reader's eyes his life as a passer has lost much of its glamour and heroic overtones. Tryon's contrition and his presumable guilt feelings about Rena's death hold the promise that John Walden's secret will continue to be safe with him. And Walden's secret is also safe with the narrator, who draws the reader's attention away from him. In summarizing his novel, Chesnutt describes it as "the story of a colored girl who passes for white" (letter to H. D. Robins, September 27, 1900, *To Be an Author* 149), emphasizing the ill-fated female passer and passing over his successful male one. In light of the metanarrative use Chesnutt makes of Frank's invisibility, his closing silence on Walden resonates eloquently, but many of Chesnutt's readers and critics seem to have paid little attention to Walden's return to the initial normative invisibility of his whiteness.

The successful male passer survives the end of the novel with a son who, presumably oblivious to his mixed heritage, joins the ranks of the future Americans whose coming of age Chesnutt has predicted. John Walden thus emerges as a direct antecedent of James Weldon Johnson's Ex-Colored Man. His stunted race consciousness, driving selfishness, and triumphant materialism provide the ironic point of departure for Johnson's characterization of his nameless first-person narrator and for the contrastive celebration of the cultures of black Americans, whose beauty and richness exceed his protagonist's power of interpretation.

4. The Mark Within: Parody in James Weldon Johnson's *The Autobiography of an Ex-Coloured Man*

The Negro author—the creative author—has arrived. . . . He appears in the lists of the best publishers. He even breaks into the lists of the best-sellers. To the general American public he is a novelty, a strange phenomenon. . . . Well, he *is* a novelty, but he is by no means a new thing. . . . What has happened is that efforts which have been going on for more than a century are being noticed and appreciated at last.
(J. W. Johnson, "Dilemma" 477)

EVEN AFTER ALL of the major all-but-white characters in *Iola Leroy* have cast their lot with their mothers' people, Harper's narrative disparagement of passing does not relent. If anything, it becomes more insistent and rhetorically tenacious,[1] in indirect recognition both of the exacting implications of the choice of blackness in a segregated society and of how much easier passing has become in a post-Emancipation era of greater mobility and potential loosening of family and community ties.

The danger Harper tries to exorcise becomes fully realized in the fictional autobiography of James Weldon Johnson's Ex-Colored Man, the 1912 descendant of a male line of determined passers that goes back through Chesnutt's John Walden to Webb's Clarence Garie.[2] In contrast with Clarence Garie's eventual exposure and pathetic death, both John Walden and the Ex-Colored Man survive the text's closure. Chesnutt diffuses the threat of his successful passer by progressively withdrawing narrative attention from him, so that by the end of the novel John Walden practically disappears in the background and implicitly into whiteness. Johnson's Ex-Colored Man, on the contrary, remains prominent throughout the text, not only as protagonist but also as narrator, having survived and prospered by his defiance of racial barriers (through passing) and sexual taboos (through intermarriage).

Published when Johnson was forty-one years old and considered by him among his "more serious work" (J. W. Johnson, *Along* 193), *The Autobiogra-phy* definitely was a novelty but not a particularly welcome one, at least not initially. Johnson's book was first published anonymously in 1912 by a small Boston house (Sherman, French and Co.) and it enjoyed a less than glamor-ous reception. *The Autobiography* did not sell well, received few reviews, and was mostly mistaken as a "human document" (*Along* 238).[3] Although Johnson originally intended it as a way of creating interest in his novel, this autobio-graphical misconception encouraged literal readings of the text, and the au-thor eventually came to regret it.[4] If this inauspicious debut links Johnson's novel with most antecedent African American fiction, the popularity it enjoyed after its republication in 1927 highlights the different cultural climate of the Harlem Renaissance. "Beautifully bound and printed" by Alfred A. Knopf (Du Bois, "Browsing Reader" 308), *The Autobiography* underwent a veritable re-birth, as the author's name was finally affixed to the book and Carl Van Vech-ten's introduction established the generic status of the text "inform[ing] the reader that the story was not the story of [the author's] life" (*Along* 239). In the making of its belated success, the novel's treatment of themes and envi-ronments characteristic of the New Negro movement and its interest in folk expressive culture coalesced with Johnson's own greater visibility as the sec-retary of the National Association for the Advancement of Colored People and with his active participation in the cultural project of the Harlem Renaissance through the publication of three important and groundbreaking anthologies.[5] As Benjamin S. Lawson notes, "Now that his [Johnson's] name could make the novel, the novel could help make Johnson's name" (98).

Fifteen years after its original publication, *The Autobiography* finally en-tered the canon of African American letters and emerged as the only pre–World War I novel to become "one of the most influential books" of the Harlem Renaissance (Fleming, *James Weldon Johnson* 19). This belated ap-preciation continued to be informed by an emphasis on the biographical and documentary aspects of the novel,[6] and even "those critics who admire[d] the novel often [did] so for the wrong reasons" (Fleming, "Irony" 83). Liter-al readings of the text have long overlooked the consummate artistry of "Mr. Johnson's objective and dispassionate treatment" ("An Ex-Coloured Man" 207) and have consequently effaced the parodic intent that makes *The Auto-biography* an unrecognized, sophisticated prototype of avant-garde modern-ist "self-conscious novels" (Alter 139).[7]

Nineteenth-century African American novels, as I have argued in the pre-vious chapters, in many ways already anticipated the relativistic and self-reflex-ive sensibility of modernism by portraying and problematizing the dramat-ically different realities and subject positions of blacks and whites. However,

Johnson's pioneer fictional play with both the autobiographical mode and an unreliable first-person narrator[8] is indicative of a new interest in portraying how reality is filtered, recreated, and mystified by individual consciousness. This difference is symptomatic of a larger shift in artistic sensibility: The modernist revolution was already beginning in the first decade of the twentieth century and came to full fruition in the 1920s. For African Americans, full fruition came with the New Negro movement. Also called the Harlem Renaissance, this new cultural climate was influenced by the innovations in philosophy, psychology, physics, and anthropology that are often mentioned with regard to Euro-American modernism but also by the mass migration, urbanization, and class differentiation the black population underwent in the years around World War I and by an unprecedented mainstream fascination with the folk and African roots of African American culture.

Johnson has long been recognized as a "contributor to and preserver of the Afro-American literary tradition, linking the nineteenth century to the Harlem Renaissance" (Kinnamon, "James Weldon Johnson" 168),[9] but only in the last twenty years have scholars discussed how his transitional status stems not only from his early thematic interest in black music and folk expressive culture but also from his modernist formal self-awareness.[10] Critics such as Robert Stepto, Lucinda MacKethan, and Valerie Smith point to the ironic relationship between Johnson's simulated autobiography and the tradition of black autobiography and the slave narrative as indispensable to the appreciation of the novel. However, little or no attention has been paid to how *The Autobiography* identifies and collects key tropes from antedating African American novels.[11] Also in this respect *The Autobiography* proves to be a "watershed" (Stepto, *From Behind the Veil* 96). It synthesizes the generic conventions and argumentative strategies of the previous sixty years of African American fiction and also recasts them in parodic ways that foreshadow the modernist concerns of the Harlem Renaissance and the self-reflexivity that characterizes postmodern "metafiction" (Hutcheon, "Historiographic" 3). Through his glaringly unreliable first-person narrator, Johnson parodies previous African American fictional tropes that were an integral part of nineteenth-century black culture, such as the race hero and heroine and the ideal of uplift.

Johnson's parodic manipulation of the African American novelistic tradition and nineteenth-century cultural values ushered in a major change in the use of the trope of passing in black fiction, a change that influenced subsequent twentieth-century treatments of this theme and critical evaluations of nineteenth-century fiction of the color line. In contrast with previous novelists of passing, in *The Autobiography* Johnson presents passing for white as the *result*, rather than the *cause*, of cultural alienation and divided racial loyalties. His emphasis shifts from physical to ideological passing, from white-ness as a mark without to whiteness as a mark within, as his narrator unwit-tingly reveals his inability to shake off his white supremacist values and prej-udices even for the short period when he decides to become a "race hero" and spokesperson for African American culture. *The Autobiography* thus performs the transition from a nineteenth-century concern with race loyal-ty and the insider's description of black life to a twentieth-century preoccu-pation with defining a distinctive African American identity. In Johnson's novel parody functions not only as ridiculing but also as reverential imita-tion: It guarantees the continued existence of the mocked conventions, and it is "the custodian of the artistic legacy" (Hutcheon, *A Theory of Parody* 75). *The Autobiography* is at once a harbinger of the Harlem Renaissance and the last articulation of post-Reconstruction cultural values in new fictional form. It is precisely its dual, Janus-like quality that leads to a new, more complex understanding of the differences and the continuities between Old and New Negro literature.

*   *   *

The plot of *The Autobiography* is an aggregate of the salient and defining topoi of previous novels of passing: the extramarital relationship between a rich white southerner and a devoted but eventually forsaken mulatta, the il-legitimate offspring's initial ignorance of his racial background, the ritual trips to the North and to a more prejudice-free Europe, the all-but-white protag-onist's decision to reconnect with his cultural roots and the difficulties of such "immersion,"[12] the moral crisis of the passer who falls in love with an unsus-pecting white person, and the sense of loneliness and alienation of the passer in a prejudiced white world. It is exactly because of the obvious ways in which "*The Autobiography* aggressively invites comparison with major antecedent Afro-American texts" (Stepto, *From Behind the Veil* 106) that the difference between the Ex-Colored Man's story and previous articulations of the theme of passing becomes so clear. The irony that stems from the contrast between the Ex-Colored Man's experiences and his motivations and rationalizations can be fully appreciated only when *The Autobiography* is read against the pre-vious literary tradition of committed novels of passing. The Ex-Colored Man's mimicry of the race loyalty characteristic of early African American protag-onists highlights the opposing ideological frameworks between which he os-cillates. His proclaimed loyalty to his "mother's people" (210) is continuous-ly undercut by his admiration for and identification with mainstream white America. When contrasted with the brave trickery or the serious life choices of previous passers, the Ex-Colored Man's oft-noted cowardice, self-commiseration, and superficial comments call attention to his lifelong estrangement from African American culture and foreground his unreliability as a first-person narrator.[13]

This unreliability is one of the formal solutions that insert *The Autobiography* among the harbingers of modernism. It induces a consistent metanarrative reflection that is more pervasive and overt but not easier to interpret than Chesnutt's in *The House Behind the Cedars* or than the one occasioned by the hermeneutic clues of earlier African American novels of the color line. Johnson's oblique approach, his parodic exposure of the narrator's contradictions and inconsistencies, underscores the constructedness of the "autobiographical" text and compels readers to become suspicious of smooth surfaces, nonthreatening statements, sentimental situations, and detached objectivity. By "highlight[ing] the narrative process" itself (V. Smith, *Self-Discovery* 45) and heightening the reader's awareness of the Ex-Colored Man's self-interested, defensive interpretive manipulations of his "black" experiences, Johnson situates his audience in a self-consciously cautious posture of reception. This distrust of the narrator mirrors, ironically, the "distrust of the reader" (Stepto, "Distrust" 300) that beguiled nineteenth-century African American authors, who were addressing a double, highly ideologically polarized black and white audience. On one hand, as a result of "directing his irony at the ex-colored man, Johnson attacks a hypothetical white audience" (Ross 199) and undermines in ironic ways superficial interpretations of African American literary and cultural texts. On the other hand, by capitalizing on his induced distrust of the narrator, Johnson provides a hermeneutic tool for interpreting not only his own text but also previous African American fiction.

The profound and parodic differences between Johnson's protagonist and the heroes and heroines of previous novels of passing become clear from the outset of *The Autobiography*. Reared in racial unawareness and assuming himself to be white, the Ex-Colored Man is easily indoctrinated into racial prejudice by other children, and he does not possess the delicacy of mind or the humanitarian bent that makes the similarly unaware Iola Leroy condemn practical instances of discrimination even while supporting the institution of slavery in principle. Johnson's narrator does not reveal any qualms of conscience about running after his black schoolmates and "pelting them with stones" (15), nor does he seem to be touched by his mother's heartfelt though vague rebuke. Even the revelation of his mixed racial background fails to engender any deep changes in his outlook or his early identification with whites. In contrast to turn-of-the-century characters such as Iola Leroy, who, upon making this same discovery, embark on a series of learning experiences that are motivated by race loyalty and lead to race consciousness, for Johnson's ex-white picaro "becoming" black is just the first of many temporary metamorphoses. In the course of the novel (which the author considered calling *The Chameleon*), the nameless narrator turns into an all-but-native speaker of Spanish, a black gambler, a black ragtime player, a racially indeterminate American expatriate in Europe, and a black musicologist and finally settles for being a white businessperson.

The least successful and most obtrusive of his metamorphoses is as an interpreter of black culture. After having recounted his shock at the revelation of his black ancestry, the protagonist periodically interrupts his narration with lengthy sociological digressions on race. These "didactic" (Levy 134) digressions represent Johnson's most obvious parodic recuperation of the stylistic features of nineteenth-century African American fiction. His proficient mimicry of earlier texts is confirmed indirectly by critical lamentations on the "loose episodic framework" (Vauthier 179) of *The Autobiography* and its "compromised" literary artistry (Kinnamon, "James Weldon Johnson" 174), which sound like belated echoes of similar critiques leveled against Brown, Harper, and Griggs. Rather than "present a problem for a reading of the narrator's portrayal as totally ironic" (Ross 204), the oft-noted accuracy of the Ex-Colored Man's descriptions of black life in different social classes and geographic areas only sharpens the strident contrast with his prejudiced readings of the material he presents. As Fleming notes, the "fact that the narrator's observations of black life in America have been so highly praised by readers and critics adds an element of irony that Johnson may not have foreseen" (*James Weldon Johnson* 35).

The Ex-Colored Man's stereotyped reflections on African America and his never-ending surprise at instances of black artistic skill or social accomplishment glaringly reveal his continued white supremacist allegiances. More subtly and pervasively, his qualities of "unconscious misreader" (Clarke, "Race" 88) emerge from the very tone of his telling, from the deceptively objective detachment against which Johnson warns his readers in his real autobiography. In *Along this Way*, which he wrote partly to correct literal readings of his novel (*Along* 239), Johnson describes in the following terms his own experiences in the "backwoods of Georgia" where the Ex-Colored Man roams only to plunder them culturally: "As I worked with my children in school and met with their parents in the homes, on the farms, and in church, I found myself studying them all with a sympathetic objectivity, as though they were something apart; but in an instant's reflection I could realize that they were me and I was they; that a force stronger than blood made us one" (*Along* 119). This "instant's reflection" escapes the Ex-Colored Man throughout the novel.

By signaling the failure of the narrator's immersion through the contrast between his superficial interpretive tools and the serious and often dramatic situations he confronts every time he plays the black man,[14] Johnson provides an obliquely critical insider's report on the power of mystification of white supremacist ideology. Whether he describes the workings of Du Boisian double consciousness (21–22), praises gifted black men (44–45), classifies the "coloured people" of the South on the basis of their socioeconomic status (76–81), or reports a debate on race he hears on a train (158–67), the Ex-Colored Man's detached sociological tone is accompanied both by a propensity to generalize on the basis of his own personal experiences, which often results in stereotyping, and by expressions of sympathy and apology for the discriminatory behavior of whites. Whereas in previous novels of the color line those digressions constituted thematic and formal sites of resistance that foregrounded the subject position of African Americans, in *The Autobiography* they are turned into spaces for articulating stereotypes and defending white supremacist beliefs.

Notwithstanding his self-proclaimed introduction into "the freemasonry of the race" (74), in his retrospective sociological digressions the narrator operates a shift from the past of events narrated, when he was "black," to the present of the writing, when he is "white," which reveals no development of his race consciousness. His continued belief in his juvenile hierarchy of authorities on the race question is transparently ironic and indicative of the ideological blinders through which he (mis)interprets African American life. Although he admits that "Frederick Douglass was enshrined in the place of honour" (46) among his "coloured" heroes, the most significant influence on his supposedly budding race consciousness as an African American derives from another text. He confesses with pride, "*Uncle Tom's Cabin* . . . opened my eyes as to who and what I was and what my country considered me; in fact, it gave me my bearing" (42). Should the irony of this declaration remain unclear, Johnson's protagonist also praises the objectivity of Stowe's novel echoing plantation tradition representations of African Americans: "We must also remember that the author depicted a number of worthless if not vicious Negroes . . . that she pictured the happy, singing, shuffling 'darky' as well as the mother wailing for her child sold 'down river'" (42).

The appreciation of the author's intertextual parody and of the ironic discrepancy between the Ex-Colored Man's proclaimed ideals and his practices, between his varying masquerades and his unwavering allegiance to the authority of whites, prompts the reader to assume the inquisitive critical pose that the protagonist himself lacks and that proves indispensable in moving beyond parody toward recuperating the political agenda of resistance that *The Autobiography* shares with previous novels of passing. As Stepto suggests, "The Ex-Colored Man's perils and travails . . . sustain the heroic proportions of the canonical types and tropes by offering what is, in effect, *a negative example of them*" (*From Behind the Veil* 104–5, emphasis added). For instance, the narrator's driving opportunism and his attempts to rationalize the lack of racial commitment that will lead to his decision to pass permanently indirectly point and give new life to that notion of "service" (*Along* 122) to the race that dominates pre–World War I African American fiction and that Johnson himself continued to value.[15] Also revealing of the interventionist subtext underlying the novel's irony is the Ex-Colored Man's seeming obliviousness to the contrast between the clear-cut sociological classifications through which he attempts to regulate "race" and especially "blackness" and his own ambiguous racial status. The protagonist's unawareness of this contrast foregrounds the constructedness of racial categories that was more explicitly critiqued in previous novels of passing. Johnson's ironic, newly oblique strategy of consciousness raising indicates his awareness of the changing cultural climate among African Americans and anticipates features of the literary production of the post–World War I writers whom Johnson praises in *The Book of American Negro Poetry* (1922): "The best of them have found an approach to 'race' that is different. Their approach is less direct, less obvious than that of their predecessors, and thereby they have secured a gain in subtlety of power and, probably, in ultimate effectiveness" (6).

The most revealing instance of the ironic discrepancy between the narrator's black experiences and his white supremacist ideology is the lynching that eventually motivates him to pass for white permanently. Protected by the fact that his "identity as a coloured man had not yet become known in the town" (185), the Ex-Colored Man becomes a spectator of ritualistic antiblack violence. In clear parodic contrast with the profound indignation and increased racial commitment that lynchings inspired in previous race heroes and heroines, the Ex-Colored Man's reactions to the spectacle of violence betray no marked sympathy for "the poor wretch" (186) who is burned alive. Although he briefly describes the "transformation of [white] human beings into savage beasts" as "terrible" (186), he spends more time detailing the "degeneracy" of the black victim, "a man only in form and stature" (186). Even as he witnesses the brutality of the lynching, his comments reveal awe and fearful respect for the power of the murderers and contempt for the victim. His ultimate concern is to reconcile what he has witnessed with his conviction that

"Southern whites are in many respects a great people" (189). Rather than an attempt to avoid stereotyping all southerners as violent racists, the Ex-Colored Man's intention to be fair soon emerges as opportunistic. He tries both to rationalize self-interest out of his subsequent decision to cut himself off from "a people that could with impunity be treated worse than animals" (191) and to minimize his own passive complicity with the organized, communal racial violence of the white society he has decided to join by passing. Within the value system implied by the novel's ironic tone, the significance of the Ex-Colored Man's effort at accommodationist self-deception looms larger than an example of individual cowardice. It becomes metonymical of the broader extratextual reality of institutionalized blindness to the pervasiveness of racial violence.[16]

The lynching occasions in the Ex-Colored Man a veritable reversion to (white) type that is highly parodic of the social Darwinism still popular when Johnson wrote his novel. As the fictional first-person narrator describes his motives for leaving the South and the race, Johnson operates a crucial shift in the use of the passing motif. Unlike his antecedents, the Ex-Colored Man claims that the primary motivation behind his decision to pass is not "discouragement or fear or [the] search for a larger field of action and opportunity" but "shame, unbearable shame" (190–91). Although this claim offers, characteristically, only a thin disguise for his opportunism, his willingness to interpret the lynching in ways that degrade the victim's people represents the most obvious symptom of the deep-seated white supremacist allegiances that beguile the Ex-Colored Man throughout the text. Johnson's protagonist thus emerges as a thoroughly self-deceiving modernist revision of Webb's Clarence, whose estrangement from and shame of the black community are the result, rather than the cause, of the externally imposed decision to hide his racial identity. Whereas Clarence initially resents passing as contrary to his inclinations and familial affections, the Ex-Colored Man's eventual decision to pass permanently is little more than the formalization of his continued estrangement from black culture and black life. Despite the Stowe-like, melodramatic tragic mulatto posture with which the Ex-Colored Man closes his narrative, passing is a decision that does not create the psychological torture Webb describes so effectively in relation to Clarence.

The uncharacteristic humility, regret, and critical self-analysis and the characteristic egotism and self-commiseration that dominate the ending of *The Autobiography* constitute the last metamorphosis of the narrator, who presents himself as a failed race hero of tragic proportions. Whereas some critics interpret these closing passages as an indication that the very act of writing leads the narrator to a first level of self-awareness,[17] I read them parodically as the Ex-Colored Man's final effort at self-fashioning that frames *The Auto-biography* and disguises how the text itself represents his most successful exploitation of the culture of his mother's people for purposes of self-aggrandizement. The Ex-Colored Man's "fast yellowing manuscripts" are not "the only tangible remnant . . . of a sacrificed talent" (211) but one of the many sentimental images instrumental to the realization of his musical ambition, albeit in a different artistic medium. *The Autobiography* itself opens up a space for the public presentation of his folk musical findings and represents the triumph of his talent as an artist as well as a masquerader. As he had calculated with regard to music, the narrator builds his autobiographical enterprise on the conviction that he has "greater chances of attracting attention as a coloured [writer] than as a white one" (147) and that his personal and sociological digressions enable him "to voice all the joys and sorrows, the hopes and ambitions, of the American Negro, in classical . . . form" (147–48).

It is before the studiedly pathetic ending of *The Autobiography* that Johnson's Ex-Colored Man voices something akin to protest or self-awareness. Finally established as a successful white businessperson, the narrator returns to the more defiant tone of the opening lines of his autobiography, admits that the "anomaly of [his] social position often appealed strongly to [his] sense of humor" (197), and appreciates passing as a "capital joke" (197), as an intrinsic refutation of the racial stereotypes he has invoked in his own narrative. For a brief moment, the text restores the traditional subversive function of the passing motif and comes to constitute the Ex-Colored Man's first act of loyalty toward his mother's people. As narrator, the passer finally declaims what the passer as protagonist never has the courage to utter: "I am a coloured man. Do I not disprove the theory that one drop of Negro blood renders a man unfit?" (197). As the narrator decentralizes his enjoyment of the disruptive joke to close his narrative on the aforementioned sentimental note, this dual ending mirrors similar double closures in nineteenth-century African American fiction and represents a parodically self-centered equivalent of the covert protest strategies characteristic of earlier novels of passing (e.g., *Clotel* and *The Garies*).

The Autobiography calls attention to the text's constructedness and "the ontological meaning of the act of telling" (V. Smith, *Self-Discovery* 45), and its autobiographical packaging of a fictional text transforms the protagonist's telling of his story into an epistemological exercise for the reader. It also foregrounds in new ways the larger extratextual threat that the theme of passing has always incorporated. In most previous African American novels, the passer's defiance of racial categorizations was only partly contained by the end of the novel by the proud determination to relinquish passing, by emigration, and less often by death. In contrast, the end of *The Autobiography* coincides with the passer's return to his undetected extratextual white existence. In an autobiography the world of the text and of the reader "are . . . in a way permeable" (Vauthier 179), and in Johnson's "autobiographical" tale of passing permeability coincides with the real-life osmosis of the races. When the narrator closes his story and returns to his anonymity as an "ordinarily successful white man" (*The Autobiography* 211), his joke on society, though couched in the language of melodramatic regret, turns into a continued threat to the group identity of the whites among whom he prospers undetected and whose racial privilege has lost some of its glamor because the narrative has foregrounded the "diminished stature of the white man who could have been black" and who could have participated in the "grandeur of black achievement" (Warren, "Troubled" 276).

Given his low level of self-awareness, however, the Ex-Colored Man, unlike previous passers, poses as serious a threat to black as to white group identity. Johnson's novel thus foreshadows the dramatically different ways in which the trope of passing was deployed during and after the Harlem Renaissance. If the very fact of the Ex-Colored Man's success at permanent passing undermines the "whiteness" of whiteness, his own misinterpretations of African American culture and white supremacist allegiances problematize the "blackness" of his blackness. By parodying previous uses of passing to undermine racial stereotypes and represent black culture, Johnson ultimately foregrounds the complex process of articulating the specific cultural and historical grounds on which "to define a black identity within the American cultural context" (Huggins 142). By parodying them, he also preserves increasingly outmoded cultural values that provide a historical perspective crucial to the definition of that very identity.

It is in the ironic interstice Johnson creates between the Ex-Colored Man's "black" experiences and his "white" (supremacist) interpretations, between his proclaimed desire for cultural memory and his de facto cultural amnesia that the crucial issue of the black "racial spirit" lies (Johnson, *The Book of American Negro Poetry* 41). Johnson recuperates and foregrounds the dual valence of Du Bois's widely influential 1903 statement that "The problem of the Twentieth Century is the problem of the color-line" (*The Souls* 41). Du Bois's prophecy obviously referred to the unsolved problem of racial inequality and black-white relations, but it also represented an insider's posing of another problem: how to define the distinctiveness of African American culture without invoking essentialist notions of blackness or prescriptive ideological standpoints, how to strengthen the bonds of race in light of the increasing internal differentiation within the black community.

Johnson's answers to these questions reveal once again the transitional status of his novel, as he looks back to the nineteenth-century values of service and uplift even as he recasts them in new ways. Like previous writers of passing, he moves beyond and ridicules the dominant Darwinian biological essentialism of his age by disintegrating "race" into its sociocultural components through a narrator who is legally black because of his ancestry, phenotypically white, and ideologically a white supremacist. Although the Ex-Colored Man's experiences, more than his explanations, reveal the class, geographic, and cultural differences between African Americans, Johnson situates his criteria for a communal, nonessentialist definition of "racial spirit" in the aspects of black culture his narrator cannot sustain or accept: in the history of resistance to the oppression that makes the Ex-Colored Man flee into whiteness permanently,[18] in the literary tradition his narrator misreads, and in such different cultural artifacts as ragtime and the spirituals, which the Ex-Colored Man cannot appreciate without attempting to recast them in the mold of European art. That the Ex-Colored Man's flight from racial violence proves coterminous with the surrender of his musical ambition indirectly attests to the close connection Johnson establishes between historical and cultural distinctiveness. Two years before *The Autobiography* came to new life at the height of the Harlem Renaissance, in his introduction to *The Book of American Negro Spirituals* (1925) Johnson comments more directly on the issue of cultural specificity in ways that clearly distinguish his notion of racial spirit from simplistic biological essentialism and bring to mind Harper's description of Iola Leroy's process of sociocultural acculturation into blackness: "Carl Van Vechten . . . declared it as his opinion that white singers cannot sing them [the Spirituals]. . . . I think white singers, concert singers, *can* sing Spirituals—if they *feel* them. But to feel them it is necessary to know the truth about their origin and history, to get in touch with the association of ideas that surround them, and to realize something of what they have meant in the experiences of the people who created them" (28–29).

The Autobiography thus culminates the process of shifting the focus of racialist discourse from biology to culture, a process that can be traced back through the post-Reconstruction emphasis on uplift to the first African American novelist's discussion of passing as paradigmatic of the artificiality of racial classifications. In the nineteenth century the emphasis was on redressing stereotypes and arguing the existence of African American culture and the agency of African Americans as subjects. In the 1920s, this order of priorities was reversed, and the focus shifted on analyzing blackness not only in its differences from mainstream culture but also in light of intraracial variations of gender, geographic provenance, class background, sexual preference, shade of color, and education. As the "subtle processes of internal reorganization" of the race (Locke xvii) foregrounded internal divisions and stratifications, passing became an extreme example of how deep such divisions could run but also remained a tool to focus on the ideological and cultural components of blackness. Johnson's parodic re-vision of previous African American fiction of the color line, his focus on whiteness as a mark within as well as without, and his use of passing as a symptom rather than a cause of cultural confusion and existential angst became as characteristic of the Harlem Renaissance as his interest in African American music and the urban scene. Similarly, Johnson's notion of the black racial spirit pioneered later discussions both on the criteria for articulating an African American literary canon and on the centrality of the vernacular to the modernist agenda of the Harlem Renaissance.

During the Harlem Renaissance the emphasis on folk forms was presented as a novelty and constituted a rebellious gesture. The determination to proudly enhance them was predicated in opposition to "the psychology of imitation and implied inferiority" (Locke 4) that supposedly characterized antecedent African American discursive forms. In his groundbreaking 1925 anthology, Locke boldly proclaims, "The Negro to-day wishes to be known for what he is, even in his faults and shortcomings, and scorns a craven and precarious survival at the price of seeming to be what he is not" (11). Although the continued reality of a white-dominated publishing industry and the need for white sponsorship qualified the realizability of this uncompromising stance, the unprecedented primitivist vogue of the 1920s made possible a different set of artistic choices, one that sustained the New Negro's agenda of radical novelty and greater outspokenness.

Within this new context, in the 1927 reprint the Ex-Colored Man is reborn with all "his faults and shortcomings" (Locke 11) as a new literary product, if not as a new hero. In his (in)capacity as a narrator, he proves instrumental in advancing the iconoclastic rationale of the New Negro movement because his low level of self-awareness, confused racial loyalties, and emphatic appreciation for all things white provide what became an influential framework for the interpretation of the supposed representational compromises and racial self-hatred of previous African American writers of passing. In the absence of an appreciation of his novel's celebratory parody, Johnson's manipulation of nineteenth-century African American fictional conventions contributed less to a recognition of the strategic maneuvering that historically was practiced by African American writers beguiled by "a double . . . [and] divided audience" (Johnson, "Dilemma" 477) than to their dismissal and patronizing critical neglect. From the vantage point of the Harlem Renaissance programmatic rupture with the very literary tradition Johnson synthesized, the lack of racial spirit that turns a potential African American musician into a white businessperson mirrors and recapitulates the proclaimed dichotomy between Old and New Negro artists.

Yet despite the Ex-Colored Man's retreat from the artistic production of his mother's people, in 1927 Johnson's 1912 presentation of the expressive culture of the folk was received as prophetic of and consistent with the cultural nationalist agenda of the Harlem Renaissance. However, it is worth repeating that the fact that the Ex-Colored Man's statements on black culture have long been taken at face value represents an irony that Johnson may not have anticipated. The Ex-Colored Man in fact constitutes a characteristically "negative" (Stepto, *From Behind the Veil* 104) parodic model for the new kind of cultural spokesperson Johnson envisioned. This becomes most obvious when the Ex-Colored Man tours the South "to catch the spirit of the Negro in his relatively primitive state" (173). Then he once again demonstrates his alienation from black culture by being surprised at the consummate artistry of black folk musicians and orators. Within the contrapuntal ironic structure of the novel, his reluctant "enthusiasm" (182) is dialogized, and it ultimately enhances the significance of his bewildered recognition of the artistic value of folk creations: "As I listened to the singing of these songs, the wonder of their production grew upon me more and more. How did the men who originated them manage to do it? The sentiments are easily accounted for; they are mostly taken from the Bible; but the melodies, where did they come from?" (181). Beyond the narrator's culturally uninformed artistic stance lies Johnson's affirmation of the uniqueness of African American artistic contributions, his respect for the "genuine folk stuff" (Johnson, *The Book of American Negro Poetry* 6), and his critique of the hierarchy of literary value that belittles the artistic potential of the folk in their vernacular medium. *The Autobiography* articulates the interest in "the classical sound of Afro-America" that Houston Baker identifies as a distinctive feature of African American modernism (*Modernism* 73).

Johnson's Ex-Colored Man foreshadows the cultural nationalist agenda of the Harlem Renaissance in another, less commented upon sense as well, because his emphasis on the vernacular mother tongue does not result in a comparable interest in the "tongue of the mother" (Gilbert and Gubar 262). The hierarchy of folk artistic authenticity is gendered in the novel, and the narrator seems to reinscribe in distinctively African American terms the modernist distinction Sandra Gilbert and Susan Gubar analyze between the male creators and the female users of language (227–71). In *The Autobiography,* the mother who plays by ear "some old Southern songs" (8) functions as a cultural mediator and vulgarizer by reproducing folk and religious melodies. However, the Ex-Colored Man has to move beyond the mother's "simple accompaniments" (8) to recuperate the complex artistry of the original folk pieces. John Brown and "Singing Johnson," respectively the preacher and the leader of singing he encounters years later at a big meeting in the South, are "a revelation" (175) to the narrator. They emerge as "archetypal" (Carroll 354) cultural figures despite the Ex-Colored Man's characteristically stereotypical comments on their "primitive poetry" (177) and "born" (175) artistic skills. The different degrees of male and female cultural agency become equally clear in the description of the call-and-response pattern of the Spirituals: The congregation, which includes a mass of faceless women, "sings the same lines over and over," whereas the male leader's "memory and ingenuity are taxed to keep the songs going" (180).

Within this gendered economy of the novel, the Ex-Colored Man's eventual rejection of cultural agency by passing "feminizes" him in ways that are reminiscent of Webb's seduced and abandoned Clarence. Clarence's hysteria finds an equivalent in the petulant, self-commiserating tone that dominates *The Autobiography*.[19] The Ex-Colored Man's short-lived project of immersion and his rhetoric of cultural uplift confirm Johnson's oblique, parodic feminization of the narrator by connecting him with the host of all-but-white race heroines that populated the novels of the Black Woman's Era. This feminization of the narrator in turn reverberates on and genders the contrast between Old and New Negroes. The novelty of the Harlem Renaissance, with its emphasis on the expressive culture of the folk and its aggressively "masculine" affirmation of race pride and self-reliance were predicated on a "feminine" definition of pre–World War I African American literature, which emphasized its gentility, "sentimental appeal," "hyper-sensitiveness," and "'touchy' nerves" (Locke 10).

The appreciation both of Johnson's parodic approach to earlier African American fiction and culture and of the proclaimed male genealogy of folk art and the vernacular lends important insight into the different set of artistic choices that characterized the supposedly more formally conservative literary output of African American women during the Harlem Renaissance.[20] A case in point is Nella Larsen. On one hand, like Johnson but with a less playful and ultimately more tragic tone, Larsen focuses on ideological as well as physical passing and constructs her novels against the familiar script of the race heroine and the ideal of uplift. By portraying Helga Crane and Irene Redfield, the protagonists respectively of *Quicksand* (1928) and *Passing* (1929), as failed, unhappy Iola Leroys who outlive the fictional happy ending and struggle with the frustrations of marriage and uplift, Larsen highlights how traditional African American cultural scripts fail to prove liberating for female characters. On the other hand, Larsen explicitly discusses the tensions between the problematics of gender and the glorification of the folk in *Quicksand* (1928). Helga Crane's marriage to the "grandiloquent" (118) Reverend Mr. Pleasant Green and her eager, condescendingly naive immersion "in the tiny Alabama town where he was pastor to a scattered and primitive flock" (118) trap her in a victimizing cycle of unwanted pregnancies. Even Zora Neale Hurston, "the outstanding exception" (Wall 155) in terms of female artistic use of the vernacular and folk themes, deals with these tensions in *Their Eyes Were Watching God* (1937), for instance, a novel that details the heroine's struggle to achieve control and assert her creative use of the vernacular in a male-dominated folk environment. The negative reception of her book by critics such as Locke and Wright highlights the gendered politics of folk representation that were already present in *The New Negro* and *The Autobiography* and that would influence so strongly the process of articulation and canonization of the African American literary tradition in the twentieth century.[21]

The Autobiography thus proves to be a precursor not only of the themes and concerns but also of the tensions and omissions that characterized the New Negro movement. The sociocultural changes that gave rise to the Harlem Renaissance altered dramatically African American modes of artistic depiction of race and of the related trope of passing. After World War I, ideological passing, often unredeemed by irony, gained center stage as a symptom of cultural confusion, existential angst, and divided racial loyalties. As a theme, passing continued to be an essential tool to foreground the dynamics of black and white group consciousness; to analyze the distinctive but far from monolithic black cultural identity in light of differences in class, gender, color, sexual preference, education, and geographic provenance; and to explore the shifting boundary between cultural change and cultural estrangement. To reconnect, without simply conflating, the nineteenth-century tradition with the profoundly different uses of the trope of passing by such Harlem Renaissance figures as Jessie Fauset, Nella Larsen, George Schuyler, and Walter White grounds the uniqueness of the African American novelistic tradition in the "changing same" of a people's distinctive sociocultural history (Jones, "The Changing Same" 112).

5. Tres-passing in African American Literary Criticism

> I want to make it perfectly clear why we can no longer subscribe to
> the common conclusion that when African American writers such as
> Phillis Wheatley, William Wells Brown, Frank Webb, or Frances Harper
> wrote, their implied or actual audiences were white or that their works
> should be read as attempts . . . to imitate the literary productions of
> Euro-Americans. And I want to be clear why we must not uncritically
> accept . . . the myth that the oral folk tradition . . . is the only
> authentically black art prior to the twentieth century. . . . Once we
> acknowledge that in the nineteenth century, as now, African
> Americans . . . could not only signify in conversation but also in
> correspondence, then some of our interpretations of early African
> American literary productions must change. (Foster, Introduction
> xxiii–xxiv)

THE PROMINENCE OF the theme of passing for white among the founders
of African American fiction has presented a disturbing and unwelcome critical puzzle for generations of scholars. This fact should come as no surprise:
The pervasive presence of light-skinned mulatto and mulatta characters must
have seemed an obvious confirmation of the power of racial hegemony to
shape not only the American social system but also the artistic imagination.
It is even less surprising that this theme, so abused and stereotyped by white
writers of tragic mulatto fictions, so difficult to reconcile with twentieth-century militant expressions of race pride, and so threatening of group boundaries, should become almost taboo among critics of African American literature, who often describe the origins of black fiction by glossing over, dismissing,
or devaluing all-but-white characters.

The present review of the critical commentary on nineteenth-century
African American fiction of passing is informed by two assumptions. First,
the awareness of the political impact of artistic and scholarly efforts is considered a constant in African American literary criticism. From this vantage
point, the various and at times opposing canon-making enterprises of Afri-

can American critics emerge as historically specific attempts to define the group's cultural identity and affirm its centrality within the American context. To the extent that this cultural identity, though variously defined, has consistently been considered distinct and identifiable, African American criticism as a whole shares nationalist concerns that stem partly from a recognition of the white supremacist, nationalistic agendas underlying the systematic and continued exclusion (or, at best, marginalization) of black texts from the American literary canon.

In this process of transforming a history of exclusion into one of the criteria for a distinct literary tradition, African American critics encountered white supremacist ideologies in the disguise of aesthetic evaluations. Confronted with continuing mainstream critical disinterest and disbelief in the artistic value of African American literature, with biased notions of critical objectivity, with widespread assumptions of their own racial partisanship, and with a dual black and white audience, African American critics had to advance their critical agendas as well as the study of African American literature as a whole. On one hand, they established an internal standard of comparison: Pre–Harlem Renaissance African American literature, especially the fiction of the color line, came to provide a negative touchstone both to measure the greater literary merits of later works and to argue the distinctiveness and relevance of specific thematic and critical agendas, such as the vernacular and the folk. On the other hand, their distrust of a white-dominated academic audience led African American critics to deploy subversive canonmaking strategies. I interpret these strategies as instances of "passing" in the metaphorical sense of the word, as a kind of tricksterism that relies on the appropriation and manipulation of hegemonic standards to circumvent, trespass, and subvert social and academic modes of exclusion.

My second working assumption is that the critical marginality of nineteenthcentury fiction of the color line within the field of African American studies is closely linked to that of black women, both as writers and as characters. Mulatta figures dominate the early works of fiction. Many of the passers in both male- and female-authored novels are women, and the post-Reconstruction period witnessed the emergence of an unprecedented number of black women writers, many of whom dealt with the trope of passing. To connect the scholarly dislike for the early novels with the male critical disinterest in gender sheds light on how these two phenomena share a common cause and have reinforced each other. To make this point from a different angle, the interest in the conflation of gender and race issues characteristic of black feminist critics has led to the recovery and reinterpretation of the early fiction as an indispensable step in articulating the literary tradition of black women.[1]

To argue for flux and change in the systematization and canonization of African American literature does not argue for formlessness: That African American literary history has been constructed and reconstructed in different ways even in the same historical period does not deny its identifiability or the distinctive continuities that characterize even its change. Analogously, to problematize racial categories, as the early writers of passing did, is not equivalent to disputing that they have been and continue to be operative. Rather, to paraphrase Morrison's *The Bluest Eye,* investigating how such categories function in African American novels of the color line and in critical works about them may lead to a new why (9).

*   *   *

By virtue of its inclusion of several writers, William Wells Brown's *The Black Man, His Antecedents, His Genius, and His Achievements* (1858) can be rightfully considered one of the earliest African American canon-making efforts.[2] In his determination to argue into scholarly existence the uniqueness of African American cultural contributions, Brown demonstrates a clear awareness of the uses of the strategy of appropriating hegemonic standards that I call passing in a broader, metaphorical sense. Brown articulates the African American literary tradition by affirming the value and importance of such varied literary figures as Martin Delany, Frederick Douglass, Phillis Wheatley, Frances Harper, himself, and others. He characterizes the tradition of African American cultural contributions as masculine, both in terms of the respective numbers of heroes (57) and heroines (3) he celebrates and also with regard to the mode of celebration.[3] Though explainable in light of a history of sexual exploitation and maligning of black women, Brown's emphasis on the refinement, chastity, and sentiment of female authors ends up depoliticizing and marginalizing them by placing them outside the male circle of trickery. The poems by women writers he chooses to include are mostly sentimental and devoted to such "female" topics as marriage advice and motherhood rather than to more outspoken and direct condemnations of slavery.

In the memoir that opens the book, on the contrary, the black man's genius (in this case Brown's) rests not only on his literary and oratorical accomplishments, which are listed rather hastily, but chiefly on incidents of resistance to and defiance of white authority in the slaveholding South, in the North, and in Europe. Helping a male slave embark to Canada by disguising him as a white woman is one instance of covert resistance that proves the gullibility of whites and grounds their defeat in the superficiality of their own racial categories. As an example of his trickery, of his success at covert manipulation, this description of passing becomes an integral part of the author's aggressive construction of the black man's genius and is paradigmatic of Brown's appropriation of the master's tools, be they skin color or scholarly expertise.

According to Brown, the black man's genius is rooted both in African culture and in his American past of resistance to the dehumanization of slavery, as proven by the impressive list of political and cultural figures that constitutes the third and last section of *The Black Man*. The conspicuous absence of activist heroines such as Sojourner Truth and Harriet Tubman from his list may be explained by reference to his aforementioned adoption of dominant standards of true womanhood. Nevertheless, it contrasts sharply with his expansion of the standards of honorable manhood to include the violent deeds of Nat Turner, "to the memory of whom the American people are not prepared to do justice" (59). Only thirty years after his rebellion, Brown describes Turner as a man "in whose soul God . . . lighted a torch of liberty that cannot be extinguished by the hand of man" (73). The author glorifies him as "a martyr to the freedom of his race, and a victim to his own fanaticism" (71).

Female trickery makes its scholarly debut a few years later in Mrs. N. F. Mossell's *The Work of the Afro-American Woman* (1894). The year before its publication, Monroe A. Majors, author of *Noted Negro Women: Their Triumphs and Their Activities* (1893), praised Mrs. Mossell as "one of the leading women of a struggling race" (129) and hoped that "when some future historian writes the history of the American Negro, it must be allowed that the Negro women did a noble share in the race development" (131). Realizing Majors's wish, *The Work* celebrates the uniqueness of African American culture by focusing on the accomplishments of black women in a variety of fields, including business, education, journalism, and drama. Mossell devotes much attention to how "the race has built up a literature of its own" (49), and the strategies she devises to record and promote female literary contributions reveal the racial and gender constraints under which she operated, as well as her subversion and tres-passing of those limitations to advance a pioneering black feminist agenda.

Interested, like Anna Julia Cooper in those same years, in promoting "the sex and race" (15), Mossell juggles a triple audience: "the budding womanhood of the race" (5), the black men who write the introduction and are acknowledged in her "Preface," and the white women of the suffrage movement (9). With the latter group of "more favored sisters" (10), Mossell's strategy is euphemistically elliptic: Implicitly accusing white women of neglect, Mossell states her intention of doing for black women the same work of recovery and celebration that her contemporary Anna Nathan Meyer performed for the "Anglo-American sisters" (10). Equally calculated is the "strategy of public modesty" (xxviii) Joanne Braxton sees at work in Mossell's book. Braxton interprets Mossell's decision to write "under the initials of her husband" (xxvii) and to accept the "seal of masculine approval" (xxx) represented by the introductory note of a bishop of the African Methodist Episcopal Church as a way to signal "her intention to defend and celebrate black womanhood without . . . challenging masculine authority" (xxviii).

Although Mossell's conciliatory intentions need not be questioned, her means of promoting a black feminist critical agenda without alienating the men of the race reveal a variation on the kinds of trickery, of tres-passing, at work in Brown's *The Black Man*. Mossell devotes two chapters to African American literature: "A Sketch of Afro-American Literature" and "The Afro-American Woman in Verse." In the first general sketch, the author traces the historical development of black male and female writing. Mossell inserts African American literature as a distinct but integral part of American literature and also expands the criteria for female inclusion in the African American literary tradition by highlighting the political aspects of women's writing. The quaintness of her own language (the adjective *small* often qualifies her descriptions) does not detract from her serious evaluation of Wheatley's poetry or Harper's prose. In her comments on the recently published *Iola Leroy* (1892), for example, although she does not mention the central theme of passing, she recognizes and appreciates the political scope of Harper's novel, which brings out "all of the open and settled questions of the so-called Negro problem" (61).

Having established the importance of African American writers and of the women among them, Mossell advances her feminist critical agenda more explicitly in the chapter devoted to poetry. Twice as long as the preceding one and exclusively dedicated to the "Afro-American woman in verse," this section articulates the female literary tradition as representative of the gifts "of the African race" (67). Mossell laments that "of the history of these sweet singers we know but little" (93) and acknowledges the limitations of her own effort of recovery using floral metaphors that foreshadow Alice Walker's black feminist essays of the 1970s: "Here and there, from this garden of poesy, we have culled a blossom; but how many gardens of beauty have we not looked upon? And yet, we must close, knowing 'the half hath not been told'" (97).

The comprehensive treatment of nineteenth-century women writers that characterizes *The Work of the Afro-American Woman* finds no equivalent in the criticism of two major intellectuals of this period: W. E. B. Du Bois and

Benjamin Brawley. For instance, in "The Negro in Literature and Art," an essay included in an issue of *The Annals of the American Academy of Political and Social Science* devoted to "The Negro's Progress in Fifty Years," Du Bois, despite his overall open-mindedness toward women's issues such as suffrage, sketches the development of African American literature mentioning dozens of men and only four women: Phillis Wheatley, Sojourner Truth, Linda Brent, and Frances E. W. Harper, "a woman of no little ability" (235) whom he praises mostly for her poetry.[4] Anonymity is the fate of most women writers also in Benjamin Brawley's work. Phillis Wheatley is the only female writer to be discussed at length in *The Negro in Literature and Art* (1910), and her verse is described "as one of the most successful of the American imitations of Pope" (13). More significant praise is lavished on her "soul," her "sterling Christian character" (13), and her pioneering role. It is mostly her chronological status as the "first Negro woman in American literature" (13) and as the mother, so to speak, of African American literature that explains her early canonization. Even in the revised and expanded 1929 edition of Brawley's book, retitled *The Negro in Literature and Art in the United States,* Wheatley remains the only woman to be granted a chapter and an illustration of her own. Although Brawley mentions other nineteenth-century female writers such as Harper, he dismisses her swiftly as one who may have indeed been "popular" but whose verse "was decidedly lacking in technique" (44). Her novel is not even mentioned, although it appears in his bibliography. Other novels of the color line, such as Brown's *Clotelle,* are cited briefly (40), and the theme of passing is referred to only with regard to Chesnutt's *The House Behind the Cedars,* and even then in euphemistic terms as the "delicate and tragic situation of those who live on the border-line of the races" (79).

A work of transition between the "encyclopedic venture[s]" (Mason, "The Academic Critic" 52) of the 1800s and the professional literary criticism of the 1920s, Brawley's study differs from William Wells Brown's in his lack of explicit appreciation for the subversive potential of passing and from Mossell's in his marginalizing remarks on black women writers. Brawley is less interested in explaining the uniqueness of African Americans by reference to their history of resistance to oppression in America than in identifying the cultural properties that make the black tradition distinctive. With Brawley, the awareness of the cultural syncretism most clearly discernible in black folk music becomes central to the discussion of African American literature (7). It leads to an increasing interest in the impact of "folk-lore and folk-music" on the "individual effort[s]" of African American writers (9) and to a preference for works influenced by folklore. Such preference is one of the most

salient characteristics of African American criticism in the twentieth century and provides an oft-invoked justification for the neglect of nineteenth-
century novelists in general and female writers in particular.

*   *   *

The assumption of cultural uniqueness that underlay the early critical
efforts and provided the rationale for arguing the importance of black literature was the explicit concern of African American criticism in the 1920s. In
Alain Locke's influential 1925 anthology, *The New Negro,* this urge to define
the meaning and role of blackness in the present takes on prescriptive overtones. The criteria for racial integrity proposed by Locke for the New Negro
exalt confrontational race pride and assertive race militancy in ways that
disparage previous strategies of resistance. Locke's famous title essay provides
a clear example of teleological criticism[5] in that the devaluation of alternative forms of race pride and artistic resistance becomes instrumental to advancing the critic's cultural agenda.[6]

Locke's New Negro is defined by contrast to the Old Negro, who was "a
creature of moral debate and historical controversy. His has been a stock
figure perpetuated as an historical fiction. . . . The thinking Negro even has
been induced to share this same general attitude, . . . to see himself in the
distorted perspective of a social problem. His shadow . . . has been more real
to him than his personality" (3–4). Locke justifies his contention of newness
by describing the sociopolitical changes that finally led to "shedding the old
chrysalis of the Negro problem" (4): the migrations toward industrial centers, the process of class differentiation, and the Northern urban segregation
that "becomes more and more . . . the laboratory of a great race-welding" (7).
As a result of these changes, "American Negroes" are no longer bonded by a
common condition, but by a common consciousness, the ideological move
being from an assumed state of passivity in the past to the race pride, "group
expression and self-determination" (7) of the present.

Despite his rhetorical depreciation of the nineteenth-century tradition,
Locke's theoretical explanation of the uniqueness of African American culture is mostly a crystallization of previous critical practices. The term "new
Negro" had been inaugurated in fiction by Sutton E. Griggs in *Imperium in
Imperio* (62). Locke's assertion that Negro culture is "separate . . . in color and
substance . . . [but] integral with the times and with its cultural setting" (xvi)
and his "sense of a mission of rehabilitating the race in world esteem" (14)
are not substantially different from Brown's and Mossell's and affirm the continuity he vocally denies. The major novelty of Locke's essay lies in the defiance
and directness with which he proclaims it. However, he does not present the

move from the subversive resistance implicit in Brown's use of passing to his own call for militant race pride as part of a historically changing critical agenda. Rather, Locke's critique of previous literary strategies, which he lumps under the category of "sentimental appeal," posits the servility of the early writers in their reliance on "charity" and their acceptance of "social dependence" (10). This indictment ultimately seems more a requirement of Locke's "iconoclastic" (10) argumentative strategy and of his desire to draw new attention to African American literature than the result of detailed analysis, as proven by the absence of specific references to early works.

William Stanley Braithwaite, in an essay titled "The Negro in American Literature" included in *The New Negro*, is even more unsympathetic than Locke in evaluating his antecedents. Whereas he devotes several pages to critiquing white-authored nineteenth-century fiction and its "sentimentalized sympathy for a down-trodden race" (30), his survey of the "achievement of Negro authorship" (36) disposes of the eighteenth- and nineteenth-century artistic production summarily. He describes Reconstruction as a "rather helpless and subservient era" (37) and asserts that "all that was accomplished between Phillis Wheatley and Paul Lawrence Dunbar, considered by critical standards, is negligible, and of historical interest only" (36). Braithwaite's exceptional praise of Charles Chesnutt stems from the critic's preference for the fiction of the color line of the 1920s, and Chesnutt is salvaged from sweeping denigration on the grounds that he was a precursor of Walter White and Jessie Fauset. Even as he focuses on the "universal" (44) quality of bourgeois characters, however, Braithwaite does not mention the connection between passing and class status that many of the authors he praises established.

In the introduction to his 1929 *Anthology of American Negro Literature*, V. F. Calverton chooses for proletarian fiction the same canon-making strategy Braithwaite uses to assert the universality of bourgeois themes. He condemns literary works that do not fit his critical agenda and searches for a legitimate and legitimizing cultural antecedent (i.e., folk music) that he proclaims at the origin of the true tradition he is writing into prominence. Calverton lavishes praise on the spirituals, blues, labor songs, and jazz because they belong to an African American folk tradition, have an "economic origin" (5), and are "distinctly and undeniably American" (4). The prescriptive and exclusionary components of his dubious praise for the "untutored zeal" (4), the "artless art" (4), the "essential irresponsibility" (10), and the "primitivisms of the Negro" (8) become apparent in his retrospective critique of nineteenth-century literature: "There is . . . an affected dignity in the work of many Negro poets. This tendency to an artificial loftiness of utterance, verging often upon the pompous, is more marked in the work of the Negro writers of the nineteenth century than of the twentieth. . . . They aspired at the stately, when they should have aimed at the simple. Their poetry . . . was hopelessly inept and sentimental. It is only with the present day . . . that this type of verse has been condemned with scorn" (10–11). Similarly, his preference for a "racialism . . . more assertive and radical" (15) and for the "proletarian types" (16) leads to a quick dismissal of works that focus on "the more enlightened and prosperous members of the race" (15). After all these selections and exclusions, Calverton's tradition of worthwhile African American literature comprises mostly twentieth-century male-authored works. The proclaimed "representative value" (vii) of the anthology (which includes selections by several important male and female nineteenth-century figures, including Chesnutt, Harper, Georgia Douglass Johnson, and Angelina Weld Grimké) is thus radically limited and qualified by Calverton's critical commentary.

Not all the critics of this period felt the need to build their new critical edifices on the ashes of the previous century or by searching the past for appropriate antecedents. *The New Negro* itself contains a lesser-known essay by Arthur A. Schomburg, "The Negro Digs Up His Past," that continues in the tradition of historical criticism initiated by Brown and Mossell. Arguing that "the American Negro must remake his past in order to make his future" (231), Schomburg proceeds to challenge the myth of nineteenth-century black passivity and argues that "the Negro has been throughout the centuries of controversy an active collaborator, and often a pioneer, in the struggle for his own freedom and advancement. This is true to a degree which makes it the more surprising that it has not been recognized earlier" (232). He focuses mostly on sociopolitical contributions, but his historical sensitivity leads to an appreciation of literary figures, such as Wheatley and Brown, that other scholars summarily dismiss as servile. The comprehensive lists of names and accomplishments that accompany his remarks reveal a historical precision that is missing in Locke's and Calverton's programmatic essays. The educational uses of the past are underlined with forcefulness in another work of this period: *Homespun Heroines and Other Women of Distinction* (1926) by Hallie Q. Brown. Brown's "anxious desire [is] to preserve for future reference" an account of the life and contributions of women (including several writers such as Wheatley, Harper, Elizabeth Keckley, and Victoria E. Matthews) in the hope "to secure . . . the interest of our youth, that they may have instructive light on the struggles endured and the obstacles overcome by our pioneer women" (vii).

In his 1926 essay titled "The Negro Artist and the Racial Mountain," Langston Hughes connects Locke's defiant race pride and Calverton's preference for the folk with a historical appreciation for the difficulties (though not necessarily the accomplishments) of nineteenth-century writers. On one hand, Hughes expresses sympathy for past writers such as Dunbar and Chesnutt who "received almost no encouragement for [their] work" (169). On the other, he recuperates William Wells Brown's interest in passing but uses the term figuratively: He warns against the dangerous "urge to pour racial individuality into the mold of American standardization" (167), a form of ideological passing that he connects with the black bourgeoisie (169). Less threatened by this kind of passing are the true repositories of African American cultural uniqueness, the "low-down folks" who "furnish a wealth of colorful, distinctive material for any artist because they still hold their own individuality" (168). More than a topic of discussion in itself, passing emerges as a tool to define by contrast Hughes's "I am a Negro—and beautiful!" agenda (171).

*   *   *

Warnings against ideological passing do not heighten the critical relevance of the trope of passing in the 1930s, despite the greater number of critical works and literary histories that include pre–World War I authors. A guarded appreciation for early African American literature characterizes two of the best-known and most influential studies of the period, Sterling Brown's *The Negro in American Fiction* (1937) and J. Saunders Redding's *To Make a Poet Black* (1939), even though their critical agendas are significantly different in many other respects. Both note "the uncommon relation of . . . letters to . . . history" (Redding, *To Make* xxix) that characterizes African American literature but evaluate it very differently. Redding sees it as tending to undermine the artistic value of literary works by turning them into propaganda, whereas Brown, like Du Bois before him, emphasizes that all literature is of necessity propaganda in that it has an ideological function.[7] These different canon-making agendas overlap, however, in their disparagement of the novels of passing.

The chapter titles of *To Make a Poet Black* reveal a teleological understanding of literary history that hypothesizes a progressive "awakening [of] artistic consciousness" (67), a move from "necessity" (3) toward art. Opening with "The Forerunners," Redding discusses the period of "Adjustment" and finally the "Emergence of the New Negro." The last lines of the book strike a prophetic note that reveals the folk telos of the critic: "It is this that must happen: a spiritual and physical return to the earth. For Negroes are yet an earthy people. . . . Their songs and stories have arisen from a loving bondage to the earth. . . . It is to this, for pride, for strength, for endurance, that they must go back" (124).

Consistent with this preference for literature dealing with the folk, Redding identifies a main line of literary development that connects Frances Harper's poetry with to Paul L. Dunbar, James Weldon Johnson, and the New Negroes. Works that do not fit the author's emphasis on folk themes are dismissed on the basis of broad evaluations such as "objective," "propagandic," and "representative." Although the theme of passing is hardly ever mentioned, the works of prose dealing with it are quickly and systematically dismissed. Harper's *Iola Leroy*, for instance, "is a poor thing as a novel, or even as a piece of prose, too obviously forced and overwritten" (43). *Clotelle*, on the other hand, is supposed to shed light on the self-hatred of its author: "William Brown's women are all octoroons, quadroons, or, at the very least, mulattoes. The unconscious irony in creating such characters is very sharp, whispering his unmentionable doubt of the racial equality he preached" (28). One partial exception to this rule of disparagement is Chesnutt's *The House Behind the Cedars* (1900), which is praised for its treatment of the protagonist's secret of Negro blood as a "moral issue" (73) but also criticized for its "sharp thrusts of ironic dialogue" that reveal how "the author lose[s] the . . . objectivity of his [dialect] short stories" (74).

Redding's undeclared but systematic rejection of passing as a legitimate theme for African American literature is accompanied by a puzzling acceptance of works that passed, such as Chesnutt's first collection of stories. To praise *The Conjure Woman* (1899) because it deals with folk themes is consistent with Redding's overall program, but the mode of his praise lends new insight into the aesthetic criteria that support his critical agenda: "The book's reception as the work of a white writer indicates much as to Chesnutt's earlier artistic objectivity and . . . signifies that he was judged by the standards of his white contemporaries" (68). The oft-used term *objectivity* becomes an indicator of Redding's seeming critical impasse, his adoption of mainstream criteria of evaluation, despite his awareness of the prejudiced use of those very criteria to deny the validity of "Negro literature of a serious vein" (88).

Comparing Redding's approach with that of his contemporary Vernon Loggins sheds important light on the former's seeming methodological inconsistency. An influential study published in 1931, *The Negro Author: His Development in America* is a sourcebook of information about African American writers between 1760 and 1900. In explaining his reasons for compiling "a general survey of a field of American literature which our literary historians almost without exception have neglected" (vii), Loggins invokes the "historical associations" of African American literature but leaves no illusions about its being "productive of little that is truly artistic" (vii). The "strongest element" (viii) of the tradition is folklore, which he discusses in the clos-

ing chapter briefly and in remarkably exoticizing terms. Opposing folklore
to "the Negro's consciously produced literature" (vii), he presents the former
as the expressive tool of the "primitive Negro" (354) and a proof that African Americans are "emotional, imaginative, musical . . . [and] expressive by
nature" (365). As for the literature based on folklore, he praises the writings
of Joel Chandler Harris, Thomas Nelson Page, Paul L. Dunbar, and Charles
W. Chesnutt (360) without highlighting any difference between the use of
folk material by plantation tradition writers and their opponents.

Redding shares several premises with his white colleague, including the
historical value of African American literature, the preference for twentieth-
century works, and the little attention devoted to women writers. However,
although he may agree with Loggins that Harper is "an author of poor stories and fair verse" (Loggins 324), in his own hands folklore does not emerge
as the expression of a "primitive mind" (Loggins 359) but rather as the central criterion for critical evaluation. Redding's depreciation of nineteenth-
century fiction in general and of works of passing in particular is instrumental to establishing the aesthetic value of folklore: By comparison with the
"propagandic" (Redding, *To Make* 43) critique of racial stereotypes operated by writers of passing, folk themes can be presented with "objectivity" as
art that stems from a distinctively black cultural soil. Redding's proposed folk
criterion for the appreciation of African American literature remains deliberately unthreatening to mainstream critical standards in that it requires from
the reader the acceptance of what one could call separate but equal artistic
materials. *To Make a Poet Black* thus emerges as a conscious attempt to trespass, to appropriate and circumvent the hegemonic aesthetic standards responsible for the marginalization (or, as in Loggins's case, the condescending appreciation) of black literature. Interested in giving "the book some
appeal to popular taste" (*To Make* xxx), Redding establishes his credibility
with the dual black and white audience he faces by adopting mainstream
criteria of "objectivity" in his critique of nineteenth-century fiction and by
manipulating those same criteria to advance an African American aesthetic
based on the artistic value of folk forms. In the process, however, "the material of an ordinary history of Negro literature is . . . cut more than half"
(Redding, *To Make* xxix–xxx).

As aware as Redding of the great resistance in the academic establishment
to recognizing the artistic value of African American literary works, Sterling
Brown adopts an argumentative strategy that is more confrontational. He
opens the introduction to *The Negro in American Fiction* (1937) by decrying
the racial prejudices of white authors and the ideological uses of American
literature: "The treatment of the Negro in American fiction, since it paral-

lels his treatment in American life, has naturally been noted for injustice. Like other oppressed and exploited minorities, the Negro has been interpreted in a way to justify his exploiters" (1). Conscious of the biases intrinsic in mainstream categories of literary analysis, and faced with the problem of assessing literary value, Brown's solution to the need to formulate alternative evaluative tools is dual. On one hand, he claims the right to be "subjective" (3) because others have been self-serving. On the other, he documents the historical development of a unique African American literary tradition by highlighting the changing but continued difference between white and black interpretive frameworks of the American experience and by conferring on "Negro novelists . . . the responsibility of being ultimate portrayers of their own" (4). In African American fiction, realism, which Brown defines as social commentary, becomes not only the principal tool to dismantle racial stereotypes but also the measure of a text's worth.

Regardless of the differences between his and Redding's critical approach and evaluation of specific nineteenth-century novels (e.g., Chesnutt's and Dunbar's), Sterling Brown also hardly mentions the theme of passing, although he dismisses on both ideological and aesthetic grounds the early novels dealing with it. According to him, William Wells Brown's characters, "though vouched for by the author, are hardly distinguishable in gentility from the heroines of 'blood and tears' romances" (40), Webb's novel is "badly overwritten" (40), and Harper's characters are "too angelic for acceptance" (76–77). His reasons for disparaging the early literature become clear when he discusses Chesnutt. Chesnutt is praised as a "pioneer" and uncompromising (78), but his racial integrity is rendered suspect by his interest in passing: "Although attacking the color line within the race, he makes great use of the hero or heroine of mixed blood, and at times seems to accept the traditional concepts of Negro character" (81). Like Redding, Brown finds it difficult to reconcile the militancy of nineteenth-century black writers with their focus on passing. Moreover, both critics are pressured by the lack of information about African American literature in the mainstream critical establishment and by contemporary racist notions that saw mulattos as better because "whiter." The approach they take is guardedly educational, and they hasten to clarify that the all-but-white characters of nineteenth-century fiction are not "representative" (Redding, *To Make* 28, 72) and "far from convincing" (Brown, *The Negro* 76).

In "Introduction: Blueprint for Negro Writing" (1937), Richard Wright addresses on a theoretical level the major methodological and ideological issues that both Brown and Redding struggle with in their critical reevaluation of African American literature. In this sophisticated nationalist mani-

festo, Wright combines ideological and aesthetic criteria in the attempt to go
beyond limiting definitions of artistic commitment and mimetic notions of
literary realism. Arguing that "a vulgarized simplicity constitutes the greatest danger" (325), Wright theorizes a way out of the art versus propaganda
dichotomy that African American critics have had to contend with. The "fluid
lore of a great people" (321), "a Marxist conception of reality" (321), and respect for the "autonomy of craft" (325) represent Wright's suggested ingredients of true art, which apparently are not to be found in works of the past.
In his comments on nineteenth-century literature, it becomes clear that his
preference for folklore as the true repository of the "nationalist character of
the Negro people" (318) forecloses the appreciation of a huge portion of early
black writing. His description of the black literary tradition is provocatively
scathing: "Generally speaking, Negro writing in the past has been confined
to humble novels, poems, and plays, prim and decorous ambassadors who
went a-begging to white America" (315). Such an all-encompassing depreciation of different literary conventions and historical contexts belies Wright's
own statement that the writer should be free to use "every iota of gain in
human thought and sensibility . . . no matter how far fetched they may seem
in their immediate implications" (322).

   Paradoxically, in light of their much-publicized literary disputes, the one
to put into practice Wright's suggestion to go beyond literal readings and
realize the "complex simplicity" (Wright, "Introduction" 322) of certain
writers is Zora Neale Hurston. She moves beyond the methodological defensiveness and prescriptiveness of her contemporaries by operating a dramatic epistemological reversal: The black experience becomes the source of interpretive criteria that she applies to the cultural tenets of other races, and
of whites in particular. In the chapter titled "My People! My People!" of *Dust
Tracks on a Road* (1942), Hurston takes readers through a pedagogical process that leads them from a conviction of the existence of fixed group characteristics to a belief in a variety of individual experiences patterned by variations in "class and culture" (216). Like Sterling Brown, she intends to explode
stereotypes and does so by focusing on the differences she sees within the
black community. By the time the reader gets to her final proclamation that
"there is no *The Negro* here" (237), Hurston has succeeded in undermining
the very analytical categories that made stereotyping possible. She applies the
concept of difference within the race first and then between races, and in the
process she pokes fun at theories of racial purity and connects that well-
known American preoccupation with Hitler's eugenics.

   As in nineteenth-century novels of passing, Hurston's deconstruction of race
does not turn blackness into an individual state of mind.[8] Group dynamics,

cultural hegemony, and racial hierarchies remain central issues, and Hurston comments on the impact of societal inequalities on individual lives through a story. Connecting race with gender as a "multiple jeopardy" (King 42), she imaginatively reconstructs her grandmother's experience of sexual abuse: "Since nobody ever told me, I give my ancestress the benefit of the doubt. She probably ran away from him just as fast as she could. But if that white man could run faster than my grandma, that was no fault of hers. Anyway, you must remember, he didn't have a thing to do but to keep on running forward. She, being the pursued, had to look back over her shoulder . . . to see how she was doing. And you know your ownself, how looking backwards slows people up" (235–36). "Race" may indeed be a "loose classification of physical characteristics" (Hurston, *Dust Tracks* 325), but it is also a criterion for oppression and a reason for "looking backwards." Only by straddling the line between the awareness of its arbitrariness and the knowledge of its underlying power relations is it possible not to be overdetermined by it.

The few comments on miscegenation that escaped the publisher's censorship and were retained in the 1942 edition of Hurston's autobiography represent only a small section of the longer discussion on the topic that appears in the original 1937 version of "My People! My People!" In the original, which appeared in print for the first time in the appendix to Robert Hemenway's 1984 edition of *Dust Tracks* (291–306), Hurston's comments on class differences within the black community are connected much more clearly with white prejudice and stereotyping. In distinguishing between "skinfolks" and "kinfolks" (294), Hurston pokes fun at the pretenses of the black bourgeoisie, but she also comments on the difference between color and racial heritage: "You can't just point out my people by skin color" (294). Not surprisingly, her aggressive challenge to racial assumptions leads her to the issue of passing: First, she notices how whites are disturbed by the very idea; second, she refuses to make commonplace comments about blacks wanting to be white and focuses instead on white people who want to pass for black (295).

It is not difficult at this point to share Hemenway's feelings about the "difficulty of fixing Hurston's thoughts" on race (288). The difficulty gives way to complexity when we realize that she challenges the very definition of race rather than limit her critique to changing its evaluation. Consciously addressing a dual audience, she questions the soundness of the term *race* in light of the variety of attitudes it is supposed to cover and suggests a proto-deconstructive definition. Once she denies the simple equation of color with race and takes color as one of the possible indicators of race, Hurston is left with a variety of cultural and political issues that are too complex to be stereotyped because they require a historically specific analysis and reveal the power relations indicated by categories of color.

Having uncovered the racial justifications for power hierarchies, Hurston recuperates her focus on group dynamics. On one hand, like Hughes, she chastises ideological passing as a denial of the "black mama" (*Dust Tracks* 302) and the black genealogy she both belongs to and symbolizes. On the other, she completes her attack against white racial stereotypes by ridiculing the concept of normative whiteness: "What we think is a race . . . could be the shade patterns of something else thrown on the ground—other folks, seen in shadow. And even if we [the Negro] do exist it's all an accident anyway. God made every-body else's color. We took ours by mistake" (*Dust Tracks* 304). By racializing whiteness Hurston anticipates the deconstructive approaches to race that took center stage in the 1980s and 1990s and also provides a critical tool for interpreting the uses of the theme of passing in early African American literature.

*   *   *

Hurston's exploration of the disruptive implications of passing is all the more remarkable for its rarity. Yet even when they are not explicitly discussed, the covert appropriation and empowering manipulation of hegemonic standards that are characteristic of passing in its broadest sense continue to make their presence felt in African American literary criticism. For instance, they can help explain the emphasis on Americanism and the ambivalent introductory declarations of the editors of *The Negro Caravan: Writings by American Negroes* (1941), Sterling Brown, Arthur P. Davis and Ulysses Lee.

Parts of their introductory indictment against the stereotyped depiction of black characters in white-authored fiction are reprinted verbatim from Sterling Brown's 1937 volume, but in 1941 Brown et al. argue more forcefully the need for self-portrayal. Their tone foreshadows the Black Aesthetic: "The validity of much of the work of white authors cannot be denied, but the belief as expressed . . . in many publishers' announcements, that white authors know the Negro best is untenable to the editors of this anthology. They believe that the 'inside view' is more likely to make possible the essential truth than 'the outside'" (4). After affirming the importance of the African American literary tradition and its ideological and thematic distinctiveness, the authors come to an unexpected conclusion: "In spite of such unifying bonds . . . writings by Negroes do not seem to the editors to fall into a unique cultural pattern. . . . The bonds of literary tradition seem to be stronger than race. The editors therefore do not believe that the expression 'Negro literature' is an accurate one. . . . 'Negro literature' has no application if it means structural peculiarity, or a Negro school of writing" (6–7). What appears to be an inconsistency is immediately qualified and explained by the authors as a precautionary measure, as a symptom of the distrust of the reader that characterized nineteenth-century black narratives and remains operative in twentieth-century literary criticism because African American intellectuals continue to be faced with a dual, highly polarized audience: "The chief cause for objection to the term is that 'Negro literature' is too easily placed by certain critics, white and Negro, in an alcove apart. The next step is a double standard of judgement, which is dangerous for the future of Negro writers" (*Negro Caravan* 7). In light of the scholarly segregation to which these statements allude, the editors' denial of a separate African American literature emerges as a tres-passing strategy finalized to promoting it. Even as "a segment of American literature" (7), African American letters still are presented as a tradition in their own right. On one hand, the editors organize the anthology by canonical genres but "explain the history of the type as used by Negro authors" (vi). On the other, they hint at an autonomous source of cultural distinctiveness when they differentiate between the literature "written under abolitionist sponsorship in the North" and the "body of folksong" in the South (5).

The critical agenda of the editors becomes clearer in the sections on specific genres where they suggest ideological and formal criteria for evaluating African American texts. In the section on the novel, the authors praise the social realism that culminates in Richard Wright's *Native Son,* which they hail as the "com[ing] of age" of African American fiction (144). They use it as a touchstone for evaluating previous literary works, and the results of this procedure with regard to nineteenth-century authors are predictable: The editors criticize both Martin Delany and William Wells Brown on aesthetic grounds (138–39), but they praise the former for his "more convincing" pictures of slavery (139), while they describe the latter as having "importance only historically" (138). They make no concession of the sort to women writers, whom they often dismiss contemptuously: For example, they classify Harper as derivative of Brown, and they describe *Iola Leroy* to be as "dull as it is pious" (139). Notwithstanding the prefatory declaration that "comprehensiveness seemed a necessity for one of the aims of the book" (v), female authors are underrepresented in the anthology, and most of those included appear in the poetry section rather than in more overtly politically charged genres such as the novel, autobiography, or essay.[9]

That *The Negro Caravan* editors' introductory denial of the distinctiveness of African American literature represents a strategy to circumvent the formidable academic resistance they expected to encounter is demonstrated by the detail with which they describe the function of an anthology of African

American literature. Their comments, whose function recalls the "authenticating documents" (Stepto, *From Behind the Veil* 4) appended to so many
nineteenth-century African American texts, find a parallel in similar signs of
distrust of the audience that Hugh Gloster betrays in his literary history *Negro
Voices in American Fiction* (1948). In his attempt to legitimize African American literature as a worthy field of study, Gloster provides a long description
of the uses of his text for both "students of social history" and "students of
literature" (viii) and also insists on the Americanness of black literature:
"Trends in . . . Negro literature . . . are neither spasmodic nor fragmentary,
but are inextricable patterns in the warp and woof of the American literary
fabric" (viii).

These parallels notwithstanding, the critical approach proposed in *Negro
Voices* is very different from that of *The Negro Caravan*. Unlike Brown et al.,
Gloster belongs to a line of aggressive canon makers in favor of literature dealing
with the black bourgeoisie that includes also Braithwaite, whom Gloster often
echoes. Gloster's treatment of pre–World War I literature is rather exhaustive
and he mentions even lesser-known writers of passing such as Webb and Hopkins, who are rarely cited in previous criticism. In terms of evaluation, however, the nineteenth century pays the price of the author's belief that "cultural
emancipation" (101) occurred only in the 1920s. He occasionally admits their
novelty and historical interest, but early African American writers are seen
mostly as extensions of their white contemporaries and as presenting "stock
characters and arguments" (29). Only when he moves away from "untalented
narrators" (34) such as Harper and Hopkins to Chesnutt does he discover "a
gifted novelist" (34) to commend. The motivation for such praise is dual: First,
echoing Redding, Gloster notes that Chesnutt demonstrates "such objectivity
and detachment that for a long time many readers were unaware that his work
was that of a Negro" (36); second, he sees Chesnutt's works as belonging to a
tradition that leads, through James Weldon Johnson, to the glorified Harlem
"Renascence [*sic*]" (113). Gloster deals with passing as a theme but reduces it
solely to a manifestation of the cultural angst of Chesnutt's Rena and Johnson's
Ex-Colored Man. He glosses over its early uses as a strategy of subversion and
highlights exclusively texts in which the passer is "more of a silent sufferer than
a social reformer" (83), a preference consistent with his optimistic assessment
of the 1920s as a period characterized by a "more unbiased attitude" toward
the artistic output of "the colored literati" (112).

* * *

As the emphasis on "Americanism" develops into a discourse of integration in the 1950s, the tendency to underplay the history of racial conflict further diminishes the relevance of nineteenth-century works and the interest

in the novels of passing wanes. The voluntaristic faith in U.S. commitment to racial equality that characterizes post-1954 (the year of the *Brown v. Board of Education* Supreme Court ruling) literary criticism emerges clearly from Langston Hughes's address to the First Conference of Negro Writers, which took place in New York in 1959. In contrast with his own declarations in "The Negro Artist and the Racial Mountain" thirty years earlier, when he chastised an artist for wanting "to be a poet—not a Negro poet" (167), Hughes advises younger writers that "this you will have to be: . . . *writer* first, *colored* second. That means losing nothing of your racial identity. . . . In the great sense of the word . . . good art transcends land, race, or nationality, and color drops away. If you are a good writer, in the end neither blackness nor whiteness makes a difference to readers" ("Writers" 43–44). However, he qualifies his optimism with playful but sarcastic comments on racist editorial politics: "To be really successful you should be white. But until you get white, *write*" ("Writers" 45).

Major critics of the period such as Margaret Just Butcher, Arthur P. Davis, and Saunders Redding also voice the new optimism and produce "good-will" criticism (Davis, "Integration" 40).[10] Butcher's *The Negro in American Culture* (1956), which is based on materials left by Alain Locke, reveals the voluntaristic aspects of this good will and its impact on the interpretation of the past. Butcher shows conflicting impulses to address but also to minimize the distinctiveness of African American culture. Her detailed study of the "Negro folk genius" (28), her assertions that American culture is most indebted to "Negro folk products" (23), her groundbreaking exploration of the slave's cultural agency and "clandestine and unforeseen effect" upon southern institutions (26) are all belittled by her final contention that "the American Negro, though forced by majority attitudes of exclusion and rejection to take on a defensive attitude of racialism, has rarely set up separate cultural values or developed divergent institutional loyalties or political objectives" (221). Similarly, although Butcher argues that African American cultural uniqueness has a "realistic social explanation" (30) and invokes surviving Africanisms to support her point, she also confirms her dedication to an integrationist agenda by cautiously postulating the "nearly complete loss of his [the Negro's] original culture" (26) in the United States. American Negro folk products are "almost wholly" the result of historically specific uses of "forms and ingredients borrowed from the majority culture" (31).

Butcher is aware of the "clandestine" (26) cultural activity of the slave, but her ambivalent critical comments, as well as her preference for literary "realism" and the texts produced after "its firm entrenchment in the early twenties" (130), inhibit a sympathetic analysis of the early fiction. With regard to nineteenth-century prose writers, Butcher refers to Brown's and Webb's novels of passing, notices their provocative treatment of the taboo topic of miscegenation (125), but dismisses them swiftly as "melodramatic and unequivocally propagandistic" (125). Harper is not even mentioned, and Chesnutt is the only nineteenth-century novelist to be praised as "an early realist, the first Negro novelist to handle social themes artistically" (130). He is a worthy antecedent for the contemporary writers Butcher celebrates: Wright, Ellison, and Baldwin (142–44). In *The Negro in American Culture* nineteenth-century fiction defines by contrast the legitimately integrated (so to speak) line of literary development that will eventually lead to the disappearance of defensive race propaganda and the "rise of a universalized theme supplementing, but not completely displacing, . . . racial mood and substance" (110).

Whereas the aforementioned major critics of the 1950s try to balance cultural distinctiveness with a concern for an integrated "universality" by underplaying the African roots of African American culture and the history of racial violence,[11] other scholars voice cautionary and dissenting positions. At the First Conference of Negro Writers (1959), Julian Mayfield goes against the grain of voluntaristic critical optimism when he emphasizes the contrast between a superficially encouraging "moral climate" and the continued reality of "racial injustice" (30). Similarly suspicious of the terms on which integration should occur, John H. Clarke urges the study of African culture and especially of the connections between African resistance to colonialism and the experience of black Americans ("Reclaiming" 23, 25). Clarke's interest in a tradition of resistance leads him to valorize the past. He contextualizes himself as a participant in the "American Negro writer's mission to reclaim his lost African heritage" (23) and traces that mission back to the nineteenth century to critique the condescending ignorance of white scholars who credit themselves with the "discovery" of Africa (22).

In Ellison's 1958 essay "Change the Joke and Slip the Yoke," this use of the past to undermine scholarly appropriations or tendentially racist misinterpretations of African American culture challenges white American cultural identity in ways that recall nineteenth-century novels of passing. Ellison connects his analysis of African American tricksterism with a dissection of the status of the oppressor. Like Hurston, he operates a dramatic reversal in perspective. He provocatively proclaims Benjamin Franklin to be a trickster and defines the cultural identity of white Americans as a political construction, as a purely oppositional concept defined by contrast with the European as well as the black American tradition. Ellison's climactic declaration that "America is a land of masking jokers" (55) and that the masking, for both blacks and whites, occurs for different historically specific purposes, collapses superficial racial distinctions, and ridicules white delusions of racial purity: "The Negro looks at the white man and finds it difficult to believe that the 'grays'—a Negro term for white people—can be so absurdly self-deluded over the true interrelatedness of blackness and whiteness. To him the white man seems a hypocrite who boasts of a pure identity while standing with his humanity exposed to the world" (55). Here Ellison echoes William Wells Brown, who in *The Black Man* quotes respected scholars such as Macauley and Hume on early British history to demystify delusions of Anglo racial purity in the United States: "The Britons lost their nationality, became amalgamated with the Romans, Saxons, and Normans, and out of this conglomeration sprang the proud Anglo-Saxon of to-day. . . . Ancestry is something which the white American should not speak of, unless with his lips to the dust" (34).

The depth of Ellison's discussion on the interconnectedness of the cultural identities of different racial groups within American society can be measured by contrast with the binarism of Robert A. Bone's *The Negro Novel in America* (1958). Bone is one of the few critics of this period to treat nineteenth-century fiction extensively and to deal explicitly with the early novels of passing. However, his interpretation of those works is marred by his Manichean opposition between "assimilationism," which for him implies "an unconscious desire to be white" and an equally "unconscious self-hatred" (4), and "nationalism," with its attendant "feeling of racial solidarity" and "process of self-magnification" (5). Armed with such imprecise critical tools, "aggrieved by what he believes to be deplorable assimilationism by the Negro middle class, and contemptuous of the literary traditions before 1920, Bone devotes considerable verbiage to an attack on both" (Turner, "*The Negro Novel*" 125). According to Bone, the "early Negro novelist had the soul of a shopkeeper" (15), early fiction as a whole constitutes a bourgeois literary heritage that "was largely negative" because it taught "only what pitfalls to avoid" (50), and the theme of passing in particular is an unmistakable symptom of self-hatred and belief in white superiority.

In the process of discarding nineteenth-century novels of passing, however, Bone reveals a pronounced fear that racial boundaries may be crossed, if only on a literary level. Very aware of the phenomenon, as well as the theme, of passing as a "racial strategy" (221), he defines it negatively and uses it metaphorically to chastise any attempt to explore the literary and cultural interconnections between blacks and whites. Assimilation, for example, is indicted as "psychological 'passing'" (4), but the apparent radicalness of this definition (which echoes Hughes's and foreshadows LeRoi Jones's) is belied by Bone's coterminous condemnation of nationalism as "extralegal" (6).

Similarly, he describes the right of black authors to deal with white characters as a "kind of literary passing" (220), but he also critiques the "art-as-weapon fallacy" (216). Bone grants African American literature a separate and unequal status that he makes contingent on artistic freedom "from the requirements of racial strategy" (221), the very conditions that novels of passing were designed to challenge.

* * *

The critical modes dominant in the 1950s continued well into the following decade, although they became increasingly more peripheral and more militant as a result of the rise of the black arts movement. Butcher, Davis, and Redding's brand of "good-will" criticism finds renewed expression in Herbert Hill's second critical anthology, *Anger, and Beyond* (1966). In Hill's introductory remarks the exaltation of folklore as a "record of . . . endurance and survival" (xix) is accompanied by a neglect of nineteenth-century literature and by the related teleological belief in the contemporary coming of age of black literature: "Today" African American writers "share all preoccupations of contemporary literature" and are engaging in universalized "protest" (xxii). Hill's proclaimed faith in integration is subtly qualified by his reiterated critique of the art-as-weapon fallacy. His urgency to undermine the artistic legitimacy of "simple protest and anger" (xxii) reveals an awareness of the emerging militant cultural movements of this period and belies the linearity of the ideological progression described by the title of his influential anthology.

The shadow of increased disillusionment with America's commitment to racial equality led Redding to a partial retraction of his previous invalidating comments on nineteenth-century fiction. In "The Negro Writer and American Literature" (1966), an expanded version of his 1959 address at the First Conference of Negro Writers and the opening essay in Hill's anthology, Redding assesses the status of African American literature in very positive terms: "What is happening seems very like a miracle" (19). However, his critical approach changed and his evaluation of Chesnutt betrays a more overtly political tone. In *To Make a Poet Black,* Redding argues that Chesnutt's claim to fame rested mostly on the dialect stories that passed with white critics, who did not recognize them as the work of a black writer and liked them. In the 1966 essay, Redding praises Chesnutt's realistic fiction and blames the failure of his novels on the "indifference to the works of culture-conscious, race-conscious Negro writers . . . [that] began to crystallyze into opposition in the first decade of this century" (6–7). However, Redding's critique of racist cultural practices does not lead to an overall appreciative reevaluation of nineteenth-century fictional strategies. It reverberates only indirectly on the present. The telling

of previous discriminations enhances the optimism of the critic's final, voluntaristic, and inspirational contention that "today" African American literature is "in an excellent state of health" (16) because the "gulf [between audi-
ences] is closed," and the Afro-American artist is finally free (19).

The legacy of disinterest in the nineteenth-century roots of African American literature that Redding passes on to the "new generation of academic
critics" (Turner, "Afro-American" 71) becomes apparent even from a cursory
glance at the table of contents of *Dark Symphony* (1968), the anthology edited by James A. Emanuel and Theodore L. Gross. Interested in reaching a
"wide audience" (ix), the editors declare, like Redding thirty years earlier, that
the "criterion for inclusion . . . is the intrinsic artistic merit of the story, the
poem, or the essay" (ix). Emanuel and Gross aim to "designate which works
by Negroes deserve to be part of the heritage of American literature" (x), a
task that leads to "selective anthologizing" (2). In the case of pre–World War
I literary works, such selection becomes a substantial erasure that spares only
excerpts from Frederick Douglass's autobiography and speeches, a short story
by Chesnutt, and poems by Dunbar and Du Bois. In their introduction, which
is supposed to illuminate "the general background which the omitted works
helped to create" (2), the editors preface the discussion of nineteenth-century
novels with the following sympathetic but broadly invalidating assessment:
"Trapped in the post-Reconstruction era of disfranchisement and multiform
repression, and suspended by literary inexperience between the Romantic
and Realistic traditions . . . early Negro novelists inevitably turned out much
aesthetically inferior work" (4). The list of fiction includes many novels of
passing, which are not explicitly identified as such, and no works by wom-
en. Harper is mentioned only as a short story writer, and even then solely as
a predecessor "of lesser ability" (3) than Chesnutt and Dunbar.

This masculinist bias and strong preference for the twentieth century continue to characterize an otherwise different kind of critical approach: the
Black Aesthetic movement. The Black Aesthetic "tendencies to denigrate
older black writers while lauding the newest" (Turner, "Afro-American" 72)
are different from previous disparagements of pre–World War I literature.
They are more direct, their list of older black writers comes to include also
some twentieth-century ones, and they substitute frankly political criteria to
aesthetic justifications for selection. Inflammatory rhetoric increases the
contrast between, for instance, Emmanuel and Gross's subdued but final
dismissal of the "literary inexperience" (4) of pre–Harlem Renaissance literature and the blunt, overarching condemnation that opens LeRoi Jones's
important 1966 essay "The Myth of a 'Negro Literature'": "From Phillis
Wheatley to Charles Chesnutt, to the present generation of American Ne-

gro writers, the only recognizable accretion of tradition readily attributable to the black producer of a formal literature in this country, with a few notable exceptions, has been of an almost agonizing mediocrity" (*Home* 105).

Jones measures the "spectacular vapidity" (106) of Negro literature by contrast with Negro music, which is "a significantly profound contribution" (106). Echoing Hughes's 1926 manifesto, he explains such opposite artistic results in terms of class: The writers "have been members of the Negro middle class" (106) and therefore promoted the "frenzied dash towards the precipice of the American mainstream" (109). Black music, on the contrary, is the creation of the "lowest classes of Negroes . . . the only consistent exhibitors of 'Negritude' . . . because [they] . . . maintained their essential identities as Negroes" (106). This clear-cut dichotomy is reinforced by Jones's critical double-standard. Whereas Jones displays remarkable historical sensitivity in appreciating the changing forms and the syncretic nature of African American music, in his comments on black literature he argues the continued, undifferentiated imitation of white middle-class values and accuses African American writers of ideological passing: "Such a literature . . . takes on the emotional barrenness of its model, and the blackness of the characters is . . . an unconvincing device. . . . It is like using black checkers instead of white. They are still checkers" (110). Even when admitting that ideological passing presents limitations when dissociated from physical passing, Jones confines to music only the impact of American color consciousness: "The Negro could not ever become white and that was his strength. . . . He had to make use of other resources, whether African, subcultural, or hermetic. And it was this boundary, this no-man's-land, that provided the logic and beauty of his music" (114). Consistent with his refusal of most preceding African American literature, Jones dedicates *Black Fire,* the anthology he edited with Larry Neal, exclusively to the newer generation of black revolutionary artists, whom he proclaims "the founding Fathers and Mothers of our nation" (xvii). However, the percentage of mothers remains disproportionately small, especially in the politically charged genre of the essay, in a parallel marginalization of the past and of women that is far from coincidental.

In the late 1960s, a noteworthy but lesser-known exception to this disparaging critical attitude toward nineteenth-century fiction was Kenny Williams's *They Also Spoke: An Essay on Negro Literature in America, 1787–1930* (1970). In the preface, dated 1969, Williams goes explicitly against the grain of contemporary critical practices: "One of the serious problems facing twentieth-century scholarship is the determination of the significance of the past. . . . This is especially true of the study of Negro literature in America which has suddenly . . . dismissed the writers of the eighteenth and nineteenth centuries because they did not subscribe to the currently-held doctrines of the mid-years of the twentieth-century" (xi). Though echoing earlier strategies of emphasizing the Americanness of African American literature to argue its national importance, Williams proposes an original reevaluation of pre–Harlem Renaissance black fiction. She voices an unprecedented outspoken appreciation for the "sensationalism and irony" (99) of *Clotel,* which she describes as "one of the first exercises in American realism" (100), and in historicizing and contextualizing literary texts she anticipates methodological concerns that characterized feminist scholarly approaches of the decades that followed. However, Williams comes to terms with the cultural climate of her own times by hardly mentioning the trope of passing even in the plot summaries of *Clotel* and *The Garies,* where it is prominent, and by describing Harper's *Iola Leroy* in uncharacteristically disparaging terms. *They Also Spoke* represents an in-between text. It does not support the contemporary Black Aesthetic critical agenda, but although it anticipates the concern with the past of later feminist scholars, it does not share their interest in recovering and reinterpreting the female literary tradition.

*   *   *

Though not as complete a break with the past as it proclaimed itself to be, the Black Aesthetic represented a significant shift in critical perspective. Previous criticism argued the uniqueness of black culture but was devoted to demonstrating its crucial role in the development of American culture as a whole. The Black Aesthetic critics of the late sixties and early seventies instead underplayed the issue of "Americanness" and concentrated on affirming the in-group relevance of an autonomous black culture. In his introduction to *The Black Aesthetic* (1971), Addison Gayle Jr. explains "the new note sounded in the art of Black people during the nineteen fifties and sixties" (xv) as resulting from the focus on Northern (rather than Southern) "white terrorism" (xviii): "The liberal ideology—both social and literary— . . . has become the primary target of the Afro-American writer and critic" (xx). This "war" (xvii) with the "duplicity" (xviii) and the subtler "humanitarian" (xix) racism of white liberals finds an antecedent, for instance, in Ellison's critiques of individual condescending white scholars (e.g., "The World and the Jug") but is now enlarged to encompass American society as a whole. Gayle affirms African American cultural uniqueness as part of the process of "de-Americanization" (xxi), which also requires an awareness that "the degree of similarity between the conditions under which blacks and whites live has been exaggerated" (385) and the conviction that African Americans are the only true interpreters of their own culture.

The impact of this separatist agenda on literary criticism and the evaluation of nineteenth-century fiction of passing becomes clear in Gayle's 1975 *The Way of the New World.* The literary rebirth Jones invoked in 1966 (*Home* 115) reemerges in Gayle as the "baptism by fire" (xix) of the 1960s riots, which the critic hails as conducive to "the catharsis . . . that gave birth to a new literary Renaissance" (xix). Keeping the Black Aesthetic as the final stage of development, Gayle identifies two other major phases: before and after the Harlem Renaissance. Before World War I, "ignoring their own history and culture, the early black writers attempted to create a literature patterned upon that of whites" (xii). After accusing them of imitativeness, "romanticism" (xii), and neglecting to "create symbols, images and metaphors anew" (xii), Gayle offers a synthetic explanation for their "failure" (xii): "They were firsts" (xii). However, this sympathetic justification does not eliminate the need to erase their supposedly servile literary legacy. In the second phase of development (1920s through the 1960s), black authors devote themselves to the "steady eroding of the romanticism . . . which plagued their predecessors" (xix). Gayle thus conceptualizes literary tradition as a process of "undoing" (xvii); the pre- and post-Renaissance periods cancel each other out and leave contemporary African American writers purified of the needs to assimilate or protest: "At long last, form and structure were recognized as little more than cousins to content, and the black novelist . . . prepared to move forward in the most monumental undertaking of the twentieth century—the task of redefining the definitions, creating new myths, symbols, and images, articulating new values, and recording the progression of a great people from social and political awareness to consciousness of their historical importance as a people and as a nation within a nation" (xx).

In "Paradigms of the Early Past," the opening essay in *The Way of the New World,* Gayle makes more detailed comments on nineteenth-century novelists. He even acknowledges a legitimate though meager line of literary descent that includes Martin Delany and Sutton Griggs as precursors of the Black Aesthetic separatist credo, a critical evaluation that a few years later was echoed by Wilson J. Moses in *The Golden Age of Black Nationalism, 1850–1925* (1978). Gayle celebrates Delany, in particular, as "the first writer to argue that Blacks were more African than American" (24). Much more numerous are the writers he disowns for their assimilationism. "Having . . . accepted their own inferiority, the black middle class . . . demanded a literature which pointed out ways in which they might become like their oppressors" (5), and Brown, Webb, and Chesnutt supposedly provided it. Gayle's list of the proscribed ones includes mostly male writers of the color line, who are accused of solving "the problem of differences between the races by pointing out that in essentials no differences exist" (10). The personal background of some of them is also brought to bear because, being mulattos, they "were in positions to profit from racial divisions" (23), according to Gayle. In his wholesale dismissal of writers of passing, however, Gayle collapses the difference between a belief in cultural distinctiveness (which the early writers of passing shared with him) and separatism and ultimately laments the artists' noncompliance with his own cultural agenda: "The inability of the black novelist to build upon the foundation laid down by Delany meant that no viable literary tradition was possible until after *Native Son*" (24).

Despite such vocal disparagements of nineteenth-century literature as Jones's and Gayle's, the vivacity of the Black Aesthetic movement, the controversies surrounding it, and the fact that the very process of disparaging also implied recording the literary production of otherwise neglected African American writers increased the interest in black literature and created the possibility for republishing several early novels, including Delany's *Blake*, Brown's *Clotelle*, and Webb's *The Garies*. In the 1970s, moreover, interest in the initial phases of the African American literary tradition was kept alive in such literary histories as *Black American Literature: A Critical History* (1973), in which Roger Whitlow makes an effort to be comprehensive and to historicize his critical evaluations, as well as in the articles featured in *CLA Journal*, the official publication of the College Language Association, which was formed in 1939 because "black scholars felt that they had . . . little opportunity to present papers at the . . . Modern Language Association meetings" (Turner, "Afro-American" 59). *CLA Journal* devoted a special issue to William Wells Brown in 1973 and regularly published essays on Chesnutt, Dunbar, Webb and, less often, on women such as Alice Dunbar-Nelson.

The impact of the Black Aesthetic movement on the subsequent course of African American criticism is fundamental in several ways. First, the distinctiveness of African American culture becomes an assumption rather than a contention. Second, the twentieth-century preference for selective teleological criticism continues, but the Black Aesthetic unapologetic emphasis on identifying a single legitimate line of predominantly male literary development intensifies the segregation by gender and, indirectly, the need for a parallel female critical tradition. Third, the reaction to the Black Aesthetic gives rise to what Houston A. Baker calls "the emergent reconstructionist generation" (*Blues* 89) of the mid- and late 1970s, which includes Robert Stepto and Henry Louis Gates Jr.

Rejecting the "absolutism" (Gates, "Preface to Blackness" 68) of Black Aesthetic critics, the reconstructionists propose a formalist approach and attempt to separate the analysis of distinctively African American literary features from the ideological implications of such distinctiveness. The critics' need to illuminate the specific historical experiences of African Americans to contextualize their literature remains at odds with their proclaimed formalism, however. To circumvent the problem, Stepto's dislike for "nonliterary structures" (*From Behind the Veil* x) and Gates's insistence that the "literary text is a linguistic event . . . [and] its explication must be an activity of close textual analysis" ("Preface to Blackness" 68) led to a preference for the study of slave narratives and African American autobiographies, where the "extraliterary" (Gates, "Preface to Blackness" 57) experiences specific to black history are an integral part of the text itself and can therefore be addressed without invalidating the critics' theoretical statements. In *From Behind the Veil* (1979), for example, the slave's "quest for freedom and literacy" (ix) becomes the "primary pre-generic myth for Afro-America" (ix), and Stepto traces the continuities of its literary forms from slave narratives to twentieth-century texts such as *Black Boy* and *Invisible Man*. This emphasis on the slave narrative as the foundational genre of the African American literary tradition dominated black literary criticism for the next two decades.

In Gates's contributions to *Afro-American Literature: The Reconstruction of Instruction* (1979), a collection of essays edited by Dexter Fisher and Robert Stepto, the preference for slave narratives seems part of a larger project reminiscent of Redding's. Gates promotes the academic study of African American literature by inserting its tradition into mainstream American literary canons and by strategically underplaying its counterhegemonic import. A clever tres-passing trickster with a profound understanding of the uses of manipulating mainstream critical standards to legitimize African American literature within the biased, white-dominated academic establishment, in "Preface to Blackness: Text and Pretext" Gates strategically depoliticizes race by arguing, " 'Blackness' is not a material object or an event but a metaphor . . . defined by a network of relations that form a particular aesthetic unity" (67). He also condemns the "extraliterary idea[s]" (57) of previous critics since the 1920s and dismisses them for confusing "art with propaganda" (54). Having rhetorically separated himself from the critical tradition, Gates calls for the reconstruction of African American scholarship by invoking an array of diverse and authoritative white critical figures such as Tzvetan Todorov, René Wellek, and Raymond Williams. To complement his legitimizing and seemingly unthreatening theoretical stance, Gates chooses as his object of study the distant slavery period, so conveniently different from the present as to support illusions of apolitical, formalist literary investigation. Blackness becomes a metaphor easier to accommodate among, or pass into, established mainstream critical concerns.

The scholarly disinterest in nineteenth-century fiction thus continues despite changing agendas, and the emphasis on past literary endeavors remains confined to the slave narrative. The work of Houston A. Baker Jr., another critic whose career bloomed in the 1980s, did not dramatically revise the trend. In *The Journey Back: Issues in Black Literature and Criticism* (1980), Baker resists the reconstructionist backlash against the Black Aesthetic movement, although he recognizes the need for a "more descriptively accurate and theoretically sophisticated" (xii) criticism. Baker posits that criticism is "in the service of goals larger than the articulation of a set of theoretical propositions" (xii), he insists on the need to clarify the relationship of literature to society by proposing an "anthropology of art" (xvi), and he qualifies the formalist approaches of Stepto and Gates by stressing the importance of "cultural context" (xvii). Like the reconstructionists, however, and consistently with his own 1971 beliefs that the literary production of the early novelists "shows poor craftmanship and a servile imitation of accepted models in both theme and content" (*Black Literature* 3–4), the only early works of prose Baker discusses at greater length are autobiographical. Nevertheless, in one of his few brief references to a nineteenth-century novelist, Baker argues that a knowledge of the African American cultural context is indispensable to evaluate Chesnutt's *The Conjure Woman* (*The Journey Back* 157–58), and this comment contains but does not articulate explicitly the critic's understanding of early African American covert fictional strategies.

*   *   *

The late 1970s witnessed the emergence not only of the reconstructionists but also of black women's studies. Feminist efforts to document and reinterpret the literary role of black women as authors and characters led to an unprecedented, sustained interest in the fictional production of the 1800s. The ideological and methodological bases for this critical movement were laid earlier in the decade. In the same year when Gayle's *The Black Aesthetic* was released (1971), Alice Walker published in *Black Collegian* "The Unglamorous but Worthwhile Duties of the Black Revolutionary Artist." This essay advanced general recommendations on the importance of preserving "what was created before" and cherishing "our old men" although they "may not all have been heroes of the kind we think of today" (*In Search* 135). The next year, Walker acted on her own recommendations and developed a groundbreaking course on black women writers that included nineteenth-century novelists such as Harper as an integral part of the tradition. Walker's comments on the black tradition also became more specific and explicitly woman-centered. In "From an Interview" (1973) she laments male critical neglect of female authors and calls for more interpretive sensitivity in analyzing the "seemingly apolitical" novels by black women (*In Search* 264). In "In Search of Our Mothers' Gardens" (1974), she reiterates even more assertively the importance of evaluating a writer's limitations within her historical context and critiques the "snickering" dismissal of "stiff, struggling, ambivalent lines" (*In Search* 237) that do not fit contemporary notions of artistic beauty or racial commitment.

Walker's dual emphases on interpreting women's strategies of literary resistance and documenting the historical roots of their tradition were not isolated or idiosyncratic phenomena. The 1970s saw the publication of anthologies that, following the lead of such earlier female anthologists as Mossell, valorize nineteenth-century women (e.g., Gerda Lerner's *Black Women in White America* [1972] and Bert Loewemberg and Ruth Bogin's *Black Women in Nineteenth-Century American Life* [1976]). These same years also witnessed a proliferation of critical studies by female scholars about early African American novels of the color line, such as Jean Fagan Yellin's *The Intricate Knot: Black Figures in American Literature, 1776–1863* (1972), Judith Berzon's *Neither White nor Black: The Mulatto Character in American Fiction* (1978), and Arlene Elder's *The "Hindered Hand": Cultural Implications of Early African-American Fiction* (1978).

The "Hindered Hand" is interesting in light of Elder's attempt to assert the importance of nineteenth-century fiction by stressing its compatibility with Black Aesthetic standards on the basis of the continued "educative, inspirational intent" (xi) of black writing. The opening lines of her introduction read, "The controversies in Black literature remain the same. William Wells Brown . . . would have agreed in principle with poet Don L. Lee, who . . . asserted in 1968 that '. . . Black poetry will give the people a future: will show visions of tomorrow'" (xi). Continuity does not imply sameness, and Elder echoes Gayle in admitting that "the majority of the early Black artists were clearly assimilationists" (201). In Elder's case, this critique does not result in dismissal. She analyzes the early writers with an appreciation for their specific historical contexts, literary strategies, forms of race pride, as well as in light of American racism: "Their failures demonstrate the limitations not only of the individual writers, in terms of talent and imagination, but of an American society that prescribed which art was acceptable, which culture, which people, and blinked at the consequences of such dogmas" (201).

Whereas Elder's "major authors" are all male and her study, like Kenny Williams's before hers, does not reveal an explicit commitment to a black feminist cause, Barbara Christian's *Black Women Novelists* (1980) gives analytical depth and historical detail to Barbara Smith's 1977 programmatic declaration that "Black women writers constitute an identifiable literary tradition" (B. Smith 7). In describing the purpose and goals of her study, Christian insists on the need to examine literary products within the ideological climate of their historical period: "This book is an attempt to describe that [novelistic] tradition, . . . to examine its origins, and to trace the development of stereotypical images imposed on black women and assess how these images have affected the works of black women artists" (x). Contextualizing the "battle of images" (Christian, *Black Women* 25), she recuperates and interprets the rationale behind nineteenth-century strategies of counterpropaganda, including the use of all-but-white characters. Eschewing critical proscriptions, Christian examines how dominant social and literary conventions regarding the class background, kind of beauty, and feminine qualities of the proper (white) heroine combined to make "the mulatta . . . the only type of black woman beautiful enough to be a popular heroine and close enough to wealth vis-à-vis her father to be well bred" (22). As such, mulatta characters became effective literary tools "to combat the negative images of black women in southern . . . literature" (22).

However, historical sensitivity does not mean uncritical acceptance. Christian expresses her belief that the artistic choices of the early novelists reflect their own personal class biases and disregard for the "richness of the folk expressions of the day" (34), but she does not propose a solution of continuity in the female tradition or the formulation of prescriptive lines of legitimate literary development. This inclusive historical approach to tradition became the trademark of black feminist criticism in the 1980s. Gloria T. Hull's comprehensive pedagogical handbook, *All the Women Are White, All the Blacks Are Men, but Some of Us Are Brave* (1982), includes bibliographies and course syllabi comprising nineteenth-century literary works and rarely mentioned early black feminist texts such as Mossell's *The Work of the Afro-American Woman* (1894). In her 1985 collection of critical essays, *Black Feminist Criticism,* Christian also features nineteenth-century women writers, as do Marjorie Pryse and Hortense J. Spillers in *Conjuring: Black Women, Fiction, and Literary Tradition* (1985) and Carole McAlpine Watson in *Prologue: The Novels of Black American Women, 1891–1965* (1985).

In *Reconstructing Womanhood* (1987), Hazel V. Carby explicitly brings together the study of nineteenth-century fiction, an interest in gender issues and literary forms of resistance, and passing. Carby's Marxist approach and examination of "racist ideologies" (18) lead to a methodological suggestion full of promise for the discussion of nineteenth-century strategies of subversion: "We need more feminist work that interrogates sexual ideologies for their racial specificity and acknowledges whiteness, not just blackness, as a racial categorization" (18). In her discussion of Hopkins's fiction, Carby demonstrates the impact of her approach on the evaluation of the early works. When connected with the "popular fictional formulas and conventions . . . of disguises and double identities" the whiteness of nineteenth-century characters becomes one of the tricks that "enabled an identity to be hidden" (148). Far from reducing literary color consciousness to a matter of exotic plot twists, Carby's distinction between passing as "narrative mechanism" and "narrative subject" (158) foregrounds the need to read early African American fiction as crafted art rather than unmediated social commentary. She questions "interpretations which consider the representation of white-looking black characters as an indication of acquiescence in dominant racist definitions of womanhood and beauty" (148).

Increasingly in the 1980s black women critics confronted the need to defend their historical, recuperative critical approaches vis-à-vis the popularity of selective and often male-centered "theoretical" paradigms. In 1987, more explicitly than in any of her previous anthologies, Mary Helen Washington insists on the importance of tradition for the feminist critic and reminds her audience of the political struggle that made her own anthologies possible. Of the ten authors included in *Invented Lives,* Washington notes, "Without exceptions these writers have been dismissed by Afro-American literary critics until they were rediscovered and reevaluated by feminist critics" (xx). The interdependence between recuperating literary works of the past and keeping alive the present commitment to black feminist criticism leads her not only to include such nineteenth-century novelists as Harper and Hopkins but also to outline the critical tradition that "has made it possible to document black women as artists, as intellectuals, as symbol makers" (xxv–xxvi).

An analogous recommendation to continue the work of recovery and reinterpretation that should accompany the formulation of comprehensive theories on the African American literary tradition characterizes Barbara Christian's "The Race for Theory" (1987). Aware of the still marginal position of black feminist criticism in the academy, conscious that the brilliant careers of past women writers too often ended in silence and poverty, and worried about the scarcity of "practical criticism" (57) even in the case of acclaimed contemporary women novelists, Christian is also wary that the current popularity of literary theory may become "prescriptive, exclusive, elitish" (58). Christian may have not given enough recognition to the ways in which the hegemonic potential of theory also is being subverted by other African American feminist critics (e.g., Deborah McDowell, Hortense Spillers, and Claudia Tate), but her suspicions are highly justified in light of the continued marginalization of black women's creative and critical writings by African American male scholars who are popularly recognized in academic circles to be "at the center of the current debates on 'race'" (Fuss 74). The active efforts of black feminist critics have led to the canonization of some nineteenth-century novelists such as Harper and Hopkins, but they have not yet resulted in a widely accepted reevaluation of the early fiction, nor have they changed the contemporary critical preference for the study of autobiographical narratives.

In the case of Henry Louis Gates Jr., probably the most publicized scholar of African American literature in the 1980s and 1990s, the study of black autobiographical narratives continues to be part of a sophisticated and multifaceted strategy to circumvent the academic resistance to the study of African American literature. A few years after his vocal renunciation of the "ideological absolutism" ("Preface to Blackness" 68) of the black arts movement, Gates continues his redefinition of "Blackness" in a controversial series of exchanges that appeared in the journal *Critical Inquiry* and were later collected in *"Race," Writing, and Difference* (1986). His bracketing of *race* within quotations marks and its definition as "a metaphor for something else and not an essence or a thing in itself, apart from its creation by an act of language" (*"Race"* 402) seem to transform a politically charged term into an abstract and less threatening intellectual category not necessarily connected with any specific cultural knowledge. Similarly building on his 1979 proclamation of loyalty to mainstream critical theorists, in *Figures in Black: Words, Signs, and the "Racial" Self* (1987) Gates argues that "black, text-specific theories" (xxi) will result from translating contemporary literary theories "into the black idiom" (xxi) and thereby reassures the white-dominated academy that the familiarity with critical theory will ensure the comprehension of the process of translation.

Gates's tres-passing attempt to promote the academic study of African American literature by emphasizing its compatibility with accepted critical frameworks is structurally similar to William Wells Brown's aforementioned strategy to secure freedom for a runaway slave by disguising him as a white woman. In both cases passing, whether in a metaphorical or a literal sense, is a mode of subversion that stems from distrust and from the awareness of opposing forces. Like Brown and the nineteenth-century writers of passing, Gates is confronted with "a 'two-toned' audience: those whose concern is black literature and those whose concern is the study of the institution of literature today" (*Figures* xxx). In a 1989 essay he refers explicitly to practices of covert resistance and sheds indirect light on his own canon-making strategies: "Lord knows that this relationship between the seen and the told—that gap of difference between what we see among and for ourselves and what we choose to tell in (a white, or integrated) public discourse—has been remarkably complex in our tradition, especially in attempts to define the canon of black literature at any given time" ("Canon-Formation" 30). Like William Wells Brown's, Gates's appropriation of hegemonic standards to circumvent modes of exclusion and canonize the African American literary tradition has met with success, as his own academic fame, the extraordinary Schomburg series on black women writers, his numerous editions of early classics, and the opening of a larger market for such works stand to prove.

With the exception of Wilson's *Our Nig*, however, which skirts the boundary between fiction and slave narrative, in his own criticism Gates makes few references to the highly political uses of "race" in the nineteenth-century female (or male, for that matter) novelistic tradition that he has helped document. His notion of canon making relies on the power to exclude and create hierarchies, often at the expense of women and the early novelists. In his introductory essay to the 1988 reprint of Saunders Redding's *To Make a Poet Black*, Gates praises the late critic for recognizing that "though a literary tradition consists of all the texts and authors that satisfy the criteria according to which that 'tradition' might be broadly defined, it was the canonical authors of the black tradition, those whose works in some way most fully represented its salient aspects, who had to be identified" (xvi). The similarities between their methods and the self-referential aspects of his praise become apparent in his description of Redding's "judgements" and "distinctions" (xvi). Gates does not seem to find fault with the fact that Redding's canon includes four women and nineteen men (xvi) or that Harper is mentioned mostly because her "poetry . . . prefigures James Weldon Johnson's use of 'dialectical patterns'" (xvii).

The essay on Redding illuminates the principles that inform Gates's conceptualization of the role of the critic in the late 1980s and early 1990s. In *Reading Black, Reading Feminist* (1990), Gates's distinction between canon making and the concern with articulating a literary tradition becomes explicitly gendered. Whereas "the task of the [male] critic . . . was to draw distinctions, to make aesthetic judgements, to chart formal lines of descent" (Introduction, *To Make* xvi), that of the female scholar is "to chart the multiplicity of experiences and perspectives" (*Reading Black* 8). However, his description of this difference does not problematize his own critical practice but rather implies the acceptance of a gendered division of labor. Despite his praise of feminist critics, Gates's commerce with the black woman's critical sphere remains that of a sympathetic promoter of marginal literary criticism. In his 1989 non-female-specific essay "Canon-Formation, Literary History, and the Afro-American Tradition: From the Seen to the Told," he nicknames those attempts "to preserve and 'resurrect' the tradition" as "the Sears Roebuck approach, the 'dream book' of black literature" (37).

Gates's interest in early women writers and feminist scholarship has been shared by other contemporary male critics such as Houston A. Baker. Baker's *Workings of the Spirit: The Poetics of Afro-American Women's Writing* (1991) includes, almost for the first time in the critic's career, a substantial discussion of nineteenth-century novelists of passing, or at least of the ones (e.g., Harper and Hopkins) whom two decades of feminist scholarship have succeeded in canonizing. Baker's comments on African American women writers reveal a complex and ambivalent relationship with black feminist criticism and its emphasis on tradition. He lavishes praise on the important contributions of female critics but then proceeds to divide and select them on the basis of a hierarchy of theoretical value that goes against black feminists' own emphasis on continuity. The scholars belonging to the more recent group of theoreticians (Valerie Smith, Hortense Spillers, Mae Henderson, Deborah McDowell, Cheryl Wall) are discussed individually and quoted repeatedly. Conversely, the members of the "first generation of Afro-American women scholars [who] began in the mid-seventies their construction of a *historical* (as opposed to a 'theoretical') basis for subjecthood and curricular subject status" (17) remain an undefined mass of names listed once and hardly ever mentioned again. Baker's curt appraisal of Washington and Christian, for example, sounds more like a posthumous eulogy than praise for productive contemporary scholars who started their academic careers when he did. Though unmentioned, the work of these critics remains central to *Workings* mostly as a result of Baker's attempt to exorcise their influence. In constructing his critique of the "resistance to theory . . . that has come . . . from the community of Afro-American women scholars, writers, and critics" (2), Baker refers to but does not quote some of the issues that coalesced in Christian's controversial "Race for Theory" (*Workings* 1, 9, 10). This essay remains Baker's invisible opponent when he accuses black feminist criticism of being "a theoretically silent body, . . . a faint echo of her master's voice" (18) on the basis that "to maintain an exclusively historical situation is . . . to remain silently and complicitously accessible to the *touch* of Euramerican discourse" (18).

His strategy to prove their "historical essentialism" (*Workings* 37) is to draw a comparison between the supposedly accommodationist politics of turn-of-the-century black women writers and contemporary women critics. Given the striking (19) similarity between turn-of-the-century writers and late-twentieth-century critics, to call the former "Washingtonian[s]" (34) is also to indict the latter as "Uncle Toms," so to speak. Although he denies any intention to "recuperate either Robert Bone's condescension towards turn-of-the-century Afro-American texts or Addison Gayle's Black Aesthetic condemnation of them *tout d'un coup*" (23), Baker's own critique of what he calls "mulatto aesthetics" (22) echoes that of his predecessors in several crucial ways. He condemns "nineteenth-century daughters" (26) for their distance from the Southern masses and the vernacular (23), and his reading of nineteenth-century conventions often is as condescending as Bone's or Gayle's. Although he is aware that "'mulatto' . . . is a sign of the legitimacy and power of . . . whitemale [*sic*] patriarchy" (36), he never questions whether that is the very reason why it was chosen as a theme and a terrain of contestation in the first place. He concludes that "what remains absent . . . in the daughter's texts . . . is a fleshing out of both the southern, vernacular, communal expressivity of black mothers and grandmothers, *and* a portrayal of the relentless whitemale hegemony . . . that threatened ceaselessly to eradicate such expressivity" (36). This conclusion can be reached because Baker glosses over Iola's search for her mother in the South or Hopkins's outspoken indictment of prebellum and postbellum sexual violence, a female site of that "relentless whitemale hegemony" (36) he wants to see addressed.

The interdependence between an interest in gender and in nineteenth-century novels could not be revealed more clearly. In the end of *Workings,* the proposed "move beyond the historical essentialism of the turn-of-the-century daughters and their Harlem Renaissance successors" (37) sounds like the most recent of a series of attempts to disregard the historical roots of contemporary black women's writing and to incorporate some writers (e.g., Zora Neale Hurston) into a male-defined and male-dominated canon. Baker's closing vision of "a poetics . . . of Afro-American discourse" centers around the "provinces of the fathers, revisions of Harlem and the Black Aesthetic," although he concedes that the center can be effectively "comprehended and transformed" (210) only by skirting what evidently remains at its periphery, that is, "through an attentive, theoretical refiguration of Afro-American women's expressivity" (210).

*   *   *

The 1990s have witnessed a proliferation of studies on pre–Harlem Renaissance African American literature, accompanied by the republication of many of the early works. The primacy of the slave narrative in critical studies remains unshaken, but scholars, especially feminist scholars, are more outspokenly questioning the methodological and exclusionary implications of that preference. On one hand, critics such as Frances Smith Foster, Jean Fagan Yellin, William L. Andrews, Nellie Y. McKay, and Deborah McDowell have expanded the definition of the slave narrative as a genre, its formal properties and thematic concerns, by focusing on a female tradition of slave narrators and autobiographers. On the other, the study of the pre–Harlem

Renaissance women's novelistic tradition by such scholars as Frances Smith Foster, Claudia Tate, Deborah McDowell, Ann duCille, and Carla Peterson has led to increasingly more vocal critiques of the existing critical consensus on the slave narrative as the foundational genre and on the vernacular and the folk tradition as the distinctive mark of authenticity of black literature.

A case in point is duCille's *The Coupling Convention* (1993), in which the author explicitly denounces both the masculinist "bias in current critical practice for vernacular theories of African American cultural production" (81) and the residual defensiveness with which black feminist criticism continues to approach the early novels even in the process of recovering and reclaiming them. According to duCille, "both black literary studies and black feminist criticism . . . [have] misread the aesthetics and the politics of much of the early work of African American authors. These authors' interventions at the level of form as well as content represent an innovative, highly political narrative strategy that African American literary history and black feminist criticism have most often seen as merely imitating the white rhetorical modes of white American writers such as Harriet Beecher Stowe" (7).[12] Not surprisingly, her proposed reinterpretation of the early fiction starts from the mulatta figure, which she describes as "both a rhetorical device and a political strategy" (7), following in the tradition of Christian, Carby, and Tate. She operates the move beyond defensiveness she has called for by renaming and appropriating Brown's *Clotel* as "woman's fiction," as a narrative that "has as much to say on the feminized subject of marriage as it does on the masculinized subject of slavery" (19).

Despite these critical moves toward its reinterpretation and a reevaluation, pre–Harlem Renaissance African American fiction has yet to overcome the critical proscription that has characterized its scholarly reception for more than a century. Its continued marginalization in the contemporary canon of African American letters emerges with clarity from two monumental volumes that are the largest and most comprehensive anthologies of African American literature ever published: *The Norton Anthology of African American Literature* (1997) and *Call and Response: The Riverside Anthology of the African American Literary Tradition* (1998). Though different in many respects, these anthologies share an outspoken emphasis on the vernacular and the folk tradition and a preference for the slave narrative that seems to inhibit and be posited in binary opposition to an appreciation of the early fiction. Both *The Norton Anthology* and *Call and Response* include a significant sample of pre–Harlem Renaissance writers, but their fictional contributions remain somewhat marginal to the larger picture of African American culture these anthologies depict.

I will provide two emblematic examples of the continued secondary status of early black fiction in the canon of African American letters. In the Preface to *The Norton Anthology,* Henry Louis Gates Jr. and Nellie Y. McKay state that they "decided to make available, where possible, texts that represent the origins of a genre" (xxix). Among these firsts, they list "Victor Séjour's *The Mulatto,* the earliest short story by an African American (published in Paris in 1837) . . . and the first African American novel, Harriet E. Wilson's *Our Nig* (1859)" (xxxix). The criteria for considering these two works as firsts are not consistent because they shift from privileging the date of Sejour's short story (regardless of the fact that it was not published in the United States) to privileging the place of publication of *Our Nig* (the United States). This inconsistency rhetorically displaces both Harper's "The Two Offers" (1859) as the first known short story published by an African American in the United States and Brown's *Clotel* (1853) as the first novel written by an African American but published in London, although both texts have been included by the period editor. It can hardly be a coincidence that the displaced works deal, respectively, with racially indeterminate characters and with the trope of passing. To replace *Clotel* with a "novelized autobiography" (Zafar 118) such as *Our Nig* as the foundational text of the African American novelistic tradition means placing great emphasis on the autobiographical mode to legitimize the rise of the African American novel by creating a generic link with the authentic African American form *par excellence,* the slave narrative.

Along similar lines, the editors of *Call and Response,* who also include a representative sampling of works of passing or mention them in the headnotes, place pre–Harlem Renaissance novelists under the heading "The Novel or Neo-Slave Narrative." In the introductory notes, general editor Patricia Liggins Hill mentions the first African American novels and explains rather defensively, "Although influenced by Stowe's classic, these fictional works were not mere imitations of it. Rather, they followed the pattern of the fugitive slave narratives found also in later black novels, including such classics as Richard Wright's *Native Son* (1940) . . . and Charles Johnson's *Middle Passage* (1990)—works that several modern critics classify as 'neo-slave narratives'" (228–29). Between the rock of *Uncle Tom's Cabin* and the hard place represented by the influential slave narrative, pre–Harlem Renaissance fiction writers are accorded very limited room indeed. That the term "neo-slave narrative," however improper, is supposed to redeem the early novels and find some space for them in the editors' proclaimed Black Aesthetic canon becomes clear from the table of contents, which lists the novelists during and after the Harlem Renaissance under a different and simpler heading: "Fiction Writers."

As postmodern, technologically advanced (e.g., the audio companion) versions of the encyclopedic ventures that characterize the beginning of African American criticism, and in light of their similarities with previous marginalizing critical assessments on nineteenth-century fiction, these anthologies open up larger issues regarding what continues to be perceived as the only authentic line of development of African American literature. And they do so in more ways than one: not only in terms of their parallel emphasis on the vernacular and marginalization of pre–Harlem Renaissance fiction but also in light of the rhetorically different notions of blackness the anthologies propose. Published the year after *The Norton Anthology* and obviously experiencing some anxiety of influence, the editors of *Call and Response* proclaim the novelty of their text by describing it as "the first comprehensive anthology of literature by African Americans presented according to the Black Aesthetic, a criteria [*sic*] for black art developed by Americans of African descent" (xxxiii).

What does an opening statement like this imply of the recently published *Norton Anthology*? Is it far-fetched to suppose that it may place *The Norton Anthology*, and its emphasis on the African American writer's participation in and subversion of the "Anglo-American belletristic tradition" (xxviii), in a position similar to that of the supposedly assimilationist early writers of passing? Does *Call and Response*'s opening emphasis on "African Survivals in Slave Folk Culture" not make *The Norton Anthology*'s opening section on "The Vernacular Tradition" seem more African *American* than *African* American? Can we not hear the faint echo of the old critical dichotomy of "assimilationism" versus "separatism," concepts that continue to underlie the critical resistance to the early novelists? And if the time has come, as it seems to have, when it is possible to accept these differences in emphasis and focus without positing them as binary opposites, without falling back on terms such as *assimilationism* and *separatism* (which are as judgmental as they seem self-explanatory), and without giving in to defensive and divisive reified notions of authenticity, may we not also expand this critical open-mindedness and sophistication to the analysis of the early novels of passing? May we not also finally admire Brown the slave narrator without wanting to apologize for Brown the novelist?

Brown and the other writers discussed in this volume imbued their novels with the same defiance of injustice and commitment to social change they revealed in their nonfiction works and in their lives as abolitionists, journalists, educators, feminists, ministers, politicians, or editors. In their fiction they expressed themselves consciously as artists, not only as activists, devising innovative and often radically new means to give literary shape to their universe as it emerged from their own lives and their people's distinctive historical and cultural heritage. The rise of the African American novel does not represent, as has often been argued, an artistically inadequate though historically important beginning but rather a key foundational moment in the development of the African American literary tradition that also changed the course of American letters as a whole in ways that to this day remain largely unexplored.

Notes

Introduction

1. Terms such as *all-but-white, white Negro, octoroon,* and *quadroon* are obsolete. I use them with an awareness both of their historical context and of how early African American writers deployed them in the very process of deconstructing the pseudobiological notions of race in which those terms were grounded.

2. For a history of literary representations of the mulatto, see Werner Sollors's recent encyclopedic volume *Neither Black Nor White Yet Both.*

3. I borrow the terms *necessity* and *extravagance* from Sau-ling Wong's *Reading Asian American Literature.* Wong explains, "The terms *Necessity* and *Extravagance* signify two contrasting modes of existence and operation, one contained, survival-driven and conservation-minded, the other attracted to freedom, excess, emotional expressiveness, and autotelism" (13).

4. Many novels of passing, by Harper and Hopkins for instance, originally appeared in black periodicals, a fact that defies long-standing notions that passing stories were aimed mostly at white audiences. On the issue of black readership, see Tate (*Domestic Allegories* 5–9, 102–4), Foster (Introduction xx–xxv), and Hopkins's 1903 reply to Cordelia A. Condict ("Reply" 594–95).

Chapter 1: The Mark Without

1. On the reception of Brown's works, see Andrews (*To Tell*) and Farrison. *Three Years in Europe* was already mentioned by way of publicity in the title page of the 1853 edition of *Clotel.*

2. In "The Novelization of Voice in Early African American Narrative," Andrews provides an insightful discussion of "the distinction between natural and fictive discourse" (27) in the first edition of *Clotel.* Whereas Andrews focuses on Brown's "narrator's 'free use' of authenticating conventions" (33), I examine how such freedom affects Brown's portrayal of slave resistance, of the free use his characters make of the racial conventions underlying the peculiar institution.

3. This connection between African American literature and historical realities is too often hastily evaluated negatively as propaganda, "polemic" (Heermance 184), or "didacticism" (R. Lewis, "Literary" 130), as if it necessarily detracted from the artistic qualities or complexity of a text.

4. Brown complicates the discussion of the controversial issue of intraracial color prejudice. On one hand, he critiques those who devalue blackness. He condemns quadroons who "have no higher aspiration than that of becoming the finely-dressed mistress of some white man" (*Clotel* 63). In the case of his character Sam, who harbors prejudices against blacks despite his being "one of the blackest men living," Brown notes that his conversation with other slaves about color gives "unmistakeable evidence that caste is owing to ignorance" (*Clotel* 133). On the other hand, he describes the negative reactions of some visibly black minor characters such as Dinah (*Clotel* 158) to the whiteness of the passer. His description gains depth in the 1864 edition, where Brown comments in greater detail on his characters' motivations: "Dinah was the mother of thirteen children, all of whom had been taken from her when young; and this, no doubt, did much to harden her feelings, and make her hate all white persons" (*Clotelle: A Tale* 41).

5. Andrews has identified a similar narrative strategy in Mark Twain's *Life on the Mississippi* (1883): "Through the experience of reading his [Twain's] book about the Mississippi, the reader is thrust into a situation analogous to that of anyone who attempts to read the 'wonderful book,' the magnificent text, of the river itself" ("Mark Twain" 9). In *Clotel,* rather than a "wonderful book," Brown wants to evoke a communal predicament of oppression, conceivably for the purpose of reducing the experiential distance between his characters and his British readers. His strategy has not been much appreciated, as critics have reacted impatiently to Brown's disregard for the reader's expectations of narrative development. The changes Brown operates in the later editions of *Clotel* seem to indicate his desire to diminish the unsettling effect of his novel to shift the reader's attention from the dynamics of the text itself to the injustices it portrays.

6. The increase in the mulatto population was noticed by other contemporary commentators, including Harriet Martineau: "I was not then aware of the extent to which all but virtuous relations are found possible between the whites and blacks . . . wherever there are masters and slaves, throughout the country. When I did become aware of this, I always knew how to stop the hypocritical talk against 'amalgamation.' I never failed to silence the cant by pointing to the rapidly increasing mulatto element of the population, and asking whether it was the priest's service which made the difference between holy marriage and abhorred 'amalgamation'" (15).

7. For a detailed account of the Crafts' escape and their lecture tours with Brown, see their narrative *Running a Thousand Miles for Freedom* (W. Craft 270–331) and Blackett.

8. As Richard Yarborough notes, "*Uncle Tom's Cabin* was the epicenter of a massive cultural phenomenon, the tremors of which still affect the relationship between blacks and whites in the United States" ("Strategies" 46). Brown aimed to revise and counteract some of the stereotypes Stowe popularized. Unfortunately, their popularity has turned Stowe's stereotypes into archetypes that continue to haunt the reading of early African American fiction and inhibit the appreciation of its oppositional force.

9. Brown appropriates for himself as author the trickery he ultimately denies to his female character. Whereas he underscores the significance of Clotel's death with a poem

that, as Edward Farrison notes, he borrowed from Grace Greenwood's 1851 *Poems,* he offsets the sentimental and pathetic thrust of Greenwood's composition by adding a final stanza infused with caustic irony (*Clotel* 220–22).

10. Mary's feelings also qualify her as a race heroine. Her reluctance to trust Devenant and her lifelong preference for the ex-slave George exempt her from Brown's puzzlingly broad indictment that "most of the slave women have no higher aspiration than that of becoming the finely-dressed mistress of some white man" (*Clotel* 63). After being reunited with George, Mary "confesses that the love she bore him was never transferred to her first husband" (244).

11. Brown himself openly acknowledges his debt to Child in chapter 29 ("Conclusion") of *Clotel* (245).

12. On the tensions between identification and appropriation that characterize white feminist-abolitionist figurations of the abused bodies of female slaves, see Karen Sanchez-Eppler's *Touching Liberty.*

13. These long-standing rumors have been confirmed recently by DNA evidence proving the existence of the descendants of an offspring of Jefferson and Sally Hemings (Murray and Duffy 58–63).

14. Mary's escape with a white man is much less problematic than Clotel's with William. Passing as the sister of the Frenchman, Mary needs no disguise.

15. Clotel decides to escape after the young man to whom she has been sold as a housekeeper starts seeking "to win her favour by flattery and presents" (*Clotel* 170).

16. Brown had already published a version of George's escape and eventual reunion with Mary on the Continent in Letter 22 ("A Narrative of American Slavery") of *Three Years in Europe* (1852). In that volume, Brown declares that the story was told to him "in France, by George Green himself" (304) in January 1852, and because *Uncle Tom's Cabin* was originally serialized between June 1851 and April 1852, the stories of Brown's George Green and Stowe's George Harris emerge as almost contemporaneous. Even if we hypothesize that Brown invented George Green and that he drew on Stowe's mulatto character, the originality of his protagonist is not undermined. Whereas Tom was "Stowe's real hero" and it was "Tom, not George, who so quickly entered the stock of American cultural archetypes" (Yarborough, "Strategies" 53), Brown decided to choose George Harris as the hero of his novel. This is not too surprising because, as black critic George T. Downing wrote reviewing *Uncle Tom's Cabin* at the time, Harris is the only black character "that really portrays any other than the subservient, submissive Uncle Tom spirit, which has been the cause of so much disrespect for the colored man" (qtd. in Gossett 173). In the attempt to differentiate his own novel from Stowe's and possibly also to underscore the independent origin of George Green's story, in the serialized and book-form American editions of his novel, Brown renames his heroic protagonist Jerome and describes him as visibly black.

17. George's combativeness does not survive his emigration to England, where Brown describes him as "somewhat ashamed of his African descent" (*Clotel* 232). This seeming inconsistency in the characterization of George reveals how Brown's Anglophilia did not blind him to the possible prejudices of his British audience. In England, George passes by omission: His employers assume he is white, and he does not disillusion them. Brown constructs George as a fully successful hero "on the road to wealth" (*Clotel* 232) and avoids

discussing color prejudice in Europe because he seems to have limited faith in the desire for critical self-examination of his British readers. He also neutralizes the threat of black male sexuality by portraying George as faithful to the long-lost Mary.

18. The intertextual dialogue between Brown, Stowe, and Melville has yet to be explored exhaustively, especially with regard to *Clotel*. Sarah Robbins reads *Benito Cereno* in the context of its original 1855 serialized publication in *Putnam's* and in terms of Melville's "appropriation of Stowe's familial sentimental markers for a multi-layered ironic critique" (555). Her argument that "for an 1850s *Putnam's* audience, seeing *Benito Cereno* as a condemnation of slavery might have been easier than for a 1990s reader less focused on Stowe's then-popular characters and the racial attitudes they embodied" (555) illuminates also the forcefulness of Brown's revisions of *Uncle Tom's Cabin*.

19. Sidney Kaplan and Robert S. Levine are among the critics who have discussed Melville's dualism. Kaplan writes, "It would be a mistake to search in Melville for the intransigent humanitarianism of a Garrison or a Weld. . . . Melville was never an abolitionist. . . . Yet it must nonetheless be . . . admitted that in forms of fiction he uttered from time to time the most powerfully democratic words of his age on the dignity of the Negro" (331). More specifically about *Benito Cereno*, Levine remarks that the text "transforms the reader into a self-conscious sea-captain desirous of restoring the ship of state even as he or she remains aware of, and mutinously identifies with, an otherness subsumed and enslaved by the 'consensual' demands of community" (223–24).

20. Critic Harry B. Henderson notes that "the events on board the *San Dominick* in a curious way seem to take place outside of history. Melville presents the revolt of the slaves as an event occurring on a floating microcosm, deliberately detached from any particularized historical context and, more significantly, bereft of genuine historical consequences" (148).

21. Brown asserts the rights of slaves to freedom, liberty, and the pursuit of happiness as a matter of justice and consistency with American democratic ideals rather than on the basis of the slaves' supposed moral superiority. It is also clear from his focus on white male and female violence against the slaves, and from his depiction of Georgiana's systematic abolitionist activism before dying, that Brown did not share Stowe's belief in the efficacy of "sentimental power" (Tompkins 81). *Clotel* and *Uncle Tom's Cabin* advance competing and often antithetical representations of blackness, and Stowe's description of little Eva's death among her affectionate slaves must have been even more offensive for Brown than it was for the "twentieth-century academic critics" whose "assumptions about power and reality" Tompkins critiques (85).

22. Some chapters of Delany's novel had already appeared in *The Anglo-African Magazine*, then a monthly, in 1859.

23. The only structural difference is the presence of a closing chapter (XXVI) in *Miralda* that is shortened and incorporated in the previous one (XXV) in the 1864 *Clotelle*.

24. Prefacing each installment and each chapter with quotes from Pope, Shakespeare, Coleridge, Dryden, Byron, T. Moore, Milton, Goldsmith, and W. L. Garrison, Brown places the antislavery struggle within a larger libertarian Western tradition. Also, on leaving the United States for England, Brown's protagonist gives vent to the "curse of a fugitive's wrath" and prophesies what was historically already happening with the outbreak of the Civil War, that "there is vengeance in store / For thy soul-crushing despots and thee"

(*Miralda*, February 23, 1861, 1). To express "the feelings that animated the heart of this noble man" (*Miralda*, February 23, 1861, 1) Brown uses a poem, confirming his deliberate manipulation of different linguistic codes and literary genres to give depth and recognizable artistic dignity to his characters.

25. Brown edits out of the 1864 *Clotelle* the detailed descriptions of the discrimination the fugitive William (Clotel's escape partner) encounters in Northern railways, hotels, courts, and churches (*Clotel* 176–81). "Even the slave who escapes from Southern plantations," Brown wrote in 1853, "is surprised when he reaches the North, at the amount and withering influence of this prejudice" (176). Similar opinions are expressed very forcefully in *Miralda* as well.

26. The chapter titled "The Negro Chase" (*Clotel* 78–82) describes the dramatic capture of a runaway male slave and includes a real newspaper clipping that provides details of his subsequent lynching. Such documentation increases the realism of an episode that "needed no romance" (Harriet Jacobs, qtd. in Carby, *Reconstructing* 49). Other violent incidents that are not included in the 1864 edition of the novel occur in the chapter "A Slave Hunting Parson" (*Clotel* 141–43), where Georgiana recounts how her father shot to death a slave who attempted to escape after being repeatedly flogged for visiting his wife on a nearby farm, and in the chapter "Truth Stranger Than Fiction" (*Clotel* 205–10), where a young Frenchman is murdered while attempting to help a slave escape from her lecherous master.

27. The elimination of Sam's song of resistance from the 1864 edition turns him into a rather shallow comic character and seems to substantiate Carby's contention that "Brown inflicted humor at the expense of his blackest character" (*Reconstructing* 81). However, Carby disregards the fact that the heroic Jerome is also described as "perfectly black" (*Clotelle: A Tale* 57). The problems in evaluating Brown's fictional presentation of folk figures stem partly from a history of publishers' neglect of the three book-form editions of the novel and from the resulting insufficient critical commentary on the substantial differences between them.

28. Compare the 1853 episode in "Escape of Clotel" (*Clotel* 169–70) with Jerome's 1864 escape (*Clotelle: A Tale* 67–68).

29. The increased emphasis on Jerome's black manhood is substantiated also by the more "masculine" and dignified mode of his escape. Like the 1853 George, Jerome resorts to cross-dressing as a woman to get out of prison, but once out he immediately finds men's clothes to wear. On this episode in relation to Brown's broader narrative construction of black manhood, see Paul Gilmore's "'De Genewine Artekil.'"

30. Clotelle's French husband belongs to a family with a centuries-long history of wealth and power (*Clotelle: A Tale* 95). After his death, Clotelle and her son become the heirs of his "large fortune" (97).

31. Rafia Zafar suggests that "Brown's later versions of the novel may . . . show the influence of Jacobs" (215n.71), whose *Incidents in the Life of a Slave Girl* appeared in 1861.

32. Brown provides a similarly happy but more cautious ending in *Miralda*. There, after Jerome's uncompromising defense of the slave's right to freedom, Brown notes, "Mr. Linwood felt the force of Jerome's reasoning, and saw very clearly his false position. *It was long before Miralda's father could eradicate from his mind, the belief of the inferiority of the negro race*" (*Miralda*, March 16, 1861, 1; emphasis mine).

33. Jerome's patriotism makes its first appearance in 1864, when the hope aroused by the Civil War informs the fugitive's speech on leaving America for England: "Though forced from my native land by the tyrants of the South, I hope I shall some day be able to return. With all her faults, I love my country still" (*Clotelle: A Tale* 88).

34. The term *protonationalist* describes nineteenth-century African American writers who did not advocate racial separatism but nevertheless emphasized race pride, autonomy, self-help, and intraracial solidarity as means of resistance against segregation.

35. Frederick Douglass's "The Heroic Slave" was published in 1853, like Brown's *Clotel*, and therefore precedes *The Garies* (1857). Yet scholars of African American fiction rarely discuss Douglass in conjunction with the other two writers. To explain this critical practice, Andrews describes "The Heroic Slave" as a "historical novella" rather than a novel proper ("Novelization" 25).

36. See also Gayle (*The Way* 11) and Davis (Introduction i).

37. In *Negro Voices in American Fiction,* Hugh M. Gloster writes, "Webb is listed as a Negro in the Schomburg Collection of the New York Public Library, but his racial identity is admittedly a matter of conjecture" (260n.3). Even Arthur P. Davis, who is "convinced . . . that Webb was a Negro," hypothesizes that he "was probably fed up with the 'Problem' and sought . . . escape . . . [like] Jean Toomer" ("*The Garies*" 29).

38. Frank J. Webb and his wife, Mary, were active and well-known participants in the cultural life of black Philadelphia. Although *The Garies* was published in England, it must have been known in America because it is cited by way of publicity in every installment of the two short stories ("Two Wolves and a Lamb" and "Marvin Hayle") Webb serialized in 1870 in the Washington *New Era,* "A National Journal, Edited by Colored Men." The Webbs are mentioned several times in Charlotte L. Forten's *Journal.* An 1855 article that appeared in the *Frederick Douglass' Paper* chastised the "disgraceful conduct" of a certain Captain Mayo, who refused passage to Rio de Janeiro to the Webbs because he discovered that the "almost white" Mrs. Webb "had African blood in her veins." Mr. Webb's complexion is described as "somewhat more brown than her own" ("Disgraceful Conduct" 1). According to Crockett, in 1856 Webb went to England, then spent some years in Jamaica, and eventually returned to the United States. He lived first in Washington, D.C., and later in Galveston, Texas, where he died on May 7, 1894.

39. The separation between the public (white) and private (black) spheres is not complete, as the "peculiar construction" of the interracial Garie family exemplifies (Webb, *The Garies* 1). Even in their case, however, Webb emphasizes the different perspectives of husband and wife on race prejudice and explains them in experiential rather than pseudobiological terms. As a wealthy slaveholder, Mr. Garie does not have any urge to leave the South despite the danger slavery poses to his family, nor does he appreciate the seriousness of Northern segregation until his house is attacked by a racist mob.

40. In keeping with Nina Baym's delineation of the generic conventions of domesticity, *The Garies* is "largely descriptive of events taking place in a home setting and . . . it espouses a 'cult of domesticity,' that is, fulfillment for women in marriage and motherhood" (26).

41. Margaret Just Butcher (126) and Henry Louis Gates Jr. (Introduction, *Our Nig* xxiii, xlii) are among the scholars who question the artistic value of Webb's novel.

42. Although they do not share Mr. Walters's glamorous wealth, most of the black

characters in the novel are skilled artisans (carpenters, seamstresses, engravers). Because of the little occupational differentiation between the free blacks in Philadelphia, artisans were a somewhat fortunate socioeconomic group (Hershberg 199).

43. The antiblack violence that dominates *The Garies* finds a referent in the history of antebellum Philadelphia. "Beginning in 1829 and continuing through the ensuing two decades, Philadelphia Negroes were the victims of half a dozen major anti-black riots and many more minor mob actions. Negro churches, schools, homes and even an orphanage were set on fire. . . . Contemporaries attributed the small net loss in the Negro population between 1840 and 1850 in large part to riots" (Hershberg 185).

44. Compare, for instance, the colloquial English the Ellises use among themselves or with their African American friends and the more formal conversations they have with sympathetic whites. In the company of the Ellises, eloquent Mr. Walters indulges in such informal addresses as "Why, Ellis, man, how came you to consent to his going?" (62). Even Charlie Ellis's best friend, Kinch (whose refractory attitude, à la Huck Finn, toward school and polite manners characterizes his interactions with his black friends), masters a more formal and distancing English when he has to deal with Mr. Stevens, the white villain.

45. Bordering on the type of the scolding wife, she is the unwitting cause of her brother Charlie's dangerous fall down the stairs. During his convalescence, Charlie is entertained by his friend Kinch, who cross-dresses as a nurse (*The Garies* 92). This extravagant and digressive episode exorcizes through ridicule Caddy's threats to African American masculinity.

46. Webb's difficulties in sustaining the separation between private and public spheres also characterized turn-of-the-century debates on the role of African American women. As historian Sharon Harley notes, "The tensions between the ideal of a full-time mother and respect for and recognition of black working women's abilities and contributions to family income existed within a set of attitudes that tended to favor traditional sex roles" (347–48).

47. The hypothesis that Webb's American dream rhetoric is to be interpreted as a strategy to undermine stereotypes of black dependence is substantiated by "Marvin Hayle," a short story Webb serialized in 1870 in *The New Era*, "A National Journal, Edited by Colored Men." The story deals with racially indeterminate European characters in England and France. Freed from the racially dichotomized discourse that overdetermines the discussion of love and wealth in an American setting, Webb advances a decidedly nonmaterialistic thesis. As the spokesperson for the high-minded, noncapitalistic values of dignity, unselfish love, artistic talent, and proud forbearance, Marvin Hayle embodies a model of true manhood that sheds retrospective light on Webb's objections to permanent passing and on his portrayal of the black male characters of *The Garies* for whom money is mostly a means of "comfortable survival in a hostile world" (Bogardus 18).

48. After she learns that Clarence is sick, Miss Bates goes to visit him. She also declares her continuing love for Clarence to her father, though using a defensive litotes: "not that I would not have gladly married, knowing what he was" (389).

49. In *North of Slavery*, Leon F. Litwack writes that "between 1832 and 1849 Philadelphia mobs set off five major anti-Negro riots" (100). Substantiating Webb's portrayal of an active and organized black community, he also notes that "in assessing the causes of the [1834] riot, a citizens' committee cited the frequent hiring of Negroes during periods

of depression and white unemployment and the tendency of negroes to protect, and even forcibly rescue, their brethren when the latter were arrested as fugitive slaves" (101).

50. Mr. Garie's anger against the priest who refuses to wed a mixed couple (136), Mrs. Bird's indignation toward Jim Crow practices on trains (110–12), and Mr. Balch's stupefaction upon discovering that even burial grounds are segregated (233) exemplify white unfamiliarity with the pervasiveness of discrimination. Webb's insistence on their bitter surprise is part of his strategy of indirect fictional argumentation. It substantiates Bakhtin's contention that "naiveté itself, under authentic novelistic conditions, takes on the nature of an internal polemic and is consequently dialogized" (278).

Chapter 2: Race Travel in Turn-of-the-Century African American Utopian Fiction

1. More than 150 utopian works were published in America between 1888 and 1900 (Roemer 8). On the popularity of such utopian writers as Edward Bellamy, Elizabeth Stuart Phelps, Charles M. Sheldon, or Ignatius Donnelly, see Hart.

2. There are a few recent and significant exceptions to this rule of neglect of African American utopian fiction. Carby in *Reconstructing Womanhood* and duCille in *The Coupling Convention* mention the utopian elements in turn-of-the-century African American women's fiction, McDowell compares African American social gospel novels with Elizabeth Stuart Phelps's "gates ajar" fiction (Introduction xxvii–xxxviii), Schrager briefly notes that *Of One Blood* combines an "American Gothic plot" with an "African utopian plot" (205), and *The Oxford Companion to African American Literature* includes an entry on "speculative fiction," an admittedly generic umbrella term "that shelters the subgenres of fantasy, science fiction, utopian and dystopian fiction, [and] supernatural fiction" (Andrews et al. 683). Much critical work is needed to transform these sparse references into a comprehensive discussion of the nineteenth-century roots of the African American utopian and science fiction tradition.

3. Griggs is the African American author most often mentioned in critical works about turn-of-the-century American utopian fiction (cf. Roemer, Bammer, and Sargent). However, even his major novel *Imperium in Imperio* has not received sustained critical attention from utopian specialists.

4. According to Bloch, the "force of anticipatory accomplishment" characterizes the utopian function (109–110). He writes, "Artistic illusion is . . . a meaning that only portrays in images what can be carried on, where *the exaggeration and the telling of stories . . . represent an anticipatory illumination of reality circulating and signifying in the active present.* . . . This elaboration, as anticipatory illumination, also remains an outward appearance, but it does not remain fantasy" (146).

5. Reilly notes this emphasis on process but interprets it as an imaginative failure: "It might be said that the utopian impulse in Afro-American literature is under compulsion to face historical forces so powerful that the impulse must spend itself on imagining the removal of oppression, rather than on utopian life afterwards" (63).

6. For an analysis of the politics of racial erasure in *Looking Backward* and the significance of Sawyer, Julian West's black servant, see Fabi ("Utopian Melting").

7. For instance, compare the description of walls and gardens in Griggs (*Imperium* 178–79) and More (34–35).

8. I borrow the terms *power* and *empowerment* from Christian's "The Race for Theory": "An approach which desires power singlemindedly must of necessity become like that which it wishes to destroy. . . . One must distinguish between the desire for power and the need to become empowered—that is, seeing oneself as capable of and having the right to determine one's life" (60–61).

9. Significantly, Griggs, like his antebellum antecedent, William Wells Brown, has been accused of "incoherence" (Reilly 69–70).

10. Belton's approach has already been tested during his university years, when he desegregates a lunch facility by organizing a sit-in, a typical instance of how the utopian imagination can foreshadow historical reality.

11. Double consciousness governs Griggs's novel from the opening "Dying Declaration," where Trout declares, "While I acknowledge that I am a traitor, I also pronounce myself a patriot" (*Imperium* 2).

12. Like many other male utopian authors, Griggs grants the potential for transformation only to male characters and fails to connect the logic of patriarchal power with white supremacy. The heroic subjectivity of his male protagonists is predicated on the subordination, blind faithfulness, or inspirational death of black women, characters for whom Griggs's utopian separatism does not open up opportunities of empowerment other than traditionally relational ones.

13. Tate's notion of "cover-plot" and "cover story" derives from Susan K. Harris's *Nineteenth-Century American Women Novels.* Tate explains, "Harris defines cover-plot and cover story as 'formulaic covering[s] . . . [for] disguis[ing] subversive discourse' in texts written by women and men. . . . In women's texts, the cover-plot is the conservative story of sanctioned patriarchal behavior and expectations for females that literally covers the radical story about the subversion of that patriarchal text" (*Domestic Allegories* 248n.2).

14. Harper chooses an unwanted kiss (103) and an attempted embrace (41) as instances of Iola's experience of sexual harassment and as metonyms for the systematic abuse of slave women. Although Harper's reticence on sexual matters is obvious, I do not share Ammons's conviction that "*Iola Leroy* is a parable about surviving rape" (31). Unless we think of the metaphorical rape of Iola's identity, which in the novel undoubtedly is emblematic of far more literal rapes, there is simply not enough textual evidence (however coded) to support that contention, as Tate also notes (*Domestic Allegories* 262n.36). Harper insists that Iola was harassed but not actually raped; her last master "had tried *in vain* to drag her down to his own low level of sin and shame" (38–39, emphasis mine), and Iola's inviolability seems to have been the reason why "she war sole seben times in six weeks, 'cause she's so putty, but . . . *she war game to de las'*" (42, emphasis mine). Harper's emphasis on Iola's purity reveals not only her oft-noted adherence to Victorian notions of true womanhood but also her reluctance to indulge in the graphic portrayals of female slave abuse that Sanchez-Eppler insightfully analyzes and critiques in *Touching Liberty.* That Iola succeeds in preserving her virtue is also part of the utopian economy of the novel.

15. Even when she extols the values of black culture, Harper eschews essentialist notions of race. She carefully contextualizes and historicizes her comments, grounding them

in a rewriting of black history that portrays African America as a nation within the nation with a history and culture that are distinctive even in their inevitable interconnections with those of white America.

16. Here I depart from Tate's otherwise convincing reading of turn-of-the-century African American women's fiction. According to Tate, "The domestic novels of Post-Reconstruction black women are not interested in representing the racial and sexual restrictions that oppress them. To the contrary, they envision, create, figure social realms of their own desire in print. The playing out . . . of fictive racial and sexual desires . . . is most importantly the author's method for indirectly reproaching the prejudicial social climate and motivating first readers to emulate the heroine's personal, domestic, and public interests" (107). In my interpretation, instead, it is precisely because Harper portrays contemporary racial and sexual restrictions that she eventually chooses a happy ending to safeguard the inspirational function of *Iola Leroy*.

17. On the different female models embodied in Iola and Lucille, see Foster (*Written by Herself* 184–85) and Tate (*Domestic Allegories* 144–49).

18. Harry's evaluation of Lucille's exceptionality is confirmed by Iola's: "Miss Lucille Delany . . . is my ideal woman. She is grand, brave, intellectual, and religious" (*Iola Leroy* 242).

19. The term "first readers" derives from Tate's *Domestic Allegories* and includes "middle- and working-class black men and women" (5).

20. Comprehending Johnson's strategy of narrative passing certainly was easier for Johnson's first black readers than for us today. On one hand, they were more familiar with and accepting of such strategies. On the other, at the time Johnson was known as a politician and as the author of a widely used black history textbook, which is also mentioned in the frontispiece of *Light Ahead for the Negro*.

21. Information on Johnson's life is scarce. See "Johnson, Edward Austin," in *Dictionary of American Biography* 390–91; "Edward Austin Johnson" 505–7; "Johnson, Edward A[ustin]," in *Dictionary of American Negro Biography* 349–50; and "The Life Work of Edward A. Johnson" 81.

22. Johnson expresses the same conviction almost verbatim in *Light Ahead for the Negro* (101).

23. Reilly, for instance, notes that Johnson's is "more documentary in style than the Bellamy novel" (60).

Chapter 3: "New People" and Invisible Men in Charles W. Chesnutt's The House Behind the Cedars

1. Craig Werner and P. Jay Delmar also notice Chesnutt's use of narrative masking techniques in *The Conjure Woman* and *The Wife of His Youth*. About the latter volume, Delmar writes, "The stories themselves tend to be masked . . . each piece working artistically through ironic or satiric structures which seek to delay the reader's perception of the last truth as long as possible" (365).

2. On Chesnutt's struggle against the limited educational opportunities available to African Americans in a segregated South, on his systematic self-education in European

and classical languages and literatures, and on his "near-obsessional commitment to the goal of becoming a novelist" (McElrath and Leitz 9), see: Chesnutt (*Journals* and *"To Be an Author"*) and Andrews (*Literary Career*).

3. To summarize it briefly, *The House Behind the Cedars* follows the adventures of two all-but-white siblings, John and Rena Walden. John moves to South Carolina, passes for white (changing his name to Warwick to make it sound more British and aristocratic), marries the unsuspecting daughter of a plantation owner, and becomes a wealthy and respected lawyer in Clarence, South Carolina. After the premature death of his wife, he convinces his sister to pass and join him and his young son in their life of privilege. In Clarence, Rena's beauty conquers George Tryon, a young blueblood friend of John. Engaged to be married, Rena goes home to Patesville, North Carolina, to visit her sick mother. There, because of a series of coincidences Tryon discovers the secret of her mixed racial heritage and immediately leaves her. This first half of the novel ends with a historical chapter that tells the story of the Walden family. In the second half of *The House Behind the Cedars* Rena, crushed, rejects her brother's advice to continue passing. John returns to Clarence, and Rena leaves Patesville to become a teacher in a black school. Her new experiences as a working woman are made more difficult by the unwelcome advances of Jeff Wain and by Tryon's attempts to see her. At the end of the novel, to avoid being overtaken by her importune suitors, Rena escapes in a forest and is caught in a storm. Distracted, she is found by her long-time friend and hopeless admirer, Frank Fowler, who takes her to her mother's home, where she dies soon thereafter.

4. On Chesnutt's difficulties in finding a publisher for "Rena Walden" and *Mandy Oxendine,* see Sedlack, Andrews (*Literary Career*), and Hackenberry.

5. There is a long-standing critical consensus that Chesnutt is the first African American novelist of serious artistic achievement, and scholars most often remark on the differences, rather than similarities, between Chesnutt and other nineteenth-century African American writers. Chesnutt himself was at times misleading in this respect, especially when writing to his white editors. He emphasized his own groundbreaking role as an African American novelist, glossing over the achievements of previous writers, although the continuities are many and significant.

6. Tom Lowrey does not have moral objections to passing, but he does "not wish . . . to be ashamed of or to blush for his origin" (*Mandy Oxendine* 46). However, he is ready to "be white or black—or blue or green" (24) to be with Mandy. At the end of the novel, Chesnutt leaves open the possibility that the two reunited lovers may seek "in the great white world such a place as their talents and their virtues merited" (112).

7. The characters of Rena and Frank were already present in the earliest version of "Rena Walden," whereas Tryon appeared in a later one. On Chesnutt's revisions of "Rena Walden" to make these characters more sympathetic in *The House Behind the Cedars,* see Andrews (*Literary Career*) and Sedlack.

8. Payne also notes that Chesnutt's "effects [are] strained" (25). Sedlack instead remarks condescendingly that *The House Behind the Cedars* reveals "a more competent, if flawed, craftsmanship" (132) and that the characters, although they may seem "flat and perhaps unconvincing" to modern readers, are "distinct improvements" for Chesnutt (134). These evaluations bespeak the critical tendency to have low expectations of the artistic craft of

early African American fiction writers. Payne, in a puzzling reading, does not even credit Chesnutt with the capacity to handle irony; according to him John Walden speaks with "unconscious irony" (16).

9. Walden's observations find a contrastive parallel in Tryon's later, much less troubled perceptions of the same scene in Patesville (*The House* 105), which foreground Chesnutt's relentless emphasis on the different subject positions of blacks and whites in American society.

10. Rena Walden seems to start her fictional career as a passer in *The House Behind the Cedars* with as promising a future as Scott's Rowena, but in the course of the novel her luck changes and she ends up as Rebecca. In *Ivanhoe,* the beautiful Rebecca cannot become Queen of Love and Beauty because she is Jewish, and for the same reason she is not a candidate to marry the heroic Ivanhoe. In the end, after Rowena and Ivanhoe's wedding, Rebecca decides to dedicate her life to God, "tending the sick, feeding the hungry, and relieving the distressed" (*Ivanhoe* 449), much as Chesnutt's Rena goes on a mission to uplift the freed blacks to express her "new-born desire to be of service to her rediscovered people" (*The House* 194). In Rena Walden are also merged the two most positive female characters of *The Last of the Barons:* the fair-haired, blue-eyed, and noble Anne, whose beauty and virtue, as in Rena's case, lead the king to try to sexually harass her, and the dark-haired Sibyll, whose love story with a nobleman ends unhappily because she, like Rena, has "love[d] beyond her state" (Bulwer-Lytton 583). By merging these opposed figures and traditional female narrative types into the same character, Chesnutt breaks the segregation of literary (and by implication social) roles and foregrounds the racial, cultural, and class prejudices that both informed the British novels he misquotes and were perpetuated in the cult of chivalry of the American South.

11. Chesnutt's range of intertextual references in *The House Behind the Cedars* is impressive and deserves more detailed study because it involves not only previous African American novelists, white contemporaries such as Howells, Albion Tourgee, and Mark Twain, and popular early-nineteenth-century British novelists such as Scott and Bulwer-Lytton but also classic epic writers such as Milton and Homer. As Carolivia Herron notices, the fact that "these associations were developed self-consciously can be seen from his journals, where we learn that in his earliest contact with the *Iliad* Chesnutt began to clarify his vocation as a writer by projecting a parallel between himself and Homer, and by choosing racism as the 'war' that would be his subject" (291).

12. Though taking a pragmatic view on passing, Walden still feels "a naturalized foreigner in the world of wide opportunity" (*The House* 66), and his sister's misadventures eventually stir up "a certain bitterness against white people—a feeling which he had put aside years ago with his dark blood" (*The House* 182). Like the white characters who learn his secret, however, Walden does not seem to link his bitterness with a more general analysis of the politics of race but only with the discomfort such politics create in his own life.

13. This is a structural similarity with *Iola Leroy,* where Harper interrupts the heroine's story to tell her family history. In both cases, the collective past is brought to bear on the heroine's individual choices.

14. Like the equally well-meaning white lawyer Mr. Balch in *The Garies,* Judge Straight simply assumes that being white is better. He tells young Walden, "You have the some-

what unusual privilege, it seems, of choosing between two races, and if you are a lad of spirit, as I think you are, it will not take you long to make your choice" (*The House* 172).

15. This is a wonderful instance of Chesnutt's skill in using the limited point of view technique for purposes of ironic characterization. Tryon reveals a lot about his racial stereotypes when he sees himself as having been "raped" by the two passers: "The more he dwelt upon the subject, the more angry he became with those who had surprised his virgin heart and deflowered it by such low trickery" (*The House* 252).

16. Tryon rationalizes his desire to see Rena again without taking any responsibility for its potential consequences: "He could not marry the other girl [Rena], of course, but they must meet again. The rest he would leave to Fate, which seemed reluctant to disentangle threads which it had woven so closely" (*The House* 265).

17. The narrator explicitly attributes Tryon's renewed passion to its being opposed (*The House* 264, 292).

18. Chesnutt's move toward more explicit polemics, as conditions for African Americans continued to worsen at the beginning of the new century, resulted from his increasing awareness of "the failure of his audience to respond to anything other than the surface of his texts" (Werner 361). He did not simply made a mistake because he "did not correctly judge the limitations of sympathy for the African-American predicament, and the need for a would-be popular author to work within those limitations" (McElrath and Leitz 23).

Chapter 4: The Mark Within

1. I borrow the notion of "rhetorical tenacity" from Hortense Spillers ("Moving on Down the Line").

2. Chesnutt's decision to name "Clarence" the town where John and Rena Walden pass is an explicit intertextual reference not only to Bulwer-Lytton's *The Last of the Barons* but also to Webb's *The Garies*. Johnson, in turn, evokes Chesnutt's *The House Behind the Cedars* in his own novel by recuperating, for instance, the ironic image of the coin with a hole in it that John Walden gives to his sister (*The House* 174) and that the Ex-Colored Man receives from his white father (*The Autobiography* 6).

3. A notable exception is Jessie Fauset, who in her 1912 review for *The Crisis* describes *The Autobiography* as "a work of fiction founded on hard fact" (38).

4. Johnson writes in his autobiography, "When the book [*The Autobiography*] was published . . . most of the reviewers . . . accepted it as a human document. This was a tribute to the writing, for I had done the book with the intention of its being so taken. But, perhaps, it would have been more farsighted had I originally affixed my name to it as a frank piece of fiction" (*Along* 238).

5. Johnson's pioneer anthologies are *The Book of American Negro Poetry* (1922), *The Book of American Negro Spirituals* (1925), and *The Second Book of American Negro Spirituals* (1926).

6. Van Vechten's introduction to the 1927 edition is paradigmatic. Although he clarifies that "*The Autobiography* . . . has little enough to do with Mr. Johnson's own life," he radically qualifies the text's fictiveness by stressing how "it is imbued with . . . his [Johnson's] *views* of the subjects discussed, so that to a person who has no previous knowledge of the

author's own history, it reads like a *real* autobiography" (v–vi). To reconcile this biographical emphasis with his previous assertion of the work's fictiveness, Van Vechten expands the documentary focus of *The Autobiography* and argues that "it reads like a composite autobiography of the Negro race" (vi). The emphasis on the nonfictional elements of *The Autobiography* also characterizes much later volumes such as *Three Negro Classics,* edited by John Hope Franklin (1965), and *Early African-American Classics,* edited by Anthony K. Appiah (1990). In both texts, Johnson's is the only novel included in a selection of such nonfiction works as Douglass's *Narrative,* Jacobs's *Incidents,* Washington's *Up from Slavery,* and Du Bois's *Souls of Black Folk.*

7. Robert Alter describes twentieth-century self-conscious novels as "deeply concerned with a particular historical moment, with the very nature of historical process, . . . as they deploy their elaborate systems of mirrors to reflect novel and novelist in the act of conjuring with reality" (139–40). The "ontological quandaries" (154), "relativistic" sensibility (157), "tongue-in-cheek narrator" (166), "parody-inventions" (168), and the "impulse of iconoclasm" (177) Alter identifies in the work of such modernist authors as Gide, Joyce, Unamuno, and Woolf also are prominent constitutive features of Johnson's novel.

8. Henry Louis Gates Jr. describes the Ex-Colored Man as "the first flawed character in Afro-American fiction," explaining that this is "the first instance where a character's fate is determined not by environmental forces such as racism but by the choices that he makes" (Introduction, *The Autobiography* xix). His unreliability and the proclaimed autobiographical purpose of his narrative differentiate the Ex-Colored Man from other first-person narrators such as Griggs's Berl Trout and E. A. Johnson's Gilbert Twitchell.

9. See also Bone (48), Kent (29), Sterling Brown (*The Negro* 132), Lawson (98), and Davis (*From the Dark Tower* 30).

10. In 1980, Joseph Skerrett assessed the currents of criticism on *The Autobiography* in the following terms: "One group, which includes Sterling Brown, Hugh Gloster, David Littlejohn, Stephen Bronz, and Nathan Huggins, feels that Johnson's narrator and his opinions are more or less direct reflections of their author. The other group, whose membership includes Robert Bone, Edward Margolies, Eugenia Collier, Robert Fleming, and Marvin Garrett, argue that Johnson's treatment of his narrator is essentially ironic" (540). Since then, critics have reached a greater agreement about the ironic tone of *The Autobiography.* See Stepto (*From Behind the Veil*), V. Smith (*Self-Discovery*), MacKethan ("*Black Boy*"), Warren ("Troubled"), C. Clarke ("Race"), and Sundquist (*Hammers*).

11. Critics such as Andrews (Introduction, *The Autobiography*) and Sundquist (*Hammers*) have recently mentioned the influence of Stowe, Twain, and Chesnutt on *The Autobiography,* but they have not focused on the consistent intertextuality that enabled Johnson to perform a feat of cultural preservation of antedating African American novels.

12. Stepto defines immersion as "a ritualized journey into a symbolic South" (*From Behind the Veil* 167). His eloquent analysis of the parodic quality of *The Autobiography* has influenced my own interpretation of Johnson's text.

13. Several critics note the cowardice, egotism, and ultimate unreliability of Johnson's narrator. See Garrett, Ross, Vauthier, C. Clarke, Andrews (Introduction, *The Autobiography*), and Sundquist (*Hammers*).

14. The narrator himself discusses his "inability to 'read'" (Stepto, *From Behind the Veil* 114) early in the novel, when he brags about how he invents stories and reproduces tunes

instead of reading books and music sheets. Even when he does become a reader at the cigar factory, his skill remains purely technical, and his duties do not require exegetical abilities but "a stock of varied information" (73). The protagonist's incapacity to read literary or racial texts becomes more obvious as he confronts more complex situations. See Lucinda MacKethan's comments on the difference between language and communication in *The Autobiography.*

15. Johnson writes in *Along This Way,* "Grown older, I occasionally meditate upon the kind of education Atlanta University gave me. . . . The central idea embraced a term that is now almost a butt for laughter—'service.' . . . The ideal constantly held up to us was of education as a means of living, not of making a living. It was impressed upon us that taking a classical course would have an effect of making us better and nobler, and of higher value to those we should have to serve. An odd, old-fashioned, naive conception? Rather" (122).

16. In light of Johnson's own early experience of near lynching (*Along* 165–70), it is hard not to read the emphasis he places on this episode in *The Autobiography* as foreshadowing his later political activism against racial violence.

17. See Fleming (*James Weldon Johnson* 40; "Irony" 96), Faulkner (151), Ross (209–10), Kinnamon ("James Weldon Johnson" 174), and Skerrett (557).

18. Some critics who have recently focused on Johnson's deconstruction of racial categories tend to underestimate his coterminous emphasis on the distinctiveness of black history and culture. See Pisiak, Kawash, and K. Pfeiffer.

19. In both cases, the "feminine" nervousness of the protagonists is not portrayed to be naturally inherent in mulattos, as contemporaneous racist discourse maintained, but constitutes the psychological result both of racial discrimination and of the characters' disloyalty to their race.

20. Bone, for instance, includes Nella Larsen and Jessie Fauset among "the rear guard" of novelists who, during the Harlem Renaissance, "lag[ged] behind" (97).

21. On the reception of Hurston's novel, Christian writes, "Locke . . . said the novel was 'folklore fiction at its best,' but asked when Hurston was going 'to come to grips with motive fiction and social document fiction.' Richard Wright called the novel counterrevolutionary and a continuation of the minstrel image" (*Black Women* 62).

Chapter 5: Tres-passing in African American Literary Criticism

1. Brown, Harper, and Chesnutt serve as the principal test cases in my examination of how and whether African American anthologies, literary histories, and criticism have discussed nineteenth-century fiction in general, novels of the color line in particular, and the contributions of women to both. Given the wealth of material, my review can be suggestive but hardly exhaustive.

2. The first known anthology of African American literature was Armand Lanusse's 1845 *Les Cenelles.* See Kinnamon, "Anthologies of African-American Literature from 1845 to 1994."

3. My comments refer to the second edition of Brown's *The Black Man,* which was published in 1863.

4. On Du Bois's relationship to women's scholarship Mary Helen Washington notes, "In a compassionate and generally progressive essay called 'On the Damnation of Wom-

en,' Du Bois sympathetically analyzes the oppression of black women, but he makes no effort to draw on the writings of black women intellectuals for their insights into the problems facing black women. In fact, in a remarkable oversight in this essay, Du Bois quotes Cooper's brilliant observation that 'only the black woman can say "when and where I enter"' and attributes the statement *not* to her but *anonymously* to 'one of our women'" (Introduction xli–xlii).

5. The terms *teleological* and *historical* indicate the critic's basic conceptualization of how to systematize his or her material. The teleological approach argues the higher legitimacy of one particular literary concern, traces its roots and antecedents, and measures the worth of individual texts on the basis of their compatibility with the critic's chosen telos. Teleological criticism theorizes the need to select and exclude as the means to assess literary value. The historical approach instead prioritizes the recovery and preservation of texts and the organization of literary works into a variegated tradition. Because the strength of historical criticism derives from demonstrating the cumulative distinctiveness of a tradition, it tends to be inclusive, although the evaluation of single works still depends on the critical agenda of the individual scholar. The teleological and historical are not posited as pure approaches or as binary opposites.

6. On the tendency toward intellectual patricide in African American male criticism, Theodore Mason writes, "Within an environment perceived to be hostile and racist, [the] debate between generations becomes an argument about credentials: who's black and who's not, who has the greater interests of black people at heart, and so on. . . . One clearly sees in the accents of their discussion the signs of an uneasy defensiveness, particularly in the need to invoke a shielding authority (the People or Science) in various guises" ("Between" 610).

7. In "Criteria of Negro Art" (1926), Du Bois writes, "All Art is propaganda and ever must be, despite the wailing of the purists. I stand in utter shamelessness and say that whatever art I have for writing has been used always for propaganda for gaining the right of black folk to love and enjoy. I do not care a damn for any art that is not used for propaganda. But I do care when propaganda is confined to one side while the other is stripped and silent" (296).

8. To my knowledge Hurston is one of the first to question the term *race* by placing it within quotation marks (*Dust Tracks* 325). In this practice, as well as in her overall discussion of the sociocultural components of "race," Hurston anticipates the argument Henry Louis Gates Jr. presents in *"Race," Writing, and Difference* (1986).

9. *The Negro Caravan* includes selections by five female poets and only two female novelists. Both the autobiographical and cultural essay sections feature only one woman author. Women are unrepresented in the sections devoted to historical and social essays.

10. In "Integration and Race Literature," Davis prophesies, "It is my belief that this period [between a world of dying segregation and one of developing integration] will produce for a while a series of 'good-will books.' . . . In an all-out effort to make integration become a reality, the Negro writer will tend to play down the remaining harshness in Negro American living and to emphasize the progress towards equality" (40).

11. Saunders Redding, for instance, briefly describes the three centuries between 1619 and 1900 as "a period that need not be rehearsed" ("The Negro Writer" 3).

12. DuCille acknowledges that her approach builds on the work of previous black feminists. In comparing Christian's discussion of the tragic mulatta in 1980 and Baker's more recent critique of early women novelists in *Workings of the Spirit* (duCille 7), however, she underestimates how Baker could have profited by more than a decade of scholarly work on early women novelists that was unavailable when Christian published *Black Women Novelists*.

Selected Bibliography

Alexander, Elizabeth. "'We Must Be About Our Father's Business': Anna Julia Cooper and the In-Corporation of the Nineteenth-Century African American Woman Intellectual." *Signs* 20.2 (1995): 336–56.

Alter, Robert. *Partial Magic: The Novel as a Self-Conscious Genre.* Berkeley: University of California Press, 1975.

Ammons, Elizabeth. *Conflicting Stories: American Women Writers at the Turn into the Twentieth Century.* New York: Oxford University Press, 1992.

Andrews, William L. "The 1850s: The First Afro-American Literary Renaissance." In *Literary Romanticism in America.* Ed. William L. Andrews. Baton Rouge: Louisiana State University Press, 1981. 38–60.

————, ed. *African American Autobiography: A Collection of Critical Essays.* Englewood Cliffs, N.J.: Prentice Hall, 1993.

————. Foreword. In *The House Behind the Cedars,* by Charles W. Chesnutt. Athens: University of Georgia Press, 1988. vii–xxii.

————. Introduction. In *The Autobiography of an Ex-Colored Man,* by James Weldon Johnson. 1912. New York: Penguin, 1990. vii–xxvii.

————. *The Literary Career of Charles W. Chesnutt.* Baton Rouge: Louisiana State University Press, 1980.

————. "Mark Twain, William Wells Brown, and the Problem of Authority in New Southern Writing." In *Southern Literature and Literary Theory.* Ed. Jefferson Humphries. Athens: University of Georgia Press, 1990. 1–21.

————. "Miscegenation in the Late Nineteenth-Century American Novel." *Southern Humanities Review* 13.1 (1979): 13–24.

————. "The Novelization of Voice in Early African American Narrative." *PMLA* 105.1 (1990): 23–34.

————. *To Tell a Free Story: The First Century of Afro-American Autobiography, 1760–1865.* Urbana: University of Illinois Press, 1986.

———. "William Dean Howells and Charles W. Chesnutt: Criticism and Race Fiction in the Age of Booker T. Washington." *American Literature* 48.3 (1976): 327–39.

Andrews, William L., Frances Smith Foster, and Trudier Harris, eds. *The Oxford Companion to African American Literature*. New York: Oxford University Press, 1997.

Appiah, Anthony, ed. *Early African-American Classics*. New York: Bantam, 1990.

"Arrival of Mr. and Mrs. Webb." *The Liberator*, 5 March 1858, 39.

Baker, Houston A., Jr. *Afro-American Poetics: Revisions of Harlem and the Black Aesthetic*. Madison: University of Wisconsin Press, 1986.

———. *Black Literature in America*. New York: McGraw-Hill, 1971.

———. *Blues, Ideology, and Afro-American Literature: A Vernacular Theory*. Chicago: University of Chicago Press, 1984.

———. *The Journey Back: Issues in Black Literature and Criticism*. Chicago: University of Chicago Press, 1980.

———. *Modernism and the Harlem Renaissance*. Chicago: University of Chicago Press, 1987.

———. *Workings of the Spirit: The Poetics of Afro-American Women's Writing*. Chicago: University of Chicago Press, 1991.

Bakhtin, M. M. *The Dialogic Imagination: Four Essays*. 1981. Ed. Michael Holquist, trans. Caryl Emerson and Michael Holquist. Austin: University of Texas Press, 1990. 259–422.

Bammer, Angelika. *Partial Visions: Feminism and Utopianism in the 1970s*. New York: Routledge, 1991.

Baym, Nina. *Woman's Fiction: A Guide to Novels by and about Women in America, 1820–1870*. Ithaca, N.Y.: Cornell University Press, 1978.

Bell, Bernard W. *The Afro-American Novel and Its Tradition*. Amherst: University of Massachusetts Press, 1987.

Bellamy, Edward. *Looking Backward, 2000–1887*. 1888. New York: Bantam, 1983.

Berzon, Judith R. *Neither White nor Black: The Mulatto Character in American Fiction*. New York: New York University Press, 1978.

Blackett, R. J. M. *Beating against the Barriers: Biographical Essays in Nineteenth-Century Afro-American History*. Baton Rouge: Louisiana State University Press, 1986.

Bloch, Ernst. *The Utopian Function in Art and Literature: Selected Essays*. Trans. Jack Zipes and Frank Mecklenburg. Cambridge, Mass.: MIT Press, 1988.

Boelhower, William. *Through a Glass Darkly: Ethnic Semiosis in American Literature*. New York: Oxford University Press, 1987.

Bogardus, R. F. "Frank J. Webb's *The Garies and Their Friends:* An Early Black Novelist's Venture into Realism." *Studies in Black Literature* 5.2 (1974): 15–20.

Bone, Robert A. *The Negro Novel in America*. New Haven, Conn.: Yale University Press, 1958.

Bontemps, Arna, ed. *Great Slave Narratives*. Boston: Beacon, 1969.

———, ed. *The Harlem Renaissance Remembered*. New York: Dodd, Mead, 1972.

Braithwaite, William Stanley. "The Negro in American Literature." In *The New Negro*. Ed. Alain Locke. 1925. New York: Atheneum, 1986. 29–44.

Brawley, Benjamin. *The Negro in Literature and Art*. N.p., 1910.

———. *The Negro in Literature and Art in the United States*. 1929. New York: AMS, 1971.

Braxton, Joanne. Introduction. In *The Work of the Afro-American Woman,* by Mrs. N. F. Mossell. New York: Oxford University Press, 1988. xxvii–xlii.

Brodhead, Richard H. Introduction. In *The Conjure Woman and Other Conjure Tales,* by Charles W. Chesnutt. Durham, N.C.: Duke University Press, 1993. 1–21.

Brown, Hallie Q. *Homespun Heroines and Other Women of Distinction.* 1926. New York: Oxford University Press, 1988.

Brown, Josephine. *Biography of an American Bondman.* 1856. In *Two Biographies by Afro-American Women.* Ed. Henry Louis Gates Jr. New York: Oxford University Press, 1991. 1–104.

Brown, Sterling A. *The Negro in American Fiction.* 1937. New York: Argosy, 1969.

Brown, Sterling A., Arthur P. Davis, and Ulysses Lee, eds. *The Negro Caravan: Writings by American Negroes.* New York: Dryden, 1941.

Brown, William Wells. *The Black Man, His Antecedents, His Genius, and His Achievements.* 1858. New York: Thomas Hamilton, 1863.

———. *Clotel; or, The President's Daughter: A Narrative of Slave Life in the United States.* 1853. New York: Carol, 1989.

———. *Clotelle; or, The Colored Heroine: A Tale of the Southern States.* 1867. Miami: Mnemosyne, 1969.

———. *Clotelle: A Tale of the Southern States.* 1864. In *William Wells Brown and Clotelle: A Portrait of the Artist in the First Negro Novel,* by J. Noel Heermance. N.p.: Archon, 1969. 1–104.

———. *Miralda; or, The Beautiful Quadroon: A Romance of American Slavery, Founded on Fact.* Serialized in *The Weekly Anglo-African,* 1 December 1860–16 March 1861.

———. *Narrative of the Life and Escape of William Wells Brown.* 1853. In *Clotel; or, The President's Daughter,* by William Wells Brown. 1853. New York: Carol, 1989. 17–55.

———. *Narrative of William Wells Brown, a Fugitive Slave, Written by Himself.* 1847. In *Puttin' On Ole Massa.* Ed. Gilbert Osofsky. New York: Harper & Row, 1969. 173–223.

———. *Three Years in Europe; or, Places I Have Seen and People I Have Met.* London: Charles Gilpin, 1852.

Browne, Ray B. *Melville's Drive to Humanism.* Lafayette, Ind.: Purdue University Studies, 1971.

Bruce, Dickson D., Jr. *Black American Writing from the Nadir: The Evolution of a Literary Tradition, 1877–1915.* Baton Rouge: Louisiana State University Press, 1989.

Bulwer-Lytton, Edward. *The Last of the Barons.* 1843. Kila, Mont.: Kessinger, 1999.

Butcher, Margaret Just. *The Negro in American Culture.* 1956. New York: New American Library, 1957.

Cable, George Washington. *The Grandissimes.* 1880. New York: Penguin, 1988.

Calverton, V. F., ed. *Anthology of American Negro Literature.* New York: Modern Library, 1929.

Campbell, James L., Sr. *Edward Bulwer-Lytton.* Boston: Twayne, 1986.

Campbell, Jane. *Mythic Black Fiction: The Transformation of History.* Knoxville: University of Tennessee Press, 1986.

Carby, Hazel V. Introduction. In *Iola Leroy; or, Shadows Uplifted,* by Frances E. W. Harper. Boston: Beacon, 1987. ix–xxx.

————. *Reconstructing Womanhood: The Emergence of the Afro-American Woman Novelist.* New York: Oxford University Press, 1987.

Carroll, Richard A. "Black Racial Spirit: An Analysis of James Weldon Johnson's Critical Perspective." *Phylon* 32.4 (1971): 344–64.

Chase, Richard. *The American Novel and Its Tradition.* 1957. Baltimore, Md.: Johns Hopkins University Press, 1986.

Chesnutt, Charles W. *The Colonel's Dream.* New York: Doubleday, Page, 1905.

————. *The Conjure Woman.* 1899. Ridgewood, N.J.: Gregg, 1968.

————. "The Future American Race." *Boston Evening Transcript,* 18 August, 25 August, 1 September 1900. Reprinted in *MELUS* 15.3 (1988): 96–107.

————. *The House Behind the Cedars.* 1900. Athens: University of Georgia Press, 1988.

————. *The Journals of Charles W. Chesnutt.* Ed. Richard Brodhead. Durham, N.C.: Duke University Press, 1993.

————. *Mandy Oxendine.* Urbana: University of Illinois Press, 1997.

————. *The Marrow of Tradition.* 1901. Ann Arbor: University of Michigan Press, 1969.

————. *The Short Fiction of Charles W. Chesnutt.* Ed. Sylvia Lyons Render. Washington, D.C.: Howard University Press, 1974.

————. *"To Be an Author": Letters of Charles W. Chesnutt, 1889–1905.* Ed. Joseph R. McElrath Jr. and Robert C. Leitz III. Princeton, N.J.: Princeton University Press, 1997.

————. *The Wife of His Youth and Other Stories of the Color Line.* 1899. Ann Arbor: University of Michigan Press, 1968.

Child, Lydia Maria. "The Quadroons" (1842). In *Fact and Fiction: A Collection of Stories,* by Lydia Maria Child. New York: C.S. Francis, 1847. 61–76.

Chopin, Kate. "Désirée's Baby." 1893. In *The Awakening and Selected Stories of Kate Chopin.* Ed. Barbara H. Solomon. New York: New American Library, 1976. 173–78.

Christian, Barbara. *Black Feminist Criticism: Perspectives on Black Women Writers.* New York: Pergamon, 1985.

————. *Black Women Novelists: The Development of a Tradition, 1892–1976.* Westport, Conn.: Greenwood, 1980.

————. Introduction. In *The Hazeley Family,* by Amelia E. Johnson. New York: Oxford University Press, 1988. xxvii–xxxvii.

————. "The Race for Theory." *Cultural Critique* 6 (1987): 51–63.

Clarke, Cheryl. "Race, Homosocial Desire, and 'Mammon' in *Autobiography of an Ex-Colored Man.*" In *Professions of Desire: Lesbian and Gay Studies in Literature.* Ed. George E. Haggerty and Bonnie Zimmerman. New York: Modern Language Association of America, 1995. 84–97.

Clarke, John Henrick. "Reclaiming the Lost African Heritage." In *The American Negro Writer and His Roots.* Selected Papers from the First Conference of Negro Writers, March 1959. New York: American Society of African Culture, 1960. 21–27.

Cooper, Anna Julia. *A Voice from the South.* 1892. New York: Oxford University Press, 1988.

Craft, William. *Running a Thousand Miles for Freedom; or, The Escape of William and Ellen Craft from Slavery.* 1860. In *Great Slave Narratives.* Ed. Arna Bontemps. Boston: Beacon, 1969. 269–331.

Crockett, Rosemary F. "Frank J. Webb: The Shift to Color Discrimination." In *The Black*

Columbiad: Defining Moments in African American Literature and Culture. Ed. Werner Sollors and Maria Diedrich. Cambridge, Mass.: Harvard University Press, 1994. 112–22.

Dandridge, Rita B. "Male Critics/Black Women's Novels." *CLA Journal* 23.1 (1979): 1–11.

Davis, Arthur P. *From the Dark Tower: Afro-American Writers, 1900 to 1960.* Washington, D.C.: Howard University Press, 1974.

———. "*The Garies and Their Friends:* A Neglected Pioneer Novel." *CLA Journal* 13.1 (1969): 27–34.

———. "Integration and Race Literature." In *The American Negro Writer and His Roots.* Selected Papers from the First Conference of Negro Writers, March 1959. New York: American Society of African Culture, 1960. 34–40.

———. Introduction. In *The Garies and Their Friends,* by Frank J. Webb. New York: Arno, 1969. i–ix.

Davis, Charles T., and Henry Louis Gates Jr., eds. *The Slave's Narrative.* New York: Oxford University Press, 1985.

Delany, Martin R. *Blake; or, The Huts of America.* 1859. Boston: Beacon, 1970.

Delmar, P. Jay. "The Mask as Theme and Structure: Charles W. Chesnutt's 'The Sheriff's Children' and 'The Passing of Grandison.'" *American Literature* 51.3 (1979): 364–75.

DeVries, James H. "The Tradition of the Sentimental Novel in *The Garies and Their Friends.*" *CLA Journal* 17.2 (1973): 241–49.

Dictionary of American Biography. Ed. Edward T. James. New York: Scribner, 1973. s.v. "Johnson, Edward Austin." 390–91.

Dictionary of American Negro Biography. Ed. Rayford W. Logan and Michael R. Winston. New York: W.W. Norton, 1982. s.v. "Johnson, Edward A[ustin]." 349–50.

"Disgraceful Conduct." *Frederick Douglass' Paper,* 10 October 1855, 1.

Donawerth, Jane L., and Carol A. Kolmerten, eds. *Utopian and Science Fiction by Women: Worlds of Difference.* Syracuse, N.Y.: Syracuse University Press, 1994.

Douglass, Frederick. "The Heroic Slave." 1853. In *Violence in the Black Imagination.* Ed. Ronald T. Takaki. New York: Capricorn, 1972. 37–77.

———. *Narrative of the Life of Frederick Douglass, an American Slave, Written by Himself.* 1845. New York: Penguin, 1986.

Du Bois, W. E. Burghardt. "The Browsing Reader." *The Crisis* 34.9 (1927): 308.

———. "Criteria of Negro Art." *The Crisis* 31–32 (1926): 290–97.

———. "The Negro in Literature and Art." *The Annals of the American Academy of Political and Social Science* 49 (1913): 233–37.

———. *The Souls of Black Folk.* 1903. New York: Fawcett, 1961.

———. "The Southerner's Problem." *The Dial,* 1 May 1905, 315–18.

duCille, Ann. *The Coupling Convention: Sex, Text, and Tradition in Black Women's Fiction.* New York: Oxford University Press, 1993.

Dunbar, Paul L. *The Uncalled.* New York: Dodd, Mead, 1898.

"Edward Austin Johnson." *The Journal of Negro History* 29.4 (1944): 505–7.

Elder, Arlene A. *The "Hindered Hand": Cultural Implications of Early African-American Fiction.* Westport, Conn.: Greenwood, 1978.

Elliott, Robert C. *The Shape of Utopia: Studies in a Literary Genre.* Chicago: University of Chicago Press, 1970.

Ellis-Fermor, Una. *The Jacobean Drama*. 1936. London: Methuen, 1965.

Ellison, Ralph. "Change the Joke and Slip the Yoke." 1958. In *Shadow and Act*. New York: Vintage, 1964. 45–59.

———. *Invisible Man*. 1952. New York: Vintage, 1972.

———. *Shadow and Act*. New York: Vintage, 1964.

———. "The World and the Jug." 1963. In *Shadow and Act*. New York: Vintage, 1964. 107–43.

Emanuel, James A., and Theodore L. Gross, eds. *Dark Symphony: Negro Literature in America*. New York: Free Press, 1968.

"An Ex-Coloured Man." Review of *The Autobiography of an Ex-Colored Man*, by James Weldon Johnson. *The Times Literary Supplement*, 22 March 1928, 207.

Fabi, M. Giulia. "'Utopian Melting': Technology, Homogeneity, and the American Dream in *Looking Backward*." In *Technology and the American Imagination*. Ed. Francesca Bisutti De Riz and Rosella Mamoli Zorzi. Venezia, Italy: Supernova, 1994. 346–54.

Farrison, William Edward. *William Wells Brown, Author and Reformer*. Chicago: University of Chicago Press, 1969.

Faulkner, Howard. "James Weldon Johnson's Portrait of the Artist as Invisible Man." *Black American Literature Forum* 19.4 (1985): 147–51.

Fauset, Jessie Redmon. *Plum Bun*. 1928. London: Pandora, 1985.

———. Review of *The Autobiography of an Ex-Colored Man*, by James Weldon Johnson. *The Crisis* 5.1 (1912): 38.

———. *There Is Confusion*. 1924. Boston: Northeastern University Press, 1989.

Ferguson, SallyAnn H. "'Frank Fowler': A Chesnutt Racial Pun." *South Atlantic Review* 50 (1985): 47–53.

———. "Rena Walden: Chesnutt's Failed 'Future American.'" *Southern Literary Journal* 15.1 (1982): 74–82.

Fisher, Dexter, and Robert B. Stepto, eds. *Afro-American Literature: The Reconstruction of Instruction*. New York: Modern Language Association of America, 1979.

Fleming, Robert E. "Humor in the Early Black Novel." *CLA Journal* 17.2 (1973): 250–62.

———. "Irony as a Key to Johnson's *The Autobiography of an Ex-Colored Man*." *American Literature* 43.1 (1971): 83–96.

———. *James Weldon Johnson*. Boston: Twayne, 1987.

———. "Sutton E. Griggs: Militant Black Novelist." *Phylon* 34.1 (1973): 73–77.

Foner, Eric. *Reconstruction: America's Unfinished Revolution, 1863–1877*. New York: Harper & Row, 1988.

Foreman, P. Gabrielle. "'Reading Aright': White Slavery, Black Referents, and the Strategy of Histotextuality in *Iola Leroy*." *Yale Journal of Criticism* 10.2 (1997): 327–54.

Forten, Charlotte L. *The Journal of Charlotte L. Forten* (1953). Ed. Ray Allen Billington. New York: W.W. Norton, 1981.

Fortunati, Vita. "Fictional Strategies and Political Message in Utopias." In *Per una definizione dell'utopia*. Ed. Nadia Minerva. Ravenna, Italy: Longo, 1992. 17–27.

Foster, Frances Smith. "Between the Sides: Afro-American Women Writers as Mediators." *Nineteenth Century Studies* 3 (1989): 53–64.

———, ed. *A Brighter Coming Day: A Frances Ellen Watkins Harper Reader*. New York: Feminist Press, 1990.

———. Introduction. In *Minnie's Sacrifice, Sowing and Reaping, Trial and Triumph: Three Rediscovered Novels by Frances E. W. Harper.* Boston: Beacon, 1994. xi–xxxvii.

———. *Written by Herself: Literary Production by African American Women, 1746–1892.* Bloomington: Indiana University Press, 1993.

Franklin, Bruce, ed. *Future Perfect: American Science Fiction of the Nineteenth Century.* New York: Oxford University Press, 1968.

Franklin, John Hope, ed. *Three Negro Classics.* New York: Avon, 1965.

Fredrickson, George M. *The Black Image in the White Mind: The Debate on Afro-American Character and Destiny, 1817–1914.* Middletown, Conn.: Wesleyan University Press, 1971.

Frye, Northrop. *The Stubborn Structure: Essays on Criticism and Society.* London: Methuen, 1970.

Fuss, Diana. *Essentially Speaking: Feminism, Nature, and Difference.* New York: Routledge, 1989.

Garrett, Marvin P. "Early Recollections and Structural Irony in *The Autobiography of an Ex-Colored Man.*" *Critique* 13.2 (1971): 5–14.

Gates, Henry Louis, Jr. "Canon-Formation, Literary History, and the Afro-American Tradition: From the Seen to the Told." In *Afro-American Literary Study in the 1990s.* Ed. Houston A. Baker Jr. and Patricia Redmond. Chicago: University of Chicago Press, 1989. 14–39.

———. *Figures in Black: Words, Signs, and the "Racial" Self.* New York: Oxford University Press, 1987.

———. Introduction. In *The Autobiography of an Ex-Colored Man,* by James Weldon Johnson. 1912. New York: Vintage, 1989. v–xxix.

———. Introduction. In *To Make a Poet Black,* by J. Saunders Redding. Ithaca, N.Y.: Cornell University Press, 1988. vii–xxviii.

———. Introduction. In *Our Nig; or, Sketches from the Life of a Free Black,* by Harriet E. Wilson. New York: Random House, 1983. xi–lv.

———. "Preface to Blackness: Text and Pretext." In *Afro-American Literature: The Reconstruction of Instruction.* Ed. Dexter Fisher and Robert B. Stepto. New York: Modern Language Association of America, 1979. 44–69.

———, ed. *"Race," Writing, and Difference.* Chicago: University of Chicago Press, 1986.

———, ed. *Reading Black, Reading Feminist: A Critical Anthology.* New York: Meridian, 1990.

Gates, Henry Louis, Jr., and Nellie Y. McKay, eds. *The Norton Anthology of African American Literature.* New York: W.W. Norton, 1997.

Gayle, Addison, Jr., ed. *The Black Aesthetic.* New York: Doubleday, 1971.

———. *The Way of the New World: The Black Novel in America.* New York: Doubleday, 1975.

Gilbert, Sandra M., and Susan Gubar. *No Man's Land: The Place of the Woman Writer in the Twentieth Century.* New Haven, Conn.: Yale University Press, 1988.

Gilmore, Paul. "'De Genewine Artekil': William Wells Brown, Blackface Minstrelsy, and Abolitionism." *American Literature* 69.4 (1997): 743–80.

Ginsberg, Elaine K., ed. *Passing and the Fictions of Identity.* Durham, N.C.: Duke University Press, 1996.

Gloster, Hugh M. *Negro Voices in American Fiction.* Chapel Hill: University of North Carolina Press, 1948.

———. "Sutton E. Griggs: Novelist of the New Negro." *Phylon* 4.4 (1943): 335–45.

Gossett, Thomas F. *"Uncle Tom's Cabin" and American Culture.* Dallas, Tex.: Southern Methodist University Press, 1985.

Griggs, Sutton E. *The Hindered Hand; or, The Reign of the Repressionist.* Nashville, Tenn.: Orion, 1905.

———. *Imperium in Imperio.* 1899. New York: Arno, 1969.

———. *Wisdom's Call.* 1911. Miami, Fla.: Mnemosyne, 1969.

Gross, Seymour L., and John Edward Hardy, eds. *Images of the Negro in American Literature.* Chicago: University of Chicago Press, 1966.

Gruesser, John Cullen, ed. *The Unruly Voice: Recovering Pauline Elizabeth Hopkins.* Urbana: University of Illinois Press, 1996.

Gunning, Sandra. *Race, Rape, and Lynching: The Red Record in American Literature, 1890–1912.* New York: Oxford University Press, 1996.

Hackenberry, Charles. Introduction. In *Mandy Oxendine,* by Charles W. Chesnutt. Urbana: University of Illinois Press, 1997. xi–xxviii.

Haraway, Donna J. *Simians, Cyborgs, and Women: The Reinvention of Nature.* New York: Routledge, 1991.

Harley, Sharon. "For the Good of Family and Race: Gender, Work, and Domestic Roles in the Black Community, 1880–1930." *Signs* 15.2 (1990): 336–49.

Harper, Frances E. W. *Iola Leroy; or, Shadows Uplifted.* 1892. Boston: Beacon, 1987.

———. *Minnie's Sacrifice.* 1869. In *Minnie's Sacrifice, Sowing and Reaping, Trial and Triumph: Three Rediscovered Novels by Frances E. W. Harper.* Ed. Frances Smith Foster. Boston: Beacon, 1994. 1–92.

———. "The Two Offers." 1859. In *A Brighter Coming Day: A Frances Ellen Watkins Harper Reader.* Ed. Frances Smith Foster. New York: The Feminist Press, 1990. 105–14.

Harris, Susan K. *Nineteenth-Century American Women Novels: Interpretive Strategies.* New York: Cambridge University Press, 1990.

Harris, Trudier. "Chesnutt's Frank Fowler: A Failure of Purpose?" *CLA Journal* 22 (1979): 215–28.

Hart, James D. *The Popular Book.* Berkeley: University of California Press, 1950.

Hattenhauer, Darryl. "Racial and Textual Miscegenation in Chesnutt's *The House Behind the Cedars.*" *Mississippi Quarterly* 47.1 (1993–94): 27–45.

Hedin, Raymond. "The Structuring of Emotion in Black American Fiction." *Novel* 16.1 (1982): 35–54.

Heermance, J. Noel. *William Wells Brown and Clotelle: A Portrait of the Artist in the First Negro Novel.* N.p.: Archon, 1969.

Hemenway, Robert, ed. Appendix. In *Dust Tracks on a Road: An Autobiography,* by Zora Neale Hurston. Urbana: University of Illinois Press, 1984. 287–89.

Henderson, Harry B. *Versions of the Past: The Historical Imagination in American Fiction.* New York: Oxford University Press, 1974.

Herron, Carolivia. "Milton and Afro-American Literature." In *Re-Membering Milton: Essays on the Texts and Traditions.* Ed. Mary Nyquist and Margaret W. Ferguson. New York: Methuen, 1987. 278–300.

Hershberg, Theodore. "Free Blacks in Antebellum Philadelphia: A Study of Ex-Slaves, Freeborn, and Socioeconomic Decline." *Journal of Social History* 5.2 (1971–72): 183–209.

Hewitt, Nancy A. "Beyond the Search for Sisterhood: American Women's History in the 1980's." *Social History* 10.3 (1985): 299–321.

Hildreth, Richard. "Complaint and Reproach." In *The Liberty Bell*. Boston: Massachusetts Anti-Slavery Fair, 1844. 52–57.

Hill, Herbert, ed. *Anger, and Beyond: The Negro Writer in the United States*. New York: Harper & Row, 1966.

Hill, Patricia Liggins, ed. *Call and Response: The Riverside Anthology of the African American Literary Tradition*. Boston: Houghton Mifflin, 1998.

Hopkins, Pauline E. *Contending Forces: A Romance Illustrative of Negro Life North and South*. 1900. New York: Oxford University Press, 1988.

———. *Of One Blood; or, The Hidden Self*. 1902–3. In *The Magazine Novels of Pauline Hopkins*. New York: Oxford University Press, 1988. 441–621.

———. "Reply to Cordelia A. Condict." March 1903. In *The Norton Anthology of African American Literature*. Ed. Henry Louis Gates Jr. and Nellie Y. McKay. New York: W.W. Norton, 1997. 594–95.

Howells, William Dean. *"Editor's Study" by William Dean Howells*. Ed. James W. Simpson. Troy, N.Y.: Whitston, 1983.

———. *An Imperative Duty*. 1891. New York: Harper & Bros., 1893.

———. *Through the Eye of the Needle*. New York: Harper & Bros., 1907.

———. *A Traveller from Altruria*. 1894. New York: Sagamore Press, 1957.

Hubbard, Dolan, ed. *Recovered Texts/Recovered Writers: Race, Class, and Gender in Black Women's Literature*. Knoxville: University of Tennessee Press, 1997.

Huggins, Nathan I. *Harlem Renaissance*. New York: Oxford University Press, 1971.

Hughes, Langston. "The Negro Artist and the Racial Mountain." 1926. In *The Black Aesthetic*. Ed. Addison Gayle Jr. New York: Doubleday, 1971. 167–72.

———. "Writers: Black and White." In *The American Negro Writer and His Roots*. Selected Papers from the First Conference of Negro Writers, March 1959. New York: American Society of African Culture, 1960. 41–45.

Hull, Gloria T., Patricia Bell Scott, and Barbara Smith, eds. *All the Women Are White, All the Blacks Are Men, but Some of Us Are Brave: Black Women's Studies*. New York: Feminist Press, 1982.

Hurston, Zora Neale. *Dust Tracks on a Road: An Autobiography*. 1942. Ed. Robert Hemenway. Urbana: University of Illinois Press, 1984.

———. *Their Eyes Were Watching God*. 1937. New York: Harper & Row, 1990.

Hutcheon, Linda. "Historiographic Metafiction: Parody and the Intertextuality of History." In *Intertextuality and Contemporary American Fiction*. Ed. Patrick O'Donnell and Robert Con Davis. Baltimore, Md.: Johns Hopkins University Press, 1989. 3–32.

———. *A Theory of Parody: The Teachings of Twentieth-Century Art Forms*. 1985. Urbana: University of Illinois Press, 2000.

Jackson, Blyden. *The Long Beginning, 1746–1895*. Baton Rouge: Louisiana State University Press, 1989.

Jackson, Miles M., Jr. "Letters to a Friend: Correspondence from James Weldon Johnson to George A. Towns." *Phylon* 29.2 (1968): 182–98.

Jacobs, Harriet. *Incidents in the Life of a Slave Girl.* 1861. New York: Harcourt Brace Jovanovich, 1973.

James, C. L. R. *Mariners, Renegades, and Castaways: The Story of Herman Melville and the World We Live In.* 1953. London: Allison & Busby, 1985.

Jauss, Hans Robert. *Toward an Aesthetic of Reception.* Minneapolis: University of Minnesota Press, 1982.

Johnson, Amelia E. *Clarence and Corinne; or, God's Way.* 1890. New York: Oxford University Press, 1988.

———. *The Hazeley Family.* 1894. New York: Oxford University Press, 1988.

———. *Martina Meriden; or, What Is My Motive?* Philadelphia: American Baptist Publication Society, 1901.

Johnson, Edward A. *Adam vs. Ape-Man and Ethiopia.* New York: J.J. Little & Ives, 1931.

———. "A Congressional Campaign." *The Crisis,* April 1929, 118.

———. *Light Ahead for the Negro.* 1904. New York: Grafton, 1975.

———. *A School History of the Negro Race in America, from 1619 to 1890.* 1893/1911. New York: AMS, 1969.

Johnson, James Weldon. *Along This Way: The Autobiography of James Weldon Johnson.* 1933. New York: Viking, 1968.

———. *The Autobiography of an Ex-Coloured Man.* 1912. New York: Hill & Wang, 1960.

———, ed. *The Book of American Negro Poetry.* 1922. New York: Harcourt, Brace & World, 1958.

———, ed. *The Book of American Negro Spirituals.* 1925. In *The Books of American Negro Spirituals.* New York: Da Capo, 1969.

———. "The Dilemma of the Negro Author." *American Mercury* 15 (1928): 477–81.

———, ed. *The Second Book of Negro Spirituals.* 1926. In *The Books of American Negro Spirituals.* New York: Da Capo, 1969.

———. *The Selected Writings of James Weldon Johnson.* Ed. Sondra Kathryn Wilson. Vols. 1–2. New York: Oxford University Press, 1995.

Jones, LeRoi. "The Changing Same (R&B and New Black Music)." 1971. In *The Black Aesthetic.* Ed. Addison Gayle Jr. New York: Anchor, 1972. 112–25.

———. *Home: Social Essays.* New York: William Morrow, 1966.

Jones, LeRoi, and Larry Neal, eds. *Black Fire: An Anthology of Afro-American Writing.* New York: William Morrow, 1968.

Kaplan, Sidney. "Herman Melville and the American National Sin: The Meaning of *Benito Cereno.*" *Journal of Negro History* 41.4 (1956): 311–38.

Karcher, Carolyn L. "Rape, Murder and Revenge in 'Slavery's Pleasant Homes': Lydia Maria Child's Antislavery Fiction and the Limits of Genre." In *The Culture of Sentiment: Race, Gender, and Sentimentality in 19th-Century America.* Ed. Shirley Samuels. New York: Oxford University Press, 1992. 58–72.

Kawash, Samira. "*The Autobiography of an Ex-Colored Man:* (Passing for) Black Passing for White." In *Passing and the Fictions of Identity.* Ed. Elaine K. Ginsberg. Durham, N.C.: Duke University Press, 1996. 59–74.

Kelley, Emma Dunham. *Four Girls at Cottage City.* 1898. New York: Oxford University Press, 1988.

———. *Megda.* 1891. New York: Oxford University Press, 1988.

Kelley, Mary. "The Sentimentalists: Promise and Betrayal in the Home." *Signs* 4.3 (1979): 434–46.

Kent, George E. "Patterns of the Harlem Renaissance." In *The Harlem Renaissance Remembered.* Ed. Arna Bontemps. New York: Dodd, Mead, 1972. 27–50.

King, Deborah K. "Multiple Jeopardy, Multiple Consciousness: The Context of a Black Feminist Ideology." *Signs* 14.1 (1988): 42–72.

Kinnamon, Keneth. "Anthologies of African American Literature from 1845 to 1994." *Callaloo* 20.2 (1997): 461–81.

———. "James Weldon Johnson." In *Dictionary of Literary Biography.* Ed. Trudier Harris. Vol. 51. Detroit: Bruccoli Clark, 1987. 168–82.

Kinney, James. *Amalgamation!: Race, Sex, and Rhetoric in the Nineteenth-Century American Novel.* Westport, Conn.: Greenwood, 1985.

Knadler, Stephen P. "Untragic Mulatto: Charles Chesnutt and the Discourse of Whiteness." *American Literary History* 8.3 (1996): 426–48.

Kramer, Victor A., ed. *The Harlem Renaissance Re-Examined.* New York: AMS, 1987.

Kumar, Krishan. *Utopia and Anti-Utopia in Modern Times.* Oxford, U.K.: Basil Blackwell, 1987.

———. *Utopianism.* Buckingham: Open University Press, 1991.

Lanusse, Armand, ed. *Les Cenelles: A Collection of Poems by Creole Writers of the Early Nineteenth Century.* 1845. Trans. Regine Latortue and Gleason R. W. Adams. Boston: G.K. Hall, 1979.

Larsen, Nella. *Passing* (1929). In *Quicksand and Passing.* Ed. Deborah E. McDowell. New Brunswick, N.J.: Rutgers University Press, 1986.

———. *Quicksand* (1928). In *Quicksand and Passing.* Ed. Deborah E. McDowell. New Brunswick, N.J.: Rutgers University Press, 1986.

Lawson, Benjamin S. "Odysseus's Revenge: The Names on the Title Page of the *Autobiography of an Ex-Colored Man.*" *Southern Literary Journal* 21.2 (1989): 92–99.

Lerner, Gerda, ed. *Black Women in White America: A Documentary History.* New York: Vintage, 1972.

Levine, Lawrence W. *Black Culture and Black Consciousness: Afro-American Folk Thought from Slavery to Freedom.* 1977. Oxford, U.K.: Oxford University Press, 1981.

Levine, Robert S. *Conspiracy and Romance: Studies in Brockden Brown, Cooper, Hawthorne, and Melville.* Cambridge, U.K.: Cambridge University Press, 1989.

Levy, Eugene. *James Weldon Johnson: Black Leader, Black Voice.* Chicago: University of Chicago Press, 1973.

Lewis, David Levering. *When Harlem Was in Vogue.* New York: Oxford University Press, 1981.

Lewis, Richard O. "Literary Conventions in the Novels of William Wells Brown." *CLA Journal* 29.2 (1985): 129–56.

"The Life Work of Edward A. Johnson." *The Crisis,* April 1933, 81.

Lipsitz, George. "The Possessive Investment in Whiteness: Racialized Social Democracy and the 'White' Problem in American Studies." *American Quarterly* 47.3 (1995): 369–87.

Littlejohn, David. *Black on White: A Critical Survey of Writings by American Negroes.* New York: Grossman, 1966.

Litwack, Leon F. *North of Slavery: The Negro in the Free States, 1790–1860.* Chicago: University of Chicago Press, 1961.

Locke, Alain, ed. *The New Negro.* 1925. New York: Atheneum, 1986.

Loewemberg, Bert J., and Ruth Bogin, eds. *Black Women in Nineteenth-Century American Life.* Philadelphia: University of Pennsylvania Press, 1976.

Loggins, Vernon. *The Negro Author: His Development in America.* New York: Columbia University Press. 1931.

Lott, Eric. *Love and Theft: Blackface Minstrelsy and the American Working Class.* New York: Oxford University Press, 1995.

MacKethan, Lucinda H. "*Black Boy* and *Ex-Coloured Man:* Version and Inversion of the Slave Narrator's Quest for Voice." *CLA Journal* 32.2 (1988): 123–47.

Majors, Monroe A. *Noted Negro Women: Their Triumphs and Their Activities.* 1893. Freeport, N.Y.: Books for Libraries Press, 1971.

Martineau, Harriet. *Autobiography.* 1877. London: Virago, 1983.

Mason, Theodore O., Jr. "The Academic Critic and Power: Trends in Contemporary Afro-American Literary Criticism." In *Culture/Criticism/Ideology.* Ed. Stuart Peterfreund. Boston: Northeastern University Press, 1986. 45–60.

———. "The African-American Anthology: Mapping the Territory, Taking the National Census, Building the Museum." *American Literary History* 10.1 (1988): 185–98.

———. "Between the Populist and the Scientist: Ideology and Power in Recent Afro-American Literary Criticism or, 'the Dozens' as Scholarship." *Callaloo* 11.3 (1988): 606–15.

Mayfield, Julian. "Into the Mainstream and Oblivion." In *The American Negro Writer and His Roots.* Selected Papers from the First Conference of Negro Writers, March 1959. New York: American Society of African Culture, 1960. 29–34.

McCarthy, Paul. *"The Twisted Mind": Madness in Herman Melville's Fiction.* Iowa City: University of Iowa Press, 1990.

McDowell, Deborah E. *"The Changing Same:" Black Women's Literature, Criticism, and Theory.* Bloomington: Indiana University Press, 1995.

———. Introduction. In *Four Girls at Cottage City,* by Emma D. Kelley-Hawkins. 1901. New York: Oxford University Press, 1988. xxvii–xxxviii.

McDowell, Deborah E., and Arnold Rampersad, eds. *Slavery and the Literary Imagination.* Baltimore, Md.: Johns Hopkins University Press, 1989.

McElrath, Joseph R., Jr., and Robert C. Leitz III. Introduction. In *"To Be an Author:" Letters of Charles W. Chesnutt, 1889–1905.* Princeton, N.J.: Princeton University Press, 1997. 3–23.

Melville, Herman. *Benito Cereno.* 1855. In *The Piazza Tales and Other Prose Pieces, 1839–1860.* Ed. Harrison Hayford, Alma A. MacDougall, and G. Thomas Tanselle. Evanston, Ill.: Northwestern University Press, 1987. 46–117.

———. *Moby-Dick.* 1851. Ed. Hershel Parker and G. Thomas Tanselle. Evanston, Ill.: Northwestern University Press, 1988.

More, Thomas. *Utopia.* 1516. Trans. Robert M. Adams. New York: Norton, 1992.

"More Novels." *Nation,* 25 February 1892, 154.

Morrison, Toni. *The Bluest Eye.* 1970. New York: Pocket Books, 1972.

———. *Paradise.* 1997. New York: Vintage, 1999.

———. *Playing in the Dark: Whiteness and the Literary Imagination.* Cambridge, Mass.: Harvard University Press, 1992.

Moses, Wilson Jeremiah. *The Golden Age of Black Nationalism, 1850–1925.* New York: Oxford University Press, 1978.

———. *The Wings of Ethiopia: Studies in African-American Life and Letters.* Ames: Iowa State University Press, 1990.

Mossell, Mrs. N. F. *The Work of the Afro-American Woman.* 1894. New York: Oxford University Press, 1988.

Mullen, Harryette. "Optic White: Blackness and the Production of Whiteness." *Diacritics* 24.2–3 (1994): 71–89.

Murray, Barbra, and Brian Duffy. "Jefferson's Secret Life." *U.S. News & World Report* 125.19 (9 November 1998): 58–63.

Nichols, William, and Charles Henry. "Imagining a Future in America: A Racial Perspective." *Alternative Futures* 1.1 (1978): 39–50.

Nowatzki, Robert C. "'Passing' in a White Genre: Charles W. Chesnutt's Negotiations of the Plantation Tradition in *The Conjure Woman.*" *American Literary Realism* 27.2 (1995): 20–36.

Patai, Daphne. "When Women Rule: Defamiliarization in the Sex-Role Reversal Utopia." *Extrapolation* 23.1 (1982): 56–69.

Payne, Ladell. *Black Novelists and the Southern Literary Tradition.* Athens: University of Georgia Press, 1981.

Penn, I. Garland. *The Afro-American Press and Its Editors.* Springfield, Mass.: Willey, 1891.

Peterson, Carla L. "Capitalism, Black (Under)development, and the Production of the African American Novel in the 1850s." *American Literary History* 4.4 (1992): 559–83.

———. *"Doers of the Word": African-American Women Speakers and Writers in the North, 1830–1880.* New York: Oxford University Press, 1995.

Pfeiffer, John. "Black American Speculative Fiction." *Extrapolation: A Journal of Science Fiction and Fantasy* 17.1 (1975): 35–43.

Pfeiffer, Kathleen. "Individualism, Success, and American Identity in *The Autobiography of an Ex-Colored Man.*" *African American Review* 30.3 (1996): 403–19.

Pisiak, Roxanna. "Irony and Subversion in James Weldon Johnson's *The Autobiography of an Ex-Colored Man.*" *Studies in American Fiction* 21.1 (1993): 83–96.

Posnock, Ross. "How It Feels to Be a Problem: Du Bois, Fanon, and the 'Impossible Life' of the Black Intellectual." *Critical Inquiry* 23.2 (1997): 323–49.

Price, Kenneth M., and Lawrence J. Oliver, eds. *Critical Essays on James Weldon Johnson.* New York: G.K. Hall, 1997.

Pryse, Marjorie, and Hortense J. Spillers, eds. *Conjuring: Black Women, Fiction, and Literary Tradition.* Bloomington: Indiana University Press, 1985.

Redding, J. Saunders. *To Make a Poet Black.* 1939. Ithaca, N.Y.: Cornell University Press, 1988.

———. "The Negro Writer and American Literature." In *Anger and Beyond: The Negro Writer in the United States.* Ed. Herbert Hill. New York: Harper & Row, 1966. 1–19.

———. "The Negro Writer and His Relationship to His Roots." In *The American Negro Writer and His Roots.* Selected Papers from the First Conference of Negro Writers, March 1959. New York: American Society of African Culture, 1960. 1–8.

Reilly, John M. "The Utopian Impulse in Early Afro-American Fiction." *Alternative Futures* 1.3–4 (1978): 59–71.

Render, Sylvia Lyons. *Charles W. Chesnutt.* Boston: Twayne, 1980.

———. Introduction. In *The Short Fiction of Charles W. Chesnutt.* Washington, D.C.: Howard University Press, 1974. 3–56.

Robbins, Sarah. "Gendering the History of the Antislavery Narrative: Juxtaposing *Uncle Tom's Cabin* and *Benito Cereno, Beloved* and *Middle Passage.*" *American Quarterly* 49.3 (1997): 531–73.

Roemer, Kenneth M. *The Obsolete Necessity: America in Utopian Writings, 1888–1900.* Kent, Ohio: Kent State University Press, 1976.

Ross, Stephen M. "Audience and Irony in Johnson's *The Autobiography of an Ex-Coloured Man.*" *CLA Journal* 18.2 (1974): 198–210.

Saks, Eva. "Representing Miscegenation Law." *Raritan* 8.2 (1988): 39–69.

Samuels, Shirley, ed. *The Culture of Sentiment: Race, Gender, and Sentimentality in 19th-Century America.* New York: Oxford University Press, 1992.

Sanchez-Eppler, Karen. "Bodily Bonds: The Intersecting Rhetorics of Feminism and Abolition." *Representations* 24 (1988): 28–59.

———. *Touching Liberty: Abolition, Feminism, and the Politics of the Body.* Berkeley: University of California Press, 1993.

Sargent, Lyman Tower. *British and American Utopian Literature, 1516–1985.* New York: Garland, 1988.

Schomburg, Arthur A. "The Negro Digs Up His Past." 1925. In *The New Negro.* Ed. Alain Locke. New York: Atheneum, 1986. 231–44.

Schrager, Cynthia D. "Pauline Hopkins and William James: The New Psychology and the Politics of Race." In *The Unruly Voice: Recovering Pauline Elizabeth Hopkins.* Ed. John Cullen Gruesser. Urbana: University of Illinois Press, 1996. 182–209.

Schweninger, Lee. "*Clotel* and the Historicity of the Anecdote." *MELUS* 24.1 (1999): 21–36.

Scott, Walter. *Ivanhoe.* 1819. London: Dent, 1970.

Sedlack, Robert P. "The Evolution of Charles Chesnutt's *The House Behind the Cedars.*" *CLA Journal* 19.2 (1975): 125–35.

Shor, Francis Robert. *Utopianism and Radicalism in a Reforming America, 1888–1918.* Westport, Conn.: Greenwood, 1997.

Skerrett, Joseph T., Jr. "Irony and Symbolic Action in James Weldon Johnson's *The Autobiography of an Ex-Colored Man.*" *American Quarterly* 32.5 (1980): 540–58.

Smith, Barbara. *Toward a Black Feminist Criticism.* New York: Crossing Press, 1977.

Smith, Stephanie A. *Conceived by Liberty. Maternal Figures in 19th-Century American Literature.* Ithaca: Cornell University Press, 1994.

Smith, Valerie. *Not Just Race, Not Just Gender: Black Feminist Readings.* New York: Routledge, 1998.

———. "Reading the Intersection of Race and Gender in Narratives of Passing." *Diacritics* 24.2–3 (1994): 43–57.

———. *Self-Discovery and Authority in Afro-American Narrative.* Cambridge, Mass.: Harvard University Press, 1987.

Sollors, Werner. *Neither Black Nor White Yet Both: Thematic Explorations of Interracial Literature.* New York: Oxford University Press, 1997.

Sollors, Werner, and Maria Diedrich, eds. *The Black Columbiad: Defining Moments in African American Literature and Culture.* Cambridge, Mass.: Harvard University Press, 1994.

Spillers, Hortense J. Introduction. In *Clarence and Corinne; or, God's Way,* by Amelia E. Johnson. New York: Oxford University Press, 1988. xxvii–xxxviii.

———. "Mama's Baby, Papa's Maybe: An American Grammar Book." *Diacritics* 17.2 (1987): 65–81.

———. "Moving on Down the Line." *American Quarterly* 40.1 (1988): 83–109.

Spingarn, Joel E. "The Negro in Art: How Shall He Be Portrayed." *The Crisis* 31–32 (1926): 278–79.

Spivak, Gayatri Chakravorty. "Can the Subaltern Speak?" In *Marxism and the Interpretation of Culture.* Ed. Cary Nelson and Lawrence Grossberg. Urbana: University of Illinois Press, 1988. 271–313.

Stepto, Robert B. "Distrust of the Reader in Afro-American Narratives." In *Reconstructing American Literary History.* Ed. Sacvan Bercovitch. Cambridge, Mass.: Harvard University Press, 1986. 300–322.

———. *From Behind the Veil: A Study of Afro-American Narrative.* Urbana: University of Illinois Press, 1979.

Stowe, Harriet Beecher. Preface. In *The Garies and Their Friends,* by Frank J. Webb. 1857. New York: Arno, 1969. v–vi.

———. *Uncle Tom's Cabin; or, Life among the Lowly.* 1852. New York: Penguin, 1986.

Strout, Cushing. *Making American Tradition: Visions and Revisions from Ben Franklin to Alice Walker.* New Brunswick, N.J.: Rutgers University Press, 1990.

Stuckey, Sterling. *Going through the Storm: The Influence of African American Art in History.* New York: Oxford University Press, 1994.

———. "Through the Prism of Folklore: The Black Ethos in Slavery." *Massachusetts Review* 9.3 (1968): 417–37.

Sundquist, Eric J. "*Benito Cereno* and New World Slavery." In *Reconstructing American Literary History.* Ed. Sacvan Bercovitch. Cambridge, Mass.: Harvard University Press, 1986. 93–122.

———. *The Hammers of Creation: Folk Culture in Modern African-American Fiction.* Athens: University of Georgia Press, 1992.

———, ed. *New Essays on Uncle Tom's Cabin.* Cambridge, U.K.: Cambridge University Press, 1986.

Suvin, Darko, ed. *Metamorphoses of Science Fiction.* New Haven, Conn.: Yale University Press, 1979.

Tate, Claudia. *Domestic Allegories of Political Desire: The Black Heroine's Text at the Turn of the Century.* New York: Oxford University Press, 1992.

———. *Psychoanalysis and Black Novels: Desire and the Protocols of Race.* New York: Oxford University Press, 1998.

Tompkins, Jane P. "Sentimental Power: *Uncle Tom's Cabin* and the Politics of Literary History" (1978). In *The New Feminist Criticism.* Ed. Elaine Showalter. New York: Pantheon, 1985. 81–104.

Tourgee, Albion W. *A Fool's Errand.* 1879. New York: Harper & Row, 1961.

Turner, Darwin T. "Afro-American Literary Critics: An Introduction." In *The Black Aesthetic.* Ed. Addison Gayle Jr. New York: Doubleday, 1971. 57–74.

————. *"The Negro Novel in America:* In Rebuttal." *CLA Journal* 10.2 (1966): 122–34.

Twain, Mark. *The Adventures of Huckleberry Finn.* 1884. New York: Penguin, 1966.

————. *Life on the Mississippi.* 1883. Oxford, U.K.: Oxford University Press, 1990.

————. *Pudd'nhead Wilson.* 1894. New York: Penguin, 1969.

Van Vechten, Carl. Introduction. In *The Autobiography of an Ex-Colored Man,* by James Weldon Johnson. 1927. New York: Knopf, 1979. v–x.

Vauthier, Simone. "The Interplay of Narrative Modes in James Weldon Johnson's *The Autobiography of an Ex-Colored Man." Jahrbuch fur Amerikastudien* 18 (1973): 173–81.

Wald, Gayle. "The Vestments and Investments of Race." *American Quarterly* 52.2 (2000): 371–80.

Walker, Alice. *In Search of Our Mothers' Gardens: Womanist Prose.* New York: Harcourt Brace Jovanovich, 1983.

Wall, Cheryl A. "Zora Neale Hurston." In *The Gender of Modernism: A Critical Anthology.* Ed. Bonnie Kime Scott. Bloomington: Indiana University Press, 1990. 170–75.

Warren, Kenneth W. *Black and White Strangers: Race and American Literary Realism.* Chicago: University of Chicago Press, 1993.

————. "Troubled Black Humanity in *The Souls of Black Folk* and *The Autobiography of an Ex-Colored Man."* In *The Cambridge Companion to American Realism and Naturalism: Howells to London.* Ed. Donald Pizer. Cambridge, U.K.: Cambridge University Press, 1995. 263–77.

Washington, Booker T. *Up from Slavery.* 1901. New York: Airmont, 1967.

Washington, Mary Helen. Introduction. In *A Voice from the South,* by Anna Julia Cooper. New York: Oxford University Press, 1988. xxvii–liv.

————, ed. *Invented Lives: Narratives of Black Women, 1860–1960.* New York: Doubleday, 1987.

Watson, Carole McAlpine. *Prologue: The Novels of Black American Women, 1891–1965.* Westport, Conn.: Greenwood, 1985.

Webb, Frank J. *The Garies and Their Friends.* 1857. New York: Arno, 1969.

————. "Marvin Hayle." Serialized in *The New Era,* 31 March, 7 April, 14 April, 21 April 1870.

————. "The Mixed School Question." *The New Era,* 27 January 1870, 1.

————. "Two Wolves and a Lamb." Serialized in *The New Era,* 13 January, 20 January, 27 January, 3 February 1870.

Welter, Barbara. "The Cult of True Womanhood: 1820–1860." *American Quarterly* 18.2 (1966): 151–74.

Werner, Craig. "The Framing of Charles W. Chesnutt: Practical Deconstruction in the Afro-American Tradition." In *Southern Literature and Literary Theory.* Ed. Jefferson Humphries. Athens: University of Georgia Press, 1990. 339–65.

Whitlow, Roger. *Black American Literature: A Critical History.* 1973. Chicago: Nelson Hall, 1976.

Williams, Kenny J. *They Also Spoke: An Essay on Negro Literature in America, 1787–1930.* Nashville, Tenn.: Townsend, 1970.

Williams, Preston N. "Black Perspectives on Utopia." In *Utopia/Dystopia?* Ed. Peyton E. Richter. Cambridge, Mass.: Schenkman, 1975. 45–56.

Wilson, Harriet E. *Our Nig; or, Sketches from the Life of a Free Black.* 1859. New York: Random House, 1983.

Wong, Sau-ling Cynthia. *Reading Asian American Literature: From Necessity to Extravagance.* Princeton, N.J.: Princeton University Press, 1993.

Wonham, Henry B. *Charles W. Chesnutt: A Study of the Short Fiction.* New York: Twayne, 1998.

———, ed. *Criticism and the Color Line: Desegregating American Literary Studies.* New Brunswick, N.J.: Rutgers University Press, 1996.

———. "Writing Realism, Policing Consciousness: Howells and the Black Body." *American Literature* 67.4 (1995): 701–24.

Wright, Richard. *Black Boy.* 1945. New York: Harper & Row, 1966.

———. "Introduction: Blueprint for Negro Writing." 1937. In *The Black Aesthetic.* Ed. Addison Gayle Jr. New York: Doubleday, 1971. 315–26.

———. *Native Son.* 1940. New York: Harper & Row, 1966.

Yarborough, Richard. *The Depiction of Blacks in the Early Afro-American Novel.* Ann Arbor: University Microfilms International, 1992.

———. "Strategies of Black Characterization in *Uncle Tom's Cabin* and the Early African American Novel." In *New Essays on Uncle Tom's Cabin.* Ed. Eric J. Sundquist. Cambridge, U.K.: Cambridge University Press, 1986. 45–84.

Yellin, Jean Fagan. *The Intricate Knot: Black Figures in American Literature, 1776–1863.* New York: New York University Press, 1972.

Zafar, Rafia. *We Wear the Mask: African Americans Write American Literature, 1760–1870.* New York: Columbia University Press, 1997.

Index

M. GIULIA FABI, who earned a Ph.D. degree from the University of California at Berkeley and has taught at the University of Rome, is an assistant professor of American literature at the University of Ferrara, Italy. She has published essays on American literature in the United States and Europe and contributed to *The Oxford Companion to African American Literature* (1977). She is the editor of a series of Italian translations of African American novels.

Composed in 10.5/13 Minion
by Celia Shapland
for the University of Illinois Press
Manufactured by Thomson-Shore, Inc.

University of Illinois Press
1325 South Oak Street
Champaign, IL 61820-6903
www.press.uillinois.edu